# SUPREME BIAS

# SUPREME BIAS

GENDER AND RACE
IN U.S. SUPREME COURT
CONFIRMATION HEARINGS

CHRISTINA L. BOYD,
PAUL M. COLLINS, JR.,
*and* LORI A. RINGHAND

STANFORD UNIVERSITY PRESS
Stanford, California

Stanford University Press
Stanford, California

Printed in the United States of America on acid-free, archival-quality paper

ISBN 9781503632691 (cloth)
ISBN 9781503636880 (paper)
ISBN 9781503636897 (electronic)

Library of Congress Control Number: 2023017623

Library of Congress Cataloging-in-Publication Data available upon request.

Cover design: Laywan Kwan
Typeset by Newgen in Garamond Premier Pro 10.75/15

# CONTENTS

# PREFACE

The appointment of a U.S. Supreme Court justice is an important political, legal, and public event. For presidents, Supreme Court nominations provide an opportunity to shape the direction of public policy long after they leave office. For nominees, being chosen to fill a vacant seat signals that they have reached the top of the legal profession and, if confirmed, will play a major role in determining the future of law and policy in the United States. For senators, their duty to provide advice and consent to a president's choice ensures that the legislative branch, as the people's elected representatives, is involved in this important process. For the rest of us, the appointments process provides an opportunity to reflect on the role of the Supreme Court in our society, and register our own opinions about the constitutional choices the Court is making on the issues that affect our lives. And we are, in fact, paying attention. Millions of Americans tune into gavel-to-gavel television coverage of the hearings, and millions more follow them on TV news, the internet, radio, social media, and newspapers, or talk about the hearings with their friends and family.

If you were one of those millions who watched the most recent confirmation hearing—that of Ketanji Brown Jackson in 2022—you would have seen many senators celebrate an exceptionally well qualified nominee who also was the first Black woman appointed to the Supreme Court. You would have seen Jackson face tough questions—especially from Republican senators—on many of the pressing issues of the day, including abortion rights, affirmative action, and immigration. And you would have seen the nominee demonstrate a sharp legal mind, a calm demeanor, and a devotion to public service.

But if you looked closer, you also might have seen something else. You might have noticed senators—frequently white, male senators—aggressively interrupt Jackson when she tried to answer their questions. You may have observed some of those same senators question whether Jackson was soft on crime, if she held radical views about race, and whether her judicial philosophy was up to snuff. You may have reflected on whether this type of questioning was the norm, whether it was just politics, or whether it was particularly harsh this time around. You may have wondered, in other words, whether female nominees and nominees of color, like Justice Jackson, faced a different type of confirmation process than do their white, male peers.

This is the topic we explore throughout this book. Combining insights from interdisciplinary work about race and gender biases with a wealth of original data and narratives drawn from the hearings themselves, we explore the role race and gender have played at Supreme Court confirmation hearings, particularly in shaping the hearing experiences of female nominees and nominees of color. We explain how race and gender biases manifest at the hearings, why it matters when they do, and what steps could be taken to reduce them in the future.

# ACKNOWLEDGMENTS

This project would not have been possible without assistance from a huge network of supportive colleagues, students, friends, and family. Previous iterations of this research were presented at a variety of academic conferences and workshops, including the 2017 Southern Political Science Association conference, the 2017 UMass Interdisciplinary Legal Studies colloquium, the 2018 and 2019 American Political Science Association conferences, the 2019 Law and Society Association conference, a 2021 George Mason University Antonin Scalia Law School faculty workshop, the 2022 Empirical Legal Studies conference, a 2022 University of Virginia School of Law faculty and student workshop, and as part of the 2022 Susquehanna University Arlin M. Adams Lecture Series. We thank the many organizers, chairs, discussants, fellow panelists, and audience members for their feedback at those events. An early version of chapter 4 appeared in *Law & Society Review* (Boyd, Collins, and Ringhand 2018).

We are grateful to so many colleagues and friends for their insightful comments on this research and willingness to act as sounding boards as we tested out the ideas that would become this book. Although there are far too many to list here, we want to acknowledge Scott Blinder, Jennifer Bowie, Roberto Carlos, James Cooper, Pam Corley, Josh Fischman, Justin Gross, Susan Haire, Rebecca Hamlin, Morgan Hazelton, Rachael Hinkle, Gbemende Johnson, Sally Kenney, Ray La Raja, Monika Lindbekk, Wendy Martinek, Lauren McCarthy,

Alison Merrill, Greg Mitchell, Paul Musgrave, Michael Nelson, Tatishe Nteta, Rachel Potter, Jesse Rhodes, Meredith Rolfe, Jamie Rowen, Geoffrey Sheagley, Barbara Spellman, Amy Steigerwalt, Susan Sterett, Art Ward, Margie Williams, and Leah Wing. We are thankful to our institutions—the University of Georgia's School of Law, School of Public and International Affairs, and Department of Political Science, and the University of Massachusetts Amherst's Legal Studies Program and Department of Political Science—for supporting our research endeavors. We send a special thanks to Doug Rice for his feedback and his willingness to lend a last-minute hand to ensure we could include Ketanji Brown Jackson's confirmation hearing in our analyses. We also thank the Dirksen Congressional Center for funding the collection of some of the data used in this book.

One of the joys of writing this book was that it gave us the opportunity to work with a large, diverse, and passionate group of undergraduate, graduate, and law students. It truly was a pleasure to have them on our research team, and we are very grateful for their work. At the University of Georgia, we thank Matt Baker, Rosa Brown, Haley Carman, Jenah Clarkson, Madison Conkel, Jordan Dyer, Gillian Gaines, Riley Grube, Grace Hayes, Julianna Hightower, Caitlyn Kinard, Kate Kostel, Chloe Levy, Alaina Moore, Katie Pitner, Kiana Powers, Emma Rowr, Adam Rutkowski, Kyle Venit, Allison Vick, Lizzy Walker, Emily Willard, and Jessie Zacune. At the University of Massachusetts Amherst, we thank Madison Alvis, Juliana Bird, Brie Bristol, Rayani Chonmany, Mitchell Director, Caroline Greenlaw, Ryan Heilmann, Emma Hupp, Telly Jacobs, Eshaa Joshi, Nadeen Jumai'an, Elisabeth Lopez, Bryce McManus, Maggie Mendoza, Brianna Owen, Moksha Padmaraju, Haley Patel, Elise Puschett, Sam Rusling-Flynn, Nora Vonmoltke-Simms, Megan Wan, and Veronica Walsh. We look forward to watching your careers and lives develop!

At Stanford University Press, we extend our sincere appreciation to our editor, Marcela Maxfield, to Sarah Rodriguez, and to the anonymous reviewers whose excellent comments significantly improved the quality of this book.

*From Christy*: During the course of this project, I have been fortunate to work with amazing students. I'm so inspired by this next generation of role models emerging before me! Speaking of role models, I am forever indebted to my mentor Andrew Martin for his support of my training and career and for believing there was a place for me in academia. Thank you to Paul and Lori for welcoming me into your confirmation hearings club. Working with you has been both rewarding and fun! Thank you to my wonderful family: Carmen, Nate, Rusan, Cindy, Steve, Dave, Nancy, Tim, Terri, John, Peppermint, and SL. I am also grateful to my academic family, Roberto Carlos, Geoff Sheagley, Michael Lynch, and Ryan Black, for their ideas, strategizing, encouragement, and support. Finally, I continue to thank my parents for believing in me. Mom was always the optimistic cheerleader, and she sweetly helped move me across the country from North Carolina to St Louis to Buffalo to Athens as I went from school to school as student and then professor. Dad was the voice of reason and sounding board for all of the big decisions, and he was also a great softball coach! I was incredibly lucky, and I dearly miss these two lights.

*From Paul:* Although writing about subject matter as important as racial and gender bias is quite challenging, it was nonetheless a pleasure to write this book. I am so grateful to my brilliant coauthors, Christy and Lori, who made the years-long process of putting this volume together one of the best experiences of my career. I am likewise thankful to the many friends, family members, and colleagues who took an interest in this research and shared their own stories of facing bias and discrimination with me. Special thanks go to my amazing wife, Lisa, and my two smart and kindhearted children, Rose and Maggie. May they never face the types of bias we uncovered in our research.

During the writing of this book, we lost my father. As a lawyer and legislator, and in other walks of life, Dad was committed to social justice. He taught us from an early age the importance of treating others with dignity and respect, and shared with us his love of politics and law. I dedicate this book to Dad's memory and to my mother, Lea, and siblings Pat, Kelly, and Katie.

*From Lori:* I am deeply grateful to my students, family, colleagues, and friends who have been my sounding boards and staunch supporters throughout the process of working on this book. I am especially glad to count my coauthors, Paul and Christy, in each of those final categories—as both colleagues and friends. From our initial brainstorming sessions, to our round-robin edits, to the rapid revision of the project when Justice Stephen Breyer announced his retirement and Ketanji Brown Jackson was nominated to the Court at a point when the manuscript was almost completed, this project, to me, represents the best of what interdisciplinary coauthorship can be. The finished book would not have been possible without our collaboration, and I am honored to have been a part of the team.

# INTRODUCTION

On January 27, 2022, Justice Stephen Breyer wrote President Biden to inform him that he would be retiring from the U.S. Supreme Court in the summer of 2022. Breyer's announcement was followed by a flurry of excitement and criticism from Court watchers anticipating that Biden would make good on his 2020 campaign promise to appoint the first Black woman justice to the U.S. Supreme Court. Less than one month later, on February 25, 2022, President Biden did just that, announcing the historic nomination of Ketanji Brown Jackson to be an associate justice of the U.S. Supreme Court (Biden 2022).

As news of the Jackson selection broke on that Friday morning in February, reactions from across the political spectrum were swift and varied. Senate Majority Leader Chuck Schumer (D-NY) praised the president's choice, saying "Judge Jackson has shown brilliance, thoughtfulness, a willingness to collaborate, and a dedication to applying the law impartially" (Senate Democrats 2022). Senate Minority Leader Mitch McConnell (R-KY) countered that Jackson was the "favored choice of far-left dark-money groups" and that "one of her prior rulings was just reversed by a unanimous panel of her present colleagues on the D.C. Circuit" (McConnell 2022). Prominent Republican member of the Senate Judiciary Committee Lindsey Graham also criticized the Jackson nomination that day, noting that it meant that "the radical Left has won President Biden over yet again" (Graham 2022a). Nonetheless, Graham predicted that the new nominee's Senate Judiciary Committee confirmation hearing would be "respectful but interesting" (Graham 2022b).

Graham's prediction was not entirely wrong: Jackson's March 2022 confirmation hearing most certainly was "interesting." It included emotional reflections on Jackson's historic nomination; dramatic moments like Senator Graham walking out of the hearing after a contentious exchange between himself, the nominee, and Senator Dick Durbin (D-IL); and heated questions about the controversial issues of the day, ranging from critical race theory to the definition of the word *woman*. But was Jackson's confirmation hearing also "respectful"? Jackson's hearing contained numerous moments of objective respectfulness toward the nominee, from both Democratic and Republican senators on the Committee who welcomed her and her family to the hearing and spoke favorably of her background. But her hearing also featured moments indicating far less respectfulness, often demonstrated in subtle yet powerful ways.

Speaking just days after Jackson's confirmation hearing ended, Senator Cory Booker (D-NJ) captured this tension, observing that while "there is legitimate questioning that went on by Republicans" on the Committee to Jackson, much of the Republican senators' questioning could be described as "deflating," "disappointing," and "a bit beyond the pale" (Diaz and Stracqualursi 2022). Booker emphasized that the nominee's treatment echoed that faced by other women and people of color, in and out of Supreme Court confirmation hearings:

> I got a chance to witness firsthand what I think many people in America can relate to, is when you show up in a room qualified, when you show up in a room with extraordinary expertise and credentials, there are a lot of Americans who know that hurt, that you are still going to be treated in a way that does not respect to you fully.... To me, it's just about the kind of way we're going to treat folk. And I think it's a kind of thing that a lot of folks, women of all races, have had to endure often when they get into a room that they're qualified to be in, but are yet questioned in ways that are disappointing. (Diaz and Stracqualursi 2022)

Jackson is hardly the first Supreme Court nominee to face a disrespectful hearing environment or one that looks different from that provided to white, male nominees. At the very end of his questioning of 2020 U.S. Supreme Court nominee Amy Coney Barrett, Senator John Kennedy (R-LA) asked, "Who does the laundry in your house?"[1] Though this query was intended as a lighthearted finale to his questioning of Barrett, it nonetheless illustrates a disturbing dynamic of Supreme Court confirmation hearings: senators treat female nominees differently than their male counterparts. No senators asked nominees Neil Gorsuch and Brett Kavanaugh, who have remarkably similar backgrounds to Barrett in almost all respects, about who does their laundry. Instead, this question was reserved for a woman. We see a similar difference in how nominees of color are questioned, relative to their white counterparts. Thurgood Marshall, the first African American nominee, was accused of being a racist and asked if he was "prejudiced against white people in the South"[2] (Ringhand 2010, 826). Sonia Sotomayor, the first Latina appointed to the Court, was portrayed as an overly emotional woman who would invoke her feelings in deciding cases (Johnson 2011). Clarence Thomas bitterly linked his hearing experience to his racial identity, describing the Committee's investigation of charges that he sexually harassed law professor and former employee Anita Hill as a "high tech lynching."[3]

Contemporary American society has become increasingly attuned to the ongoing challenges presented by these types of gender and racial disparities, as exemplified by the #MeToo and Black Lives Matter movements. But relatively little empirical work has been done on whether and how these disparities affect the Supreme Court confirmation hearings held before the Senate Judiciary Committee. The Supreme Court is one of the least open political institutions in the United States, which means the confirmation hearings provide a unique public view into this otherwise opaque entity. With sustained media attention, high levels of public interest, and gavel-to-gavel television coverage, the hearings provide a one-of-a-kind opportunity for Americans to directly observe and develop opinions about Supreme Court nominees, as well as the Court itself. The hearings also allow average citizens to see for themselves how the nominees are treated and assessed by powerful elites—in this case, the senators serving on the Judiciary Committee.

If senators treat female nominees and nominees of color differently than their white, male counterparts in this high-profile context, the effects could be quite consequential. In other words, the presence of bias matters in important and varied ways. Public displays of bias against women and people of color in highly salient professional settings may discourage ambition among young lawyers who perceive bias-based barriers to success (Williams 2008) or aggravate a sense among women and people of color that our governing institutions do not represent them or understand their concerns (Campbell and Wolbrecht 2006).

A biased Supreme Court confirmation process also may perpetuate negative stereotypes about women and people of color and cast doubt on their ability to serve in elite institutions like the Supreme Court. By shaping negative perceptions of a future justice's fitness to serve on the Court, senatorial bias toward certain nominees also could contribute to increased skepticism among the general public regarding that nominee's qualifications or foster a culture of incivility in which advocates and other justices demonstrate disrespect for and call into question the credibility of their nontraditional colleagues (Feldman and Gill 2019; Jacobi and Schweers 2017). Even if Senate Judiciary Committee members are not aware of their biases and may not be "consciously disrespectful," their behavior nonetheless could have "the 'real world' consequence of delegitimizing" the "knowledge, experience, and ultimately, leadership" of those nominees and justices who are not white men (Han and Heldman 2007, 22). Evidence of bias in such a high-profile setting also could harm the public's perceptions of the legitimacy of both the Supreme Court and the confirmation process itself (e.g., Gibson and Caldeira 2009). Beyond affecting perceptions of justices and the Supreme Court, the presence of bias during the hearings can affect the questions asked and answers given, the fate of the nominee during their Senate confirmation vote, the ideological composition of the Supreme Court, and even the crafting and interpretation of law by the Supreme Court (Collins and Ringhand 2013a; Epstein and Segal 2005; Farganis and Wedeking 2014).

This book examines how gender and racial bias can manifest at Supreme Court confirmation hearings in both explicit and implicit ways. Sometimes race and gender are discussed in uplifting and praise-filled ways—for example, as a recognition of the importance of increased inclusion on the nation's highest Court. There have been elements of this celebratory narrative in all of the Supreme Court hearings involving female nominees and nominees of color— from Thurgood Marshall through Ketanji Brown Jackson. Too often, though, discussions of race and gender at the hearings have taken a darker turn. The groundbreaking nomination of Thurgood Marshall, for example, was celebrated by some senators but aggressively disparaged by many others. In addition to accusing him of racism, some senators used their questioning time to try to make Marshall look unqualified or incompetent (S. Carter 1995). More than fifty years later, a president's promise to appoint the first Black woman to the Supreme Court generated concerns about such a nominee's qualifications before a candidate was even named (T. Johnson 2022).

Bias against female nominees and nominees of color also can occur in more subtle ways. At their core, confirmation hearings are job interviews. Nominees need to prove they have the intellectual chops to sit on the high court, while also navigating the divergent politics and preferences of the members of the Senate Judiciary Committee. Extensive earlier work examines how race and gender stereotypes can be triggered in settings like this, especially when there are disparities of power between the participants (Fiske 1993). Other research shows that partisan conflict can aggravate that tendency, meaning that when a minority group member does not share a person's values, ideals, and policy priorities, the effects of negative stereotypes may be magnified (Kawakami et al. 2000; Koch 2000; Sigelman et al. 1995; Szmer, Sarver, and Kaheny 2010). Given this existing research, we would expect the confirmation hearings, where partisanship is acute and senators hold the fate of the nominee in their hands, to be fruitful ground for the display of race and gender bias.

So what might this look like?

Think back to the 2008 presidential primary, where multiple current and former U.S. senators, among others, faced off for the Democratic nomination. Despite the identical professional titles held by Hillary Clinton, Barack Obama, Joe Biden, Chris Dodd, and John Edwards, the television media was four times more likely to refer to Clinton by her first name than any of her competitors (Uscinski and Goren 2011). Years before, in 1981, media stories and headlines about Supreme Court nominee Sandra Day O'Connor would often title her "Mrs. O'Connor" rather than using her professional titles of "Senator O'Connor" or "Judge O'Connor" (Jefferson and Johnson 2020). No *New York Times* or *Washington Post* headlines referred to other Supreme Court nominees, like William Rehnquist, Antonin Scalia, Lewis Powell, Robert Bork, Anthony Kennedy, or John Paul Stevens, as "Mr." (Brenner and Knake 2012).

Unfortunately, women and people of color routinely experience this type of discounting of their professional identities and accomplishments. Prior research shows that both race and gender are highly salient in our evaluations of the competence of others (Fiske et al. 2002). For example, women running against men for public office are often seen as less qualified than they are (Branton et al. 2018). Voters also are more likely to seek out information about the competency of female than male candidates, and their evaluation of female candidates is more influenced by that information than is their evaluation of male candidates (Branton et al. 2018). Resumes containing distinctively Black or Asian names have been found to generate up to 50 percent fewer callbacks than identical resumes without such names (Gaddis 2015). In a 2016 study, researchers created résumés for Black and Asian applicants for entry level jobs posted online (Kang et al. 2016). Some of the résumés plainly indicated the racial identity of the candidates, while other otherwise identical résumés did not. The "whitened" résumés generated significantly more interview invitations, for both Black and Asian candidates. Most dispiritingly, a large-scale meta-analysis of similar studies shows little change over time in this type of résumé-review bias, especially in regard to Black Americans (Quilian et al. 2017). Finally, both people of color and women also have been shown to receive less compensation than white men despite having identical scores on performance evaluations (Castilla 2008).[4]

High levels of achievement on objective criteria do not appear to help women or people of color escape this skepticism of their professional competence. In one of the many studies examining how employers review résumés, a group of sociologists found that high grade point averages actually *hurt* women's chances of being invited in for an interview. Résumés with female names and midlevel grade point averages were relatively attractive to potential employers, but female candidates with high grade point averages were actually called back less often than were male candidates with low grade point averages (Quadlin 2018). A follow-up survey showed that when reviewing a résumé from a male applicant with a low GPA, reviewers articulated narratives explaining away the low levels of academic achievement. But when reviewing résumés from female applicants with high GPAs, narratives shifted from skills and competence to the bane of female professionals: "likeability" (Quadlin 2018). This was demonstrative of the "double bind" so many women experience in the workplace (Chen and Bryan 2021; Gleason, Jones, and McBean 2019; Nelson 2015). That is, engaging in behaviors perceived as masculine can help women overcome gender-based skepticism of their competence, but it also increases the likelihood that they will be subject to negative judgments for behaving out of accordance with gendered expectations: they are seen as not likable enough. Studies have shown that people of color, and especially women of color, navigate different versions of this same dynamic (Livingston, Rosette, and Washington 2012; Sanchez-Hucles and Davis 2010).

These "double-binds" are one of the many ways stereotypes affect the daily experiences of women and people of color. Stereotypes—"cognitive structures that contain the perceivers' knowledge, beliefs, and expectations about human groups" (Peffley, Hurwitz, and Sniderman 1997)—shape our expectations of people's competencies and interests. Female elected officials are presumed to be interested in (and good at) formulating policies about families and children (McDermott 1998). Black elected officials are seen as more able than their white peers to handle racial equality issues (Schneider and Bos 2011). Even when postured like this—as strengths—stereotypes prime us to view people in different ways, depending on their race and gender, and leave us nonplussed when an individual's behavior deviates from those expectations. So, Clarence Thomas is criticized harshly for not supporting traditional civil rights laws, and Amy Coney Barrett is asked about the laundry.

Race, ethnicity, and gender also infuse the way we talk to and about each other. Interruptions are one example of this. Women and people of color tend to experience higher rates of interruptions when they speak (Anderson and Leaper 1998; Hancock and Rubin 2014; Leman and Ikoko 2010; Snyder 2014). These interruptions, even when intended to help the original speaker, act as assertations of power and control that have the effect of changing the direction of the dialogue and denying someone the ability to speak for themselves (Karpowitz, Mendelberg, and Mattioli 2015). The Supreme Court itself is not immune from the inequitable presence of interruptions, with recent work finding that female justices are interrupted more than male justices during oral arguments (Feldman and Gill 2019; Jacobi and Schweers 2017). Justice Sonia Sotomayor has said that "without question" she has noticed this gendered interruptions trend on the Court. "But I don't know of a woman who hasn't. Regrettably, that is a dynamic that exists not just on the court but in our society in general. Most of the time, women say things, and they're not heard in the same way as men who might say the identical thing" (Liptak 2021). Another example is the use of racialized language when talking about people of color. In a fascinating study, Foy and Ray (2019) demonstrated the racialized way sports announcers talked about male college basketball players. Announcers were more likely to talk about lighter-skinned players in terms of their mental abilities, while darker-skinned players were discussed in terms of their physical characteristics.

## BIAS AND SUPREME COURT CONFIRMATION HEARINGS

We can observe the implications of these types of stereotypes throughout the legal system. We see it in decisions police officers make about who to stop and question, the choices of prosecutors about which individuals to charge with crimes, and the deliberations of judges and juries (e.g., Baumgartner, Epp, and Shoub 2018; Boldt et al. 2021; Boyd 2016; King and Light 2019; Kutateladze et al. 2014; Mitchell et al. 2005). Given this extensive research, we can make predictions about how this type of bias might show up at Supreme Court confirmation hearings. Senators, for example, might be more likely to question the competence of nominees who are female or people of color. They might assume these nominees are more likely to be interested in the issue areas that are stereotypically associated with their race or gender. They might disrespect these nominees by interrupting them more than they interrupt white male nominees, and they might use less effusive language when talking to or about them.

These are the issues we investigate in this book. To do so, we use an original dataset based on all questions asked and answered at all public Supreme Court confirmation hearings since they began in 1939 through the 2022 hearing of Ketanji Brown Jackson. This database, which covers more than 44,000 unique statements, contains a host of information about the hearings, including the topics of conversation, the interruptions that take place between senators and nominees, and the gender, racial, and partisan identity of all nominees and senators. It also contains the text of hearing statements, allowing us to explore gender and racial distinctions in the language used by senators in questioning with nominees. And, for the first time, we introduce original data on the two "special session" hearings held to address accusations of sexual misconduct raised against Clarence Thomas in 1987 and Brett Kavanaugh in 2018.[5]

Each observation in our dataset represents a statement made at the hearings. For instance, in the example below, there are two observations: one for Senator Ted Cruz (R-TX) and one for nominee Barrett:

> SENATOR CRUZ: So, your children have been wonderfully well behaved. I think you're an amazing role model for little girls. What advice would you give little girls?
>
> JUDGE BARRETT: Well, what I'm saying is not designed—my brother now has left—I was just thinking of what my dad told me before the spelling bee about anything boys can do, girls can do better.
>
> (LAUGHTER)
>
> And, since my sons are sitting behind me, I'll also say that boys are great too.[6]

In the chapters that follow, we provide more details on our expansive data as it pertains to the focus of each chapter. For now, we note that the data allow us to investigate a wide array of topics relating to race and gender bias at the hearings. Consequently, we are able to marry normative debates related to racial and gender bias that pervade contemporary political discourse with empirical scholarship that allows us to describe and explain the extent of such bias at Supreme Court confirmation hearings. Coupling this expansive data with our rich knowledge of the hearings allows us to ground our empirical data in real world examples from decades of hearings.

We begin in Chapter 1 by examining the progress and efforts made over time to diversify the Supreme Court and the federal judiciary more generally. We describe how Supreme Court nominees historically have been chosen in part to appeal to important presidential constituencies, and how the democratic expansion of the twentieth century extended that practice to women and people of color. In doing so, we talk about the historic selections of justices such as Thurgood Marshall, Sandra Day O'Connor, Sonia Sotomayor, and Ketanji Brown Jackson. Chapter 1 also details the near selections of other women and people of color. These earlier judicial vacancy battles paved the way for future Supreme Court nominees. Chapter 1 also introduces a less celebratory narrative. This chapter tracks the gradual increase in the number of people of color and female Supreme Court nominees across time. For comparison, the chapter does the same for the lower federal courts, the "auditioning grounds" for future elevation to the U.S. Supreme Court (Black and Owens 2016; Bowie, Songer, and Szmer 2014; Dancey, Nelson, and Ringsmuth 2020; Haire and Moyer 2015). Doing so highlights just how slowly gender, ethnicity, and racial diversity reached the federal courts. It also shows how efforts to be more inclusive have not yet become a fully bipartisan effort, especially on the lower federal courts. Finally, this chapter also examines why diversity matters, for the federal judiciary and the Supreme Court.

Chapter 2 provides a comprehensive account of the Supreme Court nomination and confirmation process. We begin by discussing how vacancies arise and the considerations presidents have typically used in selecting their nominees. We then detail the first "modern" Supreme Court confirmation hearing, held in 1939, and highlight how the Senate Judiciary Committee's role in the process has evolved since that time. We explain how the senators use the hearings to grill nominees on a host of issues, including their constitutional preferences, positions on the pressing issues of the day, opinions about iconic cases, and personal backgrounds. As we explain, this questioning process not only provides important information to the senators about nominees but also serves the broader purposes of shaping public perceptions about the Supreme Court and constitutional law in the United States. In addition, we also tap our deep knowledge of the confirmation transcripts to draw out the story of how race and gender gradually began to be more present at the hearings through senatorial questioning about the role of women and people of color in American society. We discuss how gender discussions evolved from chuckling about allowing women into military combat roles to the celebration of litigator Ruth Bader Ginsburg's successful representation of female veterans, and how discussions of racial equality exploded into prominence after *Brown v. Board of Education* was decided in 1954.

In Chapter 3, we lay the theoretical groundwork for how the race, ethnicity, and gender of Supreme Court nominees may affect how these nominees are evaluated, treated, and discussed by senators during their confirmation hearings. This type of bias often arises from subconscious attitudes and stereotypes, rather than an intentional effort to discriminate (e.g., Arvey 1979; Biernat and Kobrynowicz 1997; Cuddy, Fiske, and Glick 2008; Davison and Burke 2000; Eagly and Karau 2002). In this chapter, we explain two key elements of implicit race and gender bias and explore their potential relevance to the confirmation hearing process. First, we describe how gender and race sometimes function as cues, signaling to majority group members that minority group members are of a different (and lower) status than are powerful members of the majority group (Eagly, Makhijani, and Klonsky 1992; Foschi 2000; Inesi and Cable 2015; Moyer and Haire 2015). This form of group bias can result in female and person of color nominees being perceived as "different" from the powerful and mostly male and white senators questioning them. Second, we explain how these biases and stereotypes may most readily appear in the confirmation process when they intersect with politics and partisanship. Specifically, we discuss the ways shared party affiliation (between a nominee and a questioning senator) can serve an important conditioning role on the presence and level of bias against female nominees and nominees of color (Davidson and Burke 2000; James and Clark 1993; Kawakami et al. 2000; Koch 2000; Sigelman et al. 1995; Szmer, Sarver, and Kaheny 2010). We discuss this intersection of bias and partisanship in each of the remaining chapters and explain its magnifying or mitigating effects.

Chapters 4, 5, and 6 apply these theories of bias and stereotyping to the experiences of nominees at Supreme Court confirmation hearings. In Chapter

4, we ask whether the questioning senators treat female and person of color nominees differently than their white, male counterparts. We assess whether nominees who are female or are persons of color (or both) have to do more than their white and male counterparts to prove their professional competence and defend their impartiality in the face of stereotypes. To do this for professional competence, we examine whether these nominees are asked more "judicial philosophy" questions, which senators use to interrogate nominees about how they would perform the core judicial task of interpreting the U.S. Constitution. For the analysis of subject matter stereotypes, we focus on abortion and gender discrimination (for nominee gender) and racial discrimination and crime (for nominee race).

Chapter 5 contributes to the growing body of work on power dynamics and the use of interruptions by examining the frequency and nature of interruptions during the confirmation hearings. Interrupting another speaker is a type of social control that can both demonstrate and perpetuate inequality (Aries 1996; Johnson 1994; Feldman and Gill 2019; Goldberg 1990; Jacobi and Schweers 2017; Smith-Lovin and Brody 1989). As it relates to Supreme Court confirmation hearings, senators on the Judiciary Committee may interrupt female nominees and nominees of color more often than white, male nominees because they see (consciously or not) the former as unfamiliar and lower-status minority group members who may not share their core values. We examine both intrusive interruptions—those where the interrupting speaker takes over the conversational floor, causing the original speaker to stop talking (Anderson and Leaper 1998)—and positive interruptions—those where senators interrupt their female and people of color coparticipants in the belief that doing so will aid their confirmation hearing performances.

Chapter 6 explores the vocabulary of bias during the confirmation hearings. We investigate the language used by senators in their questioning of nominees to determine if senators use less effusive language toward female nominees and nominees of color. To do this, we draw on interdisciplinary scholarship showing evidence of language bias against women and people of color in multiple contexts, from letters of recommendation to media accounts. We apply these insights to the confirmation hearings by systematically examining the language used within the question-and-answer portion of confirmation hearing transcripts. Specifically, we use computational social science techniques to explore whether senators use a harsher, more negative tone when questioning female nominees and nominees of color, and whether they tend to use more differentiation words that cast doubt on the testimony of these nominees.

In Chapter 7, we turn our attention to the special session confirmation hearings held to investigate the allegations of sexual misconduct against Clarence Thomas and Brett Kavanaugh. Using a first-of-its kind database of the dialogue that occurred during these special sessions, we explore the gender and racial dynamics of these hearings by investigating how the participants in these special sessions talked about sexual harassment and sexual assault, as well as the skepticism or respect with which the senators addressed both the nominees and their accusers. In addition, we examine the similarities and differences across the two hearings and offer insight into how societal changes likely contributed to the manner in which the Committee handled Christine Blasey Ford's accusations, compared to those of Anita Hill.

In Chapter 8, we look to the future. Race and gender biases, as we show throughout the book, have played a substantial role in Supreme Court confirmation hearings. But are we likely to continue to see this in the future? We address this question in two ways. First, we examine the growing diversity of the membership of the Senate Judiciary Committee and investigate the questioning behavior of female senators and senators of color. We show that these senators do not exhibit many of the same biases as their white, male counterparts. As a result, diversifying the makeup of the Judiciary Committee may help alleviate some of the implicit biases evidenced in our work. Second, we weigh the pros and cons of various reforms that could be taken to mitigate race and gender bias in this setting, including both institutional and individual changes in how the hearings are conducted. We conclude by reviewing the vast implications of a Supreme Court confirmation hearings process that inequitably plays out for nominees based on their race, ethnicity, and gender.

# ONE

## DIVERSIFYING THE FEDERAL COURTS

During a speech in 2001 entitled "The Supreme Court: A Place for Women," Ruth Bader Ginsburg spoke about how, historically, the Court was not a welcoming place for women. She detailed how when President Harry S. Truman began to give thought to appointing Florence Allen as the first woman to sit on the Supreme Court, he was met with resistance from all directions, including from members of the Supreme Court itself. Ginsburg recounted;

> President Truman was discouraged by the negative reaction of the Chief Justice (Fred Vinson) and the associate justices Vinson consulted. Allen had gained universal respect for her intelligence and dedicated hard work. But the Brethren feared that a woman's presence would inhibit conference deliberations where, with shirt collars open and sometimes shoes off, they decided the great legal issues of the day. (Ginsburg 2001, 423)

Allen would go on to predict, correctly, that a woman would not be appointed to the Court during her lifetime (Ginsburg 2001).

A similar fate would befall efforts to appoint the first justice of color to the Supreme Court. President John F. Kennedy considered appointing African American judge William Hastie to the Supreme Court in the early 1960s. By that time, Hastie had already served as a federal district and court of appeals judge and territory governor of the Virgin Islands. But Kennedy decided against picking Hastie, in part because "it was just too early" to put an African American on the Supreme Court (Kurland 1972, 200). It apparently remained "too early" until 1967, when President Lyndon B. Johnson finally changed the Court forever by nominating Thurgood Marshall, one of the heroes of the civil rights movement, to the high Court.

Judges Allen and Hastie's unsuccessful bids for a nomination to the U.S. Supreme Court were not isolated incidents; rather, they exemplify the challenges facing high-profile women and people of color in obtaining these rarified positions. As we explore in this chapter, the United States saw very little progress in adding women and people of color to the federal courts throughout much of the twentieth century. Even after women and people of color had overcome most voting barriers and were more or less ensconced in the legal profession, selection to the Supreme Court and other federal courts continued to be out of reach for nearly all lawyers who were not white men.

Judicial trailblazers like Allen and Hastie nonetheless laid important groundwork for later nominations, even though they were not ultimately selected to serve on the Supreme Court. With judges like Allen and Hastie on the federal bench, politicians, other judges, and the public more generally had access to a broader, more inclusive view of what a judge looks and sounds like. As we will see throughout this chapter, though, the diversification of the federal judiciary took a long time and moved slowly. There were long gaps between when the first women and people of color were appointed to the lower federal courts and when they finally achieved representation on the Supreme Court. And nearly every early appointment or potential appointment required a significant lift from the nominating White House. None of this, in other words, has been easy.

We begin our discussion of these issues by examining efforts made by presidents to diversity the Supreme Court in terms of its racial and gender composition. To do this, we recount the experiences of women and people of color who were considered for positions on the Court, including both those who were and were not appointed. Next, we examine the ways in which female nominees and nominees of color are treated differently with respect to various aspects of their confirmations, such as Senate votes supporting their nominations. We then turn to discussing broader efforts to diversify the federal bench, focusing on the confirmation process for nominees to the federal district courts and courts of appeals. This background provides important insight into the racial and gender makeup of the Supreme Court since these courts tend to function as auditioning grounds for potential Supreme Court appointees. We close this chapter with a discussion of why diversity matters for the federal judiciary and the Supreme Court.

## DIVERSIFYING THE SUPREME COURT

To many Americans, Thurgood Marshall and Sandra Day O'Connor are the most famous Supreme Court "firsts," but their stories are just part of the broader effort to diversify the U.S. Supreme Court. Figure 1.1 shows the Supreme Court's racial, ethnic, and gender diversity from 1939 to 2022. It plots all personnel changes across those years involving women and people of color serving on the Court. The vertical axis represents the number of female justices and justices of color on the Court, and the horizontal axis shows the year. Figure 1.1 displays data since 1939, the date of the first modern Supreme Court confirmation hearing. We could extend back in time to the very first justices selected in 1789, but, of course, the lines for that earlier era—the vast majority of the history of the Supreme Court—would be perfectly flat.

Figure 1.1 shows the selection of Thurgood Marshall in 1967, the Supreme Court's first person of color justice, by President Johnson. As we see, Marshall would remain on the Court until 1991, when he would be replaced by the second justice of color, Clarence Thomas. It would not be until 2009, with the arrival of Sonia Sotomayor, that the Court would see a woman of color on the bench or two justices of color serving simultaneously.

Figure 1.1 also illustrates the (lack of) gender diversity on the Court across time. It took until 1981, with O'Connor's nomination by President Ronald Reagan, for the Supreme Court to have a female justice. O'Connor would remain the only female justice on the high Court until Ruth Bader Ginsburg's appointment in 1993, and Ginsburg would be the sole female justice from 2006 to 2009. Justice Sonia Sotomayor joined Ginsburg in 2009, with Elena Kagan following her in 2010. Kagan's ascent to the bench took the number of female justices serving on the Court together to an all-time high of three. Following Justice Ginsburg's death in 2020, President Donald Trump appointed Amy Coney Barrett, keeping the number of female justices at three. With President Joe Biden's appointment of Ketanji Brown Jackson in 2022, the number of

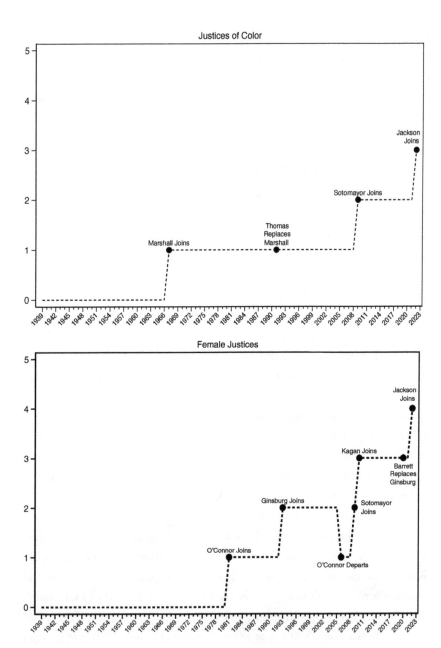

**FIGURE 1.1.** Number of U.S. Supreme Court Justices of Color and Women Justices Serving from 1939–2022

female justices serving together reached an all-time high, as did the number of justices who are people of color.

The selection of Marshall and O'Connor followed the diversification trends in professional settings across the country. As we will see, their appointments also allowed presidents to keep campaign promises and achieve personal and partisan political goals. Neither Marshall nor O'Connor, though, were the earliest women or people of color actively considered for the high Court. Over the twentieth century and into the twenty-first century, presidential administrations increasingly included nonwhite male candidates on their "short lists" for Supreme Court vacancies. In the pages that follow, we examine the stories and politics surrounding some of the short-listed women and people of color, including those who were eventually selected, for Supreme Court nominations.

### Racial and Ethnic Diversity on the Supreme Court

The path to joining the U.S. Supreme Court for people of color was paved by William Hastie. Although he never became a Supreme Court justice, Hastie achieved a number of important "firsts" in the federal judiciary that helped clear the way for Thurgood Marshall, Clarence Thomas, Sonia Sotomayor, and Ketanji Brown Jackson to later join the Court.

Hastie graduated from Harvard Law School in the early 1930s. After graduation, he went on to a successful legal and judicial career. He first made judicial history in 1937, when he was appointed by President Franklin D. Roosevelt to a judgeship on the District Court of the Virgin Islands (Hutchinson 1997). This made him the first African American to sit as a federal judge. Hastie would serve in that position for just two years, leaving to work in academia and as a civil rights attorney, where he would work alongside Thurgood Marshall, Charles Hamilton Houston, and others using the legal system to fight racial segregation (Anonymous 2004).

After a brief stint as the territory governor of the Virgin Islands (he was appointed to that post by President Truman in 1946), Hastie was selected by Truman in 1949 to serve as a judge on the U.S. Court of Appeals for the Third Circuit. While Hastie was eventually confirmed to this position, making him the first African American Article III federal judge,[1] he faced an uphill confirmation battle. The Senate delayed Hastie's nomination for more than six months, which at the time was an unprecedented delay. The delay resulted in a lapsed appointment, which in turn led Truman to appoint Hastie to the Third

Circuit through a temporary recess appointment. Truman then renominated Hastie to the Third Circuit during the next Congress (Dawson 2017; Stubbs 2016; Ware 1984).

The delay in Hastie's confirmation was largely the work of Senator James Eastland (D-MS), the chairman of the Senate Judiciary Committee. Eastland, an adamant segregationist who would go on to harass Thurgood Marshall at his hearing, was "dead set" against Hastie's Article III nomination (Ware 1984, 236). Unfortunately, Eastland was not alone in his hostility: Hastie's nomination faced "vehement" opposition of "unprecedented proportions" on account of his race, his affiliation with the National Association for the Advancement of Colored People (NAACP), and his track record of working to desegregate institutions and society (Ware 1984, 226).

Hastie was considered for seats on the Supreme Court in both 1949 and 1956, and then again in the early 1960s (Caldwell 1978; Goldman 1997). Notably, he made it as far as President Kennedy's shortlist in 1962. Hastie's nomination was pushed by President Kennedy's attorney general (and brother), Robert Kennedy. Robert Kennedy even met with the House and Senate Judiciary Committee leaders about the possible nomination. But as Eastland was the Senate Judiciary Committee chair, his resistance to Hastie loomed large, as did a more general concern about how Hastie might be treated by members of the Senate during what promised to be another bruising confirmation hearing (Hutchinson 1997).

Sitting members of the Supreme Court also opposed Hastie's candidacy. Chief Justice Warren was reportedly "violently opposed" to Hastie's nomination. Justice William O. Douglas, one of the Court's most liberal members, lamented that Hastie would vote with the Court's conservatives (Epstein et al. 2007) and argued that Hastie was "sort of a pedestrian type of person" (Anonymous 2004, 1640; O'Brien 1986, 197).[2] Despite all this, even toward the end of the nomination process, Robert Kennedy maintained his allegiance to Hastie, acting as his primary champion in the president's inner circle. Robert Kennedy argued that having an African American on the Court would be beneficial to the country and believed Hastie to be the best choice (Hutchinson 1997). Ultimately, however, Hastie would be passed over for a seat on the high Court in favor of a close ally of President Kennedy, Byron White, who served on the Court until 1993.

President Kennedy also was the first president to consider Thurgood Marshall for a Supreme Court nomination (Overby et al. 1994). Kennedy made numerous promises in his presidential campaign to appoint qualified Black Americans to high government positions. Marshall was an obvious and visible choice to fulfill those promises, having argued thirty-two cases before the Supreme Court and helping to alter virtually every corner of America's civil rights landscape (Overby et al. 1994). But this time it was Robert Kennedy who objected to putting Marshall on the Supreme Court, arguing that it would be too politically costly (Perry 1991). So in 1961 President Kennedy instead appointed Marshall to the Second Circuit Court of Appeals. Even this lower court appointment proved to be too much for some senators, however. By the time Marshall was finally confirmed to the Second Circuit by the full Senate in a 54–16 vote, his appointment, like Hastie's, had been delayed for nearly a year (Dawson 2017).

It would be President Johnson, Kennedy's vice president and successor, who would ultimately elevate Marshall to the high Court. Some describe Johnson's management of the Marshall Supreme Court appointment as "chess-like"; Johnson was a man who generally got what he wanted, and what he wanted was Marshall on the Court (Brown 2017). The process began in 1965, when Johnson convinced Marshall to leave the Second Circuit to become the solicitor general of the United States. The solicitor general is the U.S. government's chief attorney at the Supreme Court, and the position is often a stepping stone to a seat on the Court (Fried 1991; Nicholson and Collins 2008).[3] The Senate easily confirmed Marshall as solicitor general (Overby et al. 1994). As solicitor general, Marshall added fourteen victories (arguing nineteen cases during his tenure) to his record before the Supreme Court (Glass 2018a). It was clear that Johnson "fully intended" to appoint Marshall to the Court and that he "believed that a black man had to be appointed to that body" (Overby et al. 1994, 844).

But doing so would require a vacancy to fill. To facilitate that, Johnson asked Ramsey Clark, son of Associate Justice Tom Clark, to become the U.S. attorney general. By appointing Clark as attorney general, Johnson hoped (knew) that the conflict of interest between a son as attorney general and a father as a Supreme Court justice would compel Justice Clark to prematurely retire (Brown 2017). This is exactly what happened. With Justice Clark's resignation in hand, Johnson had the vacancy he needed. Within twenty-four hours of Clark's resignation, on June 13, 1967, Johnson nominated Marshall to the Supreme Court (Overby et al. 1994). When Johnson made his formal appointment of Marshall, he famously said that it was "the right thing to do, the right time to do it, the right man and the right place" (Brown 2017).[4]

Marshall's nomination received plenty of criticism. Because of his civil rights work, including arguing *Brown v. Board of Education* (1954) before the Supreme Court, Marshall was deemed "public enemy number one" in the South (Haygood 2015a). But the criticism also came from the left. Some Eastern Ivy League lawyers and far-left student groups did not think Marshall was "liberal" or "brilliant" enough for the Court (Bland 1973, 109). The theme of many attacks on Marshall was "to define the nominee as a dangerous, activist, subversive individual who might possibly damage the nation irreparably through an erosion of constitutionally protected rights" (Parry-Giles 1996, 376). As we will see in the later chapters of this book, Marshall's confirmation hearings also included controversial, racially tinged rhetoric.

The Johnson administration did everything it could to push Marshall's nomination through the Senate, both for Marshall's sake and for Johnson's legacy and upcoming reelection campaign. The White House told Marshall not to speak with the press while his nomination was pending and to avoid controversial or harsh comments (Haygood 2015b). Before the final Senate vote, Johnson convinced twenty senators who would have likely voted against Marshall to instead not vote at all. Johnson argued that if they voted against Marshall, the Johnson administration would not be able to help the senators in their next reelection campaigns (Haygood 2015a, 2015b). With this "extremely powerful" persuasion, Johnson made the final vote look a lot more favorably skewed than it otherwise would have been. The Senate's vote on the nomination was 69–11 rather than the 69–31 it would have been if these senators had voted. The historic first had an immediate and important effect: the year after the Senate confirmed Marshall to the Court, African American applications to law schools "skyrocketed" (Haygood 2015a).

Justice Marshall retired from the Court on June 28, 1991. His retirement created President George H. W. Bush's second opportunity to nominate a justice. For his first choice, he had picked an uncontroversial judge from New Hampshire, David Souter, for the seat Justice William Brennan vacated in 1990. Souter's exquisite moderation had left more conservative Republicans anxious for a "true" conservative nominee to fill any new vacancy. This put President Bush in a tough position when Justice Marshall stepped down. As explained in the *New York Times* on the day Marshall announced his retirement:

> In making his choice, Mr. Bush will have to balance pressure to cement even further the conservative grip on the Court with equal pressure to appoint a black justice at a time when the President is struggling with Congress over civil rights issues and is anxious to send a message of conciliation to blacks and other critics of his civil rights record. (Rosenthal 1991)

It was only three days later that President Bush announced the nomination of the one man he presumably thought would help him thread this needle: forty-three-year-old Clarence Thomas.

Thomas had been on Bush's radar for some time, including as a potential selection for Brennan's seat, but his nomination was not a foregone conclusion— President Bush considered other people of color and women for Marshall's seat. Potential nominees included four Hispanic men: Ricardo Hinojosa, Emilio Garza, Ferdinand Fernandez, and Jose Cabranes. Of these, the most serious consideration appears to have been given to Emilio Garza, a fifty-seven-year-old Fifth Circuit judge (ABC News 2006; Perry 1991). Looking toward the upcoming 1992 reelection campaign, leaders in the Bush administration recognized the "political advantages of appointing a Hispanic . . . since important states as California, Texas, and Florida had large populations of Hispanic voters. But the ideal Hispanic candidate proved elusive" (Mayer and Abramson 1994, 170). Bush also had two women on his shortlist: Edith H. Jones and Pamela A. Rymer (Nemacheck 2007; Perry 1991).

The immediate reaction to the Thomas pick was mixed. The NAACP opposed his confirmation. The organization disagreed with Thomas over the role of institutional racism in Black American lives and found his judicial philosophy to be "inconsistent with the historic positions taken by the NAACP" (Miller 2005, 183). During Thomas's Senate Judiciary Committee hearings, the NAACP urged the Senate to put "reason above race, principle above pigmentation, and conscience above color" (Miller 2005, 184). But there was also plenty of support for Thomas. Thirteen Democratic senators announced support for Thomas during the confirmation process (Hutchings 2001). This was important, because the Democrats controlled the Senate at the time, so a successful nomination would require at least some Democratic support. Conservatives, as expected, "greeted the nomination with delight" (Dowd 1991), undoubtedly in part because, like the Bush administration, they recognized "what a paralyzing predicament a conservative black nominee would present to liberal Democrats" (Mayer and Abramson 1994, 170). Despite rejecting some or many of Thomas's views, prominent Black elites and local leaders, such as Virginia governor Douglas Wilder, Reverend Joseph Lowery of the Southern Christian Leadership Conference, and poet Maya Angelou, also supported Thomas (Hutchings 2001). And while the NAACP opposed Thomas's confirmation, some high-profile individual members of the organization, including its previous chairwoman Margaret Wilson, did support him (Miller 2005).

The complex dynamics of a Black conservative nominee facing a Democratically controlled Senate became even more intense when sexual harassment allegations emerged against Thomas. The allegations, made by his former employee at the Department of Education and the Equal Employment Opportunity Commission, Professor Anita Hill, became public after the Judiciary Committee had finished questioning Thomas but before the nomination had been reported out to the full Senate. Under pressure to address Hill's allegations, the Democrats, led by Judiciary Committee Chair Senator Joe Biden (D-DE), reopened the hearings to take testimony on the matter from Hill and Thomas. We will return to this special session, including the racial and gender dynamics within and surrounding it, in greater detail in Chapter 7. For now, we note that the allegations altered the final vote on Thomas's nomination, changing what seemed likely to be confirmation by a significant and largely bipartisan vote to confirmation by a mainly partisan and narrow one. The final vote on Thomas was held on October 15, 1991, with a bare majority of 52 senators voting in favor of his confirmation.

For nearly twenty years, Justice Thomas was the only person of color serving on the Supreme Court. That changed in 2009, with the confirmation of Justice Sonia Sotomayor. With Sotomayor's appointment, the Supreme Court for the first time would see two justices of color serving simultaneously, and the first female justice of color. Like many modern justices, Sotomayor had a distinguished lower federal court judicial career before being nominated for the high Court. She was a federal district judge for the Southern District of New York from 1992 to 1998 and a federal appellate court judge for the U.S. Court of Appeals for the Second Circuit from 1998 to 2009. In her legal career and during her time as a judge in the lower federal courts, Sotomayor was recognized for her "intelligence, assertiveness, and organization" (Marrero-Otero 2011, 185). So when David Souter announced his retirement from the Supreme Court in 2009, Sotomayor was Obama's "presumptive front-runner" to fill the vacancy (Rosen 2009). The increasing Hispanic population in the United States and its "critical voting block" in the 2008 election (and future elections) also likely influenced Obama's selection of Sotomayor (Johnson 2011). She received a well-qualified rating from the American Bar Association (ABA)—an important signal of how she was likely to fare in the Senate (Sen 2014; Smelcer, Steigerwalt, and Vining 2012)—and was confirmed by a largely partisan vote of 68–31.

No woman of color had previously been nominated, much less confirmed, to sit on the Supreme Court. As such, Sotomayor's story cannot be exclusively situated in histories of either person of color or female nominees (Cassese 2019; Collins 1990; Crenshaw 1989). But as happened with race for Marshall and Thomas, Sotomayor's ethnicity became a major point of discussion and strategy during her confirmation saga. Sotomayor was strongly supported among Hispanic Americans, with one 2009 poll indicating that 74 percent of Hispanic Americans supported her confirmation, compared to just 54 percent among Americans overall (Steigerwalt, Vining, and Stricko 2013). Sotomayor also received endorsements from Hispanic interest groups, including the Hispanic Bar Association, the U.S. Hispanic Chamber of Commerce, and the Mexican-American Legal Defense Fund (Steigerwalt, Vining, and Stricko 2013). Conservative media pundits, in contrast, criticized Sotomayor as "an anti-white liberal judicial activist," a "reverse racist," and not likely be able to meet the "demanding standard" for a justice (Buchanan 2009; Barr 2009; Rosen 2009).

Ketanji Brown Jackson, the Court's second female nominee of color, joined the Court in 2022 following her lengthy service as a federal lower court judge (including the U.S. District Court for the District of Columbia from 2013 to 2021 and the U.S. Court of Appeals for the District of Columbia from 2021 to 2022). As a 2020 candidate for president, Joe Biden said that he was "looking forward to making sure there's a black woman on the Supreme Court, to make sure we in fact get every representation" (CBS News 2020). In another nod to the political considerations of Supreme Court appointments, Biden's pledge to finally put a Black woman on the Court came during the primary debate in South Carolina, where, according to exit polls, African Americans made up 56 percent and women 59 percent of eventual voters during the 2020 state Democratic primary (Clement et al. 2020; Martin 2020). Biden took the first chance he had to fulfill that promise, nominating and appointing Jackson to the vacancy created in 2022 by the retirement of Justice Stephen Breyer.

Even before Biden announced the selection of Ketanji Brown Jackson, Republican senators and prominent conservatives suggested that the nominee would not be qualified (Serwer 2022). For instance, Senator Roger Wicker (R-MS) said she would be a "beneficiary" of affirmative action (Swire and Stracqualursi 2022). And Illya Shapiro of the Cato Institute, a libertarian think tank, wrote, in a series of tweets that were eventually deleted, that Biden's nominee would be a "lesser black woman" who "will always have an asterisk attached" (Taaffe and Gingerich 2022).

Following Jackson's nomination, the attacks would continue. Conservative Fox News host Tucker Carlson used his platform to mount an attack against Jackson by mocking her name and casting doubt on her qualifications. He went as far as to suggest the Biden administration was hiding the results of her law school admissions test (the LSAT, which she took as an undergraduate student at Harvard):

> So is Ketanji Brown Jackson, a name that even Joe Biden has trouble pronouncing, one of the top legal minds in the entire country? We certainly hope so, it's Biden's right, appointing her is his one of his gravest constitutional duties. So it might be time for Joe Biden to let us know what Ketanji Brown Jackson's LSAT score was. Wonder how she did on the LSATs, why won't he tell us that? (Waldman 2022)

To our knowledge, no prior nominee had been pressed (by the media or otherwise) for their LSAT score as a means of proving their status as a "top legal mind."[5] Despite these and other challenges, Jackson was successfully confirmed to the Court in April 2022 by a close vote of 53–47. Just three Republican senators joined the 50 Democrats to cast votes to confirm Jackson: Susan Collins (R-ME), Lisa Murkowski (R-AK), and Mitt Romney (R-UT).

### Gender Diversity on the Supreme Court

Florence Allen never sat on the Supreme Court but was instrumental to diversifying it in terms of the gender of its justices. Sex-based discrimination in voting became unconstitutional in the United States in 1920, following passage of the Nineteenth Amendment. Just two years later, Allen was elected as the first female justice to sit on the Ohio Supreme Court (Jefferson and Johnson

2020, 22). Allen would go on to earn a number of other achievements in the legal and political fields. She was nominated by President Franklin D. Roosevelt to the U.S. Court of Appeals for the Sixth Circuit in 1934 and was unanimously confirmed by the Senate. Until the 1940s, Allen was the only female Article III federal judge, and one of just a few female appellate court judges in the entire country. So it is not a surprise that she also was the first woman to receive serious shortlist consideration from a White House for a Supreme Court appointment (Jefferson and Johnson 2020).

As Jefferson and Johnson (2020) document, Allen was first shortlisted for the high Court by President Franklin D. Roosevelt. She continued to be a serious contender through the Truman administration, but President Truman's successor, Dwight D. Eisenhower, was reportedly less interested in her. President Eisenhower focused his Supreme Court appointments on justices whose views "reflect a middle-of-the-road political and governmental philosophy" (Goldman 1997, 124). Allen was not that. She was a vocal member of the female suffrage movement and a loyal Democrat who ran for numerous political offices in the 1920s, even while serving on the Ohio Supreme Court.[6]

Later presidents would seriously consider nominating other women to the high Court, including Soia Mentschikoff (considered by Presidents Kennedy and Johnson), Sylvia Bacon (considered by Presidents Richard Nixon and Gerald Ford), and Carla Hills and Cornelia Kennedy (both considered by President Ford) (Jefferson and Johnson 2020). None of these women were ultimately chosen, however, for a variety of reasons. President Ford selected the perceived moderate John Paul Stevens in 1975 instead of Carla Hills to fill the seat vacated by Justice Douglas—a decision Ford may have later regretted (reflecting on his 1976 election loss, Ford apparently said that "a woman might have helped, but who can say") (O'Brien 1991, 111). The handwritten notes on Ford's shortlist, shown in Figure 1.2 and prepared by Attorney General Edward Levi, indicate that Kennedy and Hills were late additions to another all-male list. No Supreme Court vacancy arose during President Jimmy Carter's single term, but had he had the opportunity, he may well have selected Shirley Hufstedler, an appellate judge then sitting on the Ninth Circuit Court of Appeals (Biskupic 2005).

From Allen to Kennedy to Hufstedler, these shortlisted women were successful and qualified legal thinkers, even if they were never nominated for the high Court. Mentschikoff, who was one of the first women to be named partner at a Wall Street law firm (Bowman 2014), was described as "an outstanding

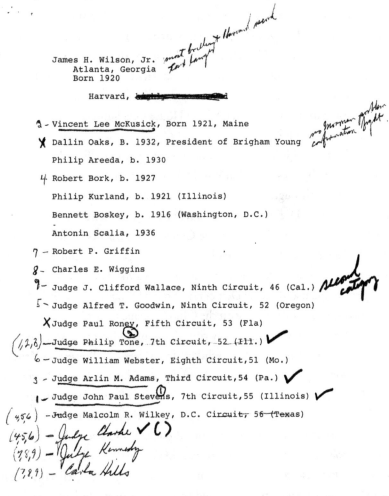

**FIGURE 1.2.** President Ford's Shortlist for the Seat Vacated by William Douglas in 1975

woman" (Jefferson and Johnson 2020, 39). Hufstedler, who former colleagues called "brilliant," "incisive," and "the best and brightest," was praised for "her reasoning and its persuasiveness" as a federal appellate judge (Ninth Circuit Public Information Office 2016). But probably the most famous shortlisted woman prior to the O'Connor selection was Mildred Lillie, considered for a seat on the Supreme Court by President Nixon and his attorney general, John Mitchell.

Nixon and Mitchell saw numerous benefits in selecting Lillie for one of the two open Supreme Court seats created in 1971 by the retirements of Justices John Marshall Harlan II and Hugo Black. In a conversation with Nixon in September 1971, Mitchell said: "There are just two women who could fit . . . your philosophy. And I'm a little doubtful about one of them [Sylvia Bacon] because we don't have all of the record. The one that, obviously because she's been on the court for so many years, has expressed her philosophy, is this Judge [Mildred] Lillie in California. She was on the Superior Court out there. She's now on the intermediate Court of Appeals. She's fifty-five years old. She is solidly backed by Reagan, the prosecutors . . . and well recommended by all of the police officers" (Dean 2001, 110).

Nixon and Mitchell's conversation about Lillie reveals the tension in their deliberations. Nixon did not want to put a woman on the Court: "I don't think a woman should be in any government job whatever. I mean, I really don't. The reason why I do is mainly they are erratic. And emotional" (Dean 2001, 113). At the same time, though, Nixon recognized the political advantages of putting a woman on the Court: "If a woman were appointed, it could affect one or two percent, who would say because he appointed a woman, I am for him. Now it's as cold as that. [It would show everybody] that we care about women. My God, we've put a woman on the Supreme Court. . . . So I lean to a woman only because, frankly, I think at this time, John, we got to pick up every half a percentage point we can" (Dean 2001, 113). So long as her conservative credentials checked out, it thus seemed that Nixon was ready to appoint Lillie to the high Court. But the Nixon administration received word in mid-October 1971 that Lillie would be rated as "not qualified" by the American Bar Association, which had been rating judicial nominees since 1957.[7] This created a major risk that Lillie's nomination would fail in the Senate, so Nixon and his staff abandoned plans to nominate her. The open Supreme Court seats would ultimately be filled, as had every seat before, by two men: Lewis Powell and William Rehnquist.

But as the debate in the Nixon White House made clear, by the late 1970s it was a matter of when—not if—a woman would sit on the Supreme Court. President Carter may not have had the opportunity to take this step, but his commitment to diversifying the lower federal courts likely provoked Reagan's 1980 presidential campaign pledge to put a woman on the Court himself. In the waning days of his presidential campaign, Reagan came out strong on this issue, noting that he was very aware that "appointments can carry enormous symbolic significance," that "it is time for a woman to sit among our highest jurists," and that he intended to "appoint a woman to the Supreme Court" (Cannon 1980).

Reagan would win the election and make good on his promise. In July 1981, Reagan announced Sandra Day O'Connor as his choice to replace retiring justice Potter Stewart. O'Connor was a "conservative, cloth-coat-Republican" with significant political experience (McFeatters 2006, 14). This service included working as an aid to Republican Barry Goldwater's presidential campaign in 1964 and two terms in the Arizona Senate (McFeatters 2006). O'Connor also had a lengthy legal and judicial resume. She attended Stanford Law School (graduating third in her class) and went on to serve as the Arizona assistant attorney general. Later, she would serve as an Arizona state trial court and appellate court judge.

O'Connor's nomination generated some criticism and skepticism, including thousands of negative messages sent to the White House (Jefferson and Johnson 2020, 95). Much of that opposition came not from Democrats, but from the far-right wing of Reagan's own Republican Party, including from activists Jerry Falwell, Howard Phillips, and Peter Gemma (Glass 2018b). O'Connor also faced extensive criticism for what was perceived as her lack of judicial experience and her political background, even though earlier male judges—such as Earl Warren—had similar backgrounds as elected officials with limited or no judicial experience.

For Reagan, however, both O'Connor's qualifications and her background were appealing. As one author put it, "She was definitely from the conservative wing of the Arizona Republican Party, but nothing in her judicial opinions was controversial enough to derail her—or cause the White House embarrassment" (McFeatters 2006, 9). Reagan worked for the nomination behind the scenes, writing to and calling Republican senators to assure them about his confidence in O'Connor's judicial philosophy and pro-life views (Goldman 1997, 316). During O'Connor's hearing, California judge Joan Dempsey Klein detailed O'Connor's legal and judicial career and described her judicial opinions as "concise and cogent, orderly, lucid and logical."[8] Judge Klein continued by explicitly calling out the double-standard O'Connor was being held to:

> Judge O'Connor's experience on the appellate bench serves to prepare her for the work ahead. By contrast, at least 15 of the prior 101 Supreme Court justices had no judicial experience whatsoever, or a bare minimum prior to

their appointments. These numbers include three of the justices currently serving with distinction.[9]

Reagan's pressure campaign for O'Connor's appointment succeeded, and the Senate unanimously confirmed O'Connor to the Court in relatively short order.

O'Connor would serve as the Court's only female justice until 1993, when President Bill Clinton appointed the nation's second female justice, Ruth Bader Ginsburg. With the Ginsburg pick, Clinton secured a legacy for himself by nominating the second woman to the Supreme Court, and the first who had been made a career of advocating for women's rights, including successful litigation before the Supreme Court. The ABA rated Ginsburg as "well qualified," the highest rating available. This made Ginsburg the first female nominee or prospective nominee up to that point to receive this high mark (O'Connor had only been given a rating of "qualified").

In July 2005, almost twenty-five years after her historic appointment, Justice O'Connor announced her plan to retire, pending the confirmation of a new associate justice to replace her. Mirroring the debate that happened when Justice Marshall retired, there was a great deal of discussion about whether President George W. Bush should appoint another female justice to replace her. First Lady Laura Bush wanted that result: "I know that my husband will pick somebody who has a lot of integrity and strength" she said, and "I would really like him to name another woman" (BBC 2005).[10] Despite these appeals, Bush choose a man, federal judge John Roberts, to replace the retiring O'Connor. O'Connor herself was not entirely pleased. Following the announcement, she said "He's good in every way, except he's not a woman" (Desmon 2005).

When Chief Justice Rehnquist died on September 3, 2005, President Bush found himself with an unexpected second nomination, this time for the position of chief justice. Bush responded by withdrawing the existing Roberts nomination so Roberts instead could be nominated for the Chief Justice spot. Although unanticipated, this gave Bush a second chance to retain O'Connor's seat as the "woman's seat." The Bush administration, in an internal search run by White House Counsel (and longtime Bush lawyer) Harriet Miers, considered but rejected several women serving on the federal courts of appeals. As one outlet reported, "Some [of the female judges] were appealing but intellectually undistinguished (Edith Brown Clement), others were too politically inflammatory to get through the Senate (Janice Rogers Brown and Edith Jones), others were dismissed as too moderate (Consuelo M. Callahan of the Ninth Circuit)" (Toobin 2007, 331).

Unhappy with these choices, Bush and his inner circle decided to nominate Miers herself. President Bush had great trust and confidence in her—in the press conference formally announcing her nomination, he said "I know her heart. I know her character" (Bush 2005). Moreover, leading Democrats in the Senate, including Harry Reid and Patrick Leahy, supported Miers as a nominee (West 2005). But the conservative wing of the Republican Party was concerned. Unlike many nominees before her, Miers did not have judicial writings or political activities to provide hints as to her views on issues important to them (West 2005). With many Senate Democrats poised to vote in favor of the nominee, Miers likely would have been confirmed, but her nomination created a risk of substantial discord within the Republican Party. Rather than allow that to happen, Miers withdrew herself from consideration (Toobin 2007). In the wake of this internal Republican dispute, a more traditional (white, male, federal judge) conservative nominee, Samuel Alito, was nominated and successfully confirmed for O'Connor's seat. So by January 2006, the U.S. Supreme Court was once again back to having just one sitting female justice. That justice—Justice Ginsburg—would serve as the only female justice on the Court from early 2006 to Sonia Sotomayor's confirmation in the summer of 2009.

Sotomayor's selection was not a surprise. All signs had indicated that Obama would select a woman to fill David Souter's seat. Most prominently, the four people he interviewed for the Supreme Court vacancy were all women (along with Sotomayor, this included Solicitor General Elena Kagan, Homeland Security Secretary Janet Napolitano, and U.S. Courts of Appeals judge for the Seventh Circuit, Diane Wood) (Martin and Allen 2009). His pick, of course, was Sonia Sotomayor. As noted above, Sotomayor's confirmation battle, along with her legal and judicial journey more generally, sits at the intersection of race and gender. Sotomayor herself has said, famously, that, "based on [her] gender and [her] Latina heritage," she may be a different type of judge than others (Sotomayor 2002, 92). As Johnson (2011) observed, "the race and gender of Justice Sotomayor proved to be a volatile mix" during her confirmation battle, leading to dramatic differences at her hearing "in tone and substance from those of the first two women Justices" (106), a point we will return to throughout this book.

The year after Sotomayor's confirmation, following the retirement of John Paul Stevens, Obama would put another woman, his then solicitor general and friend Elena Kagan, on the Supreme Court. Prior to her service as the solicitor general, Kagan was a law professor and dean at Harvard Law School and also had worked as an advisor to the Clinton administration. Kagan's nomination did generate some controversy. Like Harriet Miers, she had no judicial experience and had not authored any appellate court opinions. She also had limited courtroom experience (she had none until her recent year as solicitor general). In addition, some members of the more liberal wing of the Democratic Party worried that Kagan, as an "Obama person" was too centrist (van Diggelen 2010).

None of these concerns would derail Kagan's nomination. Like Sotomayor, Kagan received a "well qualified" rating from the ABA and was confirmed to the Court by a mainly partisan vote in the Senate of 63–37. One Democrat, Ben Nelson from Nebraska, voted against her confirmation. Five Republicans—Susan Collins (R-ME), Lindsey Graham (R-SC), Judd Gregg (R-NH), Richard Lugar (R-IN), and Olympia Snowe (R-ME)—voted for her. With Elena Kagan's confirmation secured, the U.S. Supreme Court had for the first time in its history three sitting women judges. President Obama reflected on this important moment: "[Elena Kagan's confirmation is] a sign of progress that I relish not just as a father who wants limitless possibilities for my daughters, but as an American proud that our Supreme Court will be a little more inclusive, a little more representative, and more reflective of us as a people than ever before" (Obama 2010).

The next opportunity to expand and diversify female representation on the Court would come in the fall of 2020, following the death of Ruth Bader Ginsburg. Having already placed two conservative white men on the Supreme Court, President Trump was eager to seat a third justice on the Court, especially since the Republican Party controlled the Senate and the 2020 election was just weeks away. Trump did not waste any time. The day after Ginsburg died, Trump announced: "I will be putting forth a nominee next week. It will be a woman" (BBC 2020). Politics were definitely on the president's mind as he considered the nomination. Some commentators observed that nominating a woman could help Trump appeal to female voters—something he had struggled to do (BBC 2020). Others observed that a female conservative nominee could avoid the spectacle of an all-male majority overturning *Roe v. Wade*, the case recognizing a constitutional right to abortion that had long been a target of conservatives. Trump considered several women, including Barbara Lagoa, a Cuban American former Florida state appellate and state supreme court judge who Trump had placed on the Eleventh Circuit Court of Appeals in late 2019. Speaking about Lagoa in September 2020, Trump ticked through her various advantages, saying: "She's excellent. She's Hispanic. She's a terrific woman from everything I know. . . . We love Florida" (Cole, de Vogue, and Polantz 2020).

The other serious candidate for this vacancy was Amy Coney Barrett. Barrett was a 2017 Trump-appointed federal appellate court judge whom Trump had seriously considered for the Supreme Court seat that eventually went to Brett Kavanaugh. Unlike Harriet Miers, Barrett had strong conservative credentials. She was a Notre Dame Law School graduate who had later joined the Notre Dame faculty as a professor, had served as a law clerk to conservative icon justice Antonin Scalia, and her many prior writings and speeches highlighted her Catholic faith and pro-life views (Hollis-Brusky and Wilson 2020; Wolf and Groppe 2020). She also had close ties to the Federalist Society, which was used by the Trump administration to help select its judicial nominees (Hollis-Brusky 2015; Talbot 2022). Additionally, Barrett was rated as "well qualified" by the ABA. She won the nod from President Trump, and her nomination was confirmed by the Senate along party lines, 52–48, just days before the 2020 election would remove Trump from office and flip partisan control of the U.S. Senate. As the first Republican-appointed woman to be nominated to the high Court since 1981, she was celebrated in conservative circles as an important role model for conservative girls, demonstrating that all women, not just liberal women, "deserve the opportunity to rise."[11]

As we have detailed already, the most recent Supreme Court appointee, Ketanji Brown Jackson, continued this trend toward increased gender diversification on the high Court. Upon taking her seat in 2022, Jackson, for the first time in history, brought the U.S. Supreme Court's number of sitting female justices to four.

## BROADER FEDERAL JUDICIAL DIVERSITY EFFORTS

As this history shows, female nominees and nominees of color have had to overcome significant barriers before joining the ranks of U.S. Supreme Court justices. One way they, like other judges, have overcome these barriers is to serve for a time on the lower federal courts, which often serve as "auditioning grounds" for potential future elevation to the U.S. Supreme Court (Black and Owens 2016; Bowie, Songer, and Szmer 2014; Dancey, Nelson, and Ringsmuth 2020;

Haire and Moyer 2015). Indeed, of the justices confirmed to the Supreme Court from 1970 to the present, only four of them (Powell, Rehnquist, O'Connor, and Kagan) never served as lower federal court judges. Given the importance of these courts as gateways to a Supreme Court nomination, we next examine presidents' lower court judicial selection agendas and strategies.

We begin by diving more deeply into efforts by various presidents to place women and people of color on the lower federal courts. Figures 1.3 and 1.4 provides this information from the administrations of Franklin D. Roosevelt through Donald Trump, for both the federal district courts and the courts of appeals.[12] As these data show, there were very few nonwhite, nonmale judges selected across all of the pre-Carter presidential administrations. From 1933 to 1976, there were over 800 judges selected to the federal district courts, and only 6 were women. During that same period nearly 250 courts of appeals judges were appointed, with just 2 being women. The numbers are slightly better for judges of color but are still dismal: 28 judges of color were selected to the federal district courts in this time, and only 5 were selected for the courts of appeals.[13]

It was Jimmy Carter who decisively broke through this stagnation. President Carter was very open about his commitment to diversifying the federal courts. In his State of the Union address in 1979, he spoke about his plans:

> I am determined . . . to increase the low representation on the Federal bench of women, Blacks, Hispanics, and other minorities. These goals are within our reach, if we work together cooperatively and recognize the importance our country places in the selection of these new judges. (Carter 1979)

Carter faced multiple hurdles in his efforts to diversify the lower courts, including the difficulties posed for nonwhite male nominees by the ABA's ratings process. In particular, research shows that female nominees and nominees of color systematically receive lower ABA ratings than white, male nominees, likely because their paths to the bench take different routes than white men (Clark 2003; Haire 2001; Sen 2017). Despite these challenges, during his four years in office Jimmy Carter far surpassed the combined efforts of all prior presidential administrations in bringing more genuine diversity to the federal courts. During his single term as president, he appointed 29 women and 44 people of color to the federal district courts and 11 women and 12 people of color to the federal courts of appeals.

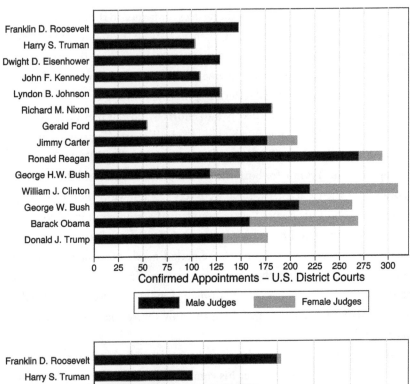

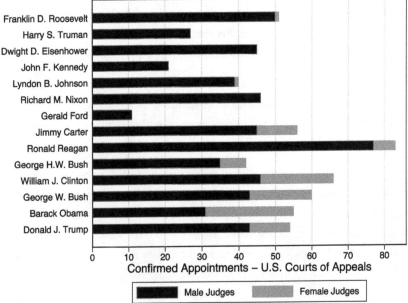

**FIGURE 1.3.** Gender Distribution of Confirmed Judges to Federal District and Circuit Courts, by Appointing President (Roosevelt to Trump)

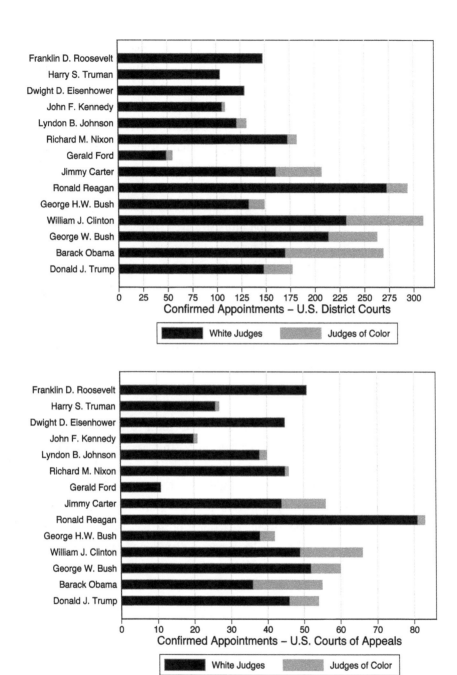

FIGURE 1.4. Race and Ethnicity Distribution of Confirmed Judges to Federal District and Circuit Courts, by Appointing President (Roosevelt to Trump)

What led to Carter's determination and ultimate success in adding people of color and women to the federal bench when prior administrations had done so little? Undoubtedly, multiple factors were at play, but two are particularly noteworthy for our purposes: political will and political opportunity. Carter clearly had the political will to diversify the federal courts. He had a sincere interest in achieving more societal representation in the judiciary (Clark 2003), and his focus on appointing women and person of color judges aligned with the priorities of the Democratic Party and its voting base (Carter 1995; Clark 2003).

Perhaps more importantly, though, Carter had the political opportunity to make good on his judicial selection promises. Even the most aggressive presidential appointment strategy will have no effect without judicial vacancies to fill. Luckily for Carter, the stars aligned for him on this front. After years of pleas from the federal judiciary to relieve the burdens imposed by burgeoning federal court caseloads (Barrow, Zuk, and Gryski 1996), Congress finally passed legislation in 1978 authorizing a large number of new federal judgeships. The timing—with a unified, Democratically controlled Congress and a Democrat in the White House—was not coincidental. Elected officials are not blind to the political stakes behind staffing the judiciary (Barrow, Zuk, and Gryski 1996) and often try to do so in ways that provide a partisan advantage to their political party. The Omnibus Judgeship Act enacted in October 1978 created 117 new district court and 35 new circuit court judgeships. This was "an unprecedented number of new positions in the Federal judiciary" that increased "the size of the Federal bench by over one-quarter" (Carter 1978b). Carter would be able to use these new seats to achieve his political and personal goals. "This act," he wrote in a signing statement accompanying enactment of the legislation, "provides a unique opportunity to begin to redress another disturbing feature of the Federal judiciary: the almost complete absence of women or members of minority groups" (Carter 1978b).

Subsequent presidents did not always follow Carter's lead in prioritizing gender and racial diversity in judicial appointments, as Figures 1.3 and 1.4 show. While there was no going back to the days when the number of nonwhite male appointees could be counted on one hand per presidential administration, a partisan difference is apparent in the data. Knowing that they could "score points" with left-leaning voters (Scherer 2011, 612) by diversifying the federal courts, Democratic presidents after Carter would be much more focused on appointing women and judges of color than would their Republican counterparts.

Presidents Clinton and Obama used strong political rhetoric about the need for judicial diversification and worked to back up their words with action. Clinton, in his 1992 presidential campaign, promised that his judicial selections would help make the courts "look like America" (Scherer 2011, 601). Obama lauded his focus on inclusiveness in his judicial appointments: "We have appointed judges all across the country who understand the importance of keeping the doors of justice open to everybody . . . and by the way, the most diverse Federal appointees that we've ever seen" (Obama 2011). President Biden's early lower federal court nomination efforts, which are excluded from Figures 1.3 and 1.4,[14] showed a concerted commitment to placing women and people of color on the federal district and circuit courts. In 2021 alone, the Biden administration saw 32 women and 27 people of color successfully confirmed to the lower federal courts. This represented a stunningly high 80 percent and 67.5 percent of the administration's confirmed judicial picks, respectively, in its first year, more than any previous president.

Prioritizing judicial diversity has presented a more complicated issue for Republican presidents in the post-Carter era. President Reagan committed to putting a woman on the Supreme Court during his 1980 election campaign, and he fulfilled that promise with the appointment of Sandra Day O'Connor. But Reagan did not extend this commitment to judicial diversity to the lower federal courts. Incremental increases in focus on judicial diversity can be observed with subsequent Republican administrations (compare, for example, Reagan's 10 percent female judicial appointments to George W. Bush's 20 percent[15]), albeit at a slower pace than their Democratic administration counterparts.

Despite these differences between Republican and Democratic presidents in their efforts to diversify the federal courts, it is worth pausing to acknowledge the bigger picture seen in these figures: the cross-time increase in number of women and people of color in the federal judiciary has had an effect in successfully bringing more diversity to the federal courts. Today, the United States "has the most diverse federal bench to date" (Sen 2017, 369). Because experience on the federal bench is something that historically many presidents have looked for in their Supreme Court nominees, this increased diversity on the lower federal courts means the current pool of female candidates and candidates of color who can count this important experience among their formal credentials is historically deep.

## WHY JUDICIAL DIVERSITY?

As we conclude this chapter, we step back to consider why gender and racial diversity, or the lack thereof, matters for the judiciary. Doing so helps highlight what is at stake, now and in the future, when elected officials decide whether to appoint more women and people of color to high-profile courts like the U.S. Supreme Court. It can also provide insight into the consequences of a Supreme Court confirmation process that unfolds differently for women and people of color than it does for other nominees.

First, a descriptively diverse judiciary can increase the legitimacy of and support for our judges and judicial institutions. Increasing trust and confidence in courts and the legal system helps ensure that people seek to resolve their disputes in those forums, follow the decisions made by courts and judges, and support their continued existence (Gibson and Caldeira 2009; Gibson, Caldeira, and Spence 2003; Means, Eslich, and Prado 2019). But, at the same time, evidence indicates that institutions like courts, along with the outcomes and processes within them, "cannot be legitimate when certain social groups remain systematically excluded" (Clayton, O'Brien, and Piscopo 2018, 113). As Goldman (1978, 253) noted, "a pluralistic judiciary is more likely to win the confidence of the diverse groupings in a pluralistic society . . . [than is] a judiciary overwhelmingly composed of one race, one social class, and one political orientation." Social science research confirms the presence of this effect: an increase in representation of African Americans on the courts results in a strong positive growth in African American views of the institutional legitimacy of the courts (Scherer and Curry 2010) and the equal presence of women in decision-making bodies "grants legitimacy to political decisions and democratic procedures" (Clayton, O'Brien, and Piscopo 2018, 126).[16] This descriptive, representation-based positivity can also extend to perceptions of individual judges. Badas and Stauffer (2018), for example, find that shared gender and racial identity between Supreme Court nominees and the public increase support for the nominee, even in the face of sharp ideological distance.

Political figures echo this idea when defending their efforts to diversify the judiciary. When he nominated Ketanji Brown Jackson to the Supreme Court in 2022, President Biden remarked, "For too long, our government, our courts, haven't looked like America. I believe it's time that we have a court that reflects the full talents and greatness of our nation" (Ruger 2022). Similarly, in 2013, Senior

White House Counsel Chris Kang argued that the Obama administration's efforts to appoint more women, people of color, and other underrepresented groups to the courts was important "because a judiciary that better resembles our nation instills even greater confidence in our justice system, and because these judges will serve as role models for generations of lawyers to come" (Kang 2013).[17] Years before, Attorney General Robert Kennedy argued that putting William Hastie on the Supreme Court in the early 1960s would have a similar effect that would extend well beyond the borders in the United States: "I thought it would mean so much overseas and abroad" if an African American were on the Supreme Court (Cray 1997, 383).

In addition to these legitimating effects, there also can be behavioral differences among judges based on their gender, race, and ethnicity. As Harris and Sen (2019, 242) note: "Judges have policy preferences, shaped by factors that include their race, gender, and most importantly, ideology or partisanship (which themselves could be influenced by race or gender). In other words, judges are nuanced decision makers who bring their preferences and experiences to bear on what are sometimes difficult questions lacking objectively correct answers." Social science evidence confirms race and gender differences among judges may affect decision making on the court, particularly in certain contexts.[18]

For judges of color, Washington details why Black judges might behave differently from other judges:

> The Black jurist has a unique vantage point from which to critique the quality of the justice in America both in terms of the justice system's daily operations and of the development of the law within the system. Unlike their nonminority counterparts on the bench, most Black jurists have not only battled injustices in society on behalf of their clients as lawyers, but, in order to attain their positions, most have themselves had to confront and conquer racism in the legal system. (Washington 1994, xviii)

Means's qualitative study of Black judges in the United States uncovers powerful evidence of the "personal experiences and perspectives" of Black judges emerging in decision making (2016, 199). Means reveals that Black judges "consciously and unconsciously behaved in ways that represented Black interests and Black Americans" (199). Quantitative studies further indicate that in certain cases Black judges decide differently from their white colleagues.[19] This includes race and other employment discrimination cases (Boyd 2016; Chew and Kelly 2009;

Morin 2014; Weinberg and Nielsen 2012), Voting Rights Act cases (Cox and Miles 2008), pretrial detention in criminal cases (Boldt et al. 2021), disability cases (Boyd and Rutkowski 2020), and affirmative action cases (Kastellec 2013).

A similar pattern of findings of consistent differences in judicial decision making has been found in studies comparing female and male judges, particularly in cases involving sex discrimination claims. This research reveals that female federal trial and appellate judges are more supportive of sex discrimination plaintiffs relative to their male judge counterparts (e.g., Boyd 2016; Boyd, Epstein, and Martin 2010; Davis, Haire, and Songer 1993; Farhang and Wawro 2004; Haire and Moyer 2015; Peresie 2005). Justice Ginsburg put it well when asked if some discrimination cases might turn out differently as the Court adds more women: "I would suspect that, because the women will relate to their own experiences" (Bazelon 2009). Given how many legal standards turn not just on the facts of what happened, but what the facts mean in in a particular context—was the behavior "reasonable," was it severe or pervasive enough to create a "hostile" environment—it is not surprising that people with different backgrounds and life experiences will bring different insights to these determinations.

There also is emerging evidence that race and gender can play a role beyond the voting patterns of individual judges. This includes studies finding powerful collegial effects in settings where multiple judges serve on courts together. Often termed "panel effects," this research indicates that, again in race- and gender-related cases where we would expect judges to bring unique information to the cases before them, the presence of a Black (female) judge on a multijudge panel can cause her white (male) colleague to rule in favor of the minority party's position on the race or gender-specific issue before them (Boyd, Epstein, and Martin 2010; Cox and Miles 2008; Kastellec 2013; Mak et al. 2021).[20] In addition to this type of panel effect, Haire and Moyer (2015) and Moyer et al. (2021) reveal that female judge–authored appellate court opinions are longer than those authored by their male counterparts. And, in trial courts, Boyd (2013) finds that cases supervised by female judges settle more often and more quickly than those supervised by male judges. Boyd argues that this effect may stem from women in managerial positions being "more likely than their male colleagues to foster collaboration, bridge building, and negotiation in their case management environments" (Boyd 2013, 211).

The implications of these studies are clear: "More women on the courts would lead to more decisions favorable to women" and "more people of color on the courts would lead to more decisions favorable to people of color" (Harris and Sen 2019, 241–42). Or, to put it slightly differently, more diverse courts may result in fewer cases in which exclusively white and male judges issue decisions opposed to the interests of women and people of color. But the effects may well go further. As one study put it, the "push to make the federal bench more diverse, both in terms of gender and ethnicity" may result in the Supreme Court having a "more inclusive institutional culture" that extends to the attorneys, parties, and outputs of the Court (Gleason, Jones, and McBean 2019, 514–15).

## CONCLUSION

In this chapter, we have explored the history and importance of diverse representation on our federal courts, and the Supreme Court in particular. In the following chapters, we turn to a more direct examination of the Supreme Court confirmation hearings, the treatment of female nominees and nominees of color in that process, and the potential consequences of treating these nominees differently than their white or male counterparts. Specifically, a selection process for Supreme Court justices that plays out unequally for nominees based on race or gender can affect who gets selected, can undermine selected justices' effectiveness among their colleagues, and can even extend to public perceptions of the justices and the Court itself. We turn to these issues next, beginning with an in-depth examination of how the process begins.

# TWO

# THE SUPREME COURT CONFIRMATION PROCESS

On September 18, 2020, Supreme Court Justice Ruth Bader Ginsburg died at her home in Washington, D.C., from complications related to pancreatic cancer. Appointed by President Bill Clinton in 1993, Ginsburg was only the second woman to serve on the Supreme Court. During her tenure on the nation's highest bench, Ginsburg was a leader of the Court's liberal bloc and wrote key opinions in cases related to gender and mental disability discrimination, environmental protection, voting rights, and religious freedom (Wolf 2020). Outside of the Court, Ginsburg was a pop culture and feminist icon who appeared in children's books, film, and television and was affectionately known as the "Notorious R.B.G." (Aridi 2020).

The death of a sitting Supreme Court justice is far from a rare event—almost as many justices have died in office as have retired (Stolzenberg and Lindgren 2010; Ward 2012). Yet, replacing Ginsburg was complicated by the fact she died only 46 days from the 2020 presidential election between Republican incumbent Donald Trump and Democratic challenger Joe Biden. At issue was a "norm," used by the Republican-controlled Senate just four years earlier, that the Senate would not move Supreme Court appointments forward in a presidential election year (in that case, following the death of Justice Antonin Scalia 270 days before the 2016 election). At the time of Scalia's death, Senate Majority Leader Mitch McConnell (R-KY) had explained that the purpose of this was to ensure that the American people have a say in the appointment of the next Supreme Court justice, which they could express through their vote in the upcoming presidential election. The result of this in 2016 was that President Obama's nomination of Merrick Garland to replace Scalia in 2016 was not considered by the Senate (Elving 2018).

If the Republican-controlled Senate followed its 2016 standard in 2020, the Senate would not act on any presidential nomination to replace Ginsburg until after the November 2020 election. But that is not what happened. Instead, the Senate quickly took up President Trump's nomination of U.S. court of appeals judge Amy Coney Barrett, which was made only eight days after Ginsburg's death. After being nominated on September 29, Barrett's nomination was immediately moved to the Senate Judiciary Committee, which engaged in rigorous and occasionally contentious questioning of the nominee on October 13–14. During the almost twenty hours of questioning, Barrett was interrogated on a wide range of topics, including her views on the Affordable Care Act, reproductive rights, presidential pardons, and the scope of the Second Amendment. While Republicans saw her performance at the hearings as demonstrative of her keen intellect and sound judicial temperament, Democrats were frustrated by her refusal to answer many of their questions (Collins 2020; Walsh 2020).

Following these hearings, a Judiciary Committee vote was scheduled for October 22. The Senate's rules require that at least two members of the minority party, plus a majority of the Committee, be present in order to proceed on a nomination (Senate Judiciary Committee 2021). In an attempt to block Barrett's confirmation, all ten Democrats on the Judiciary Committee boycotted the Committee vote. As a result, the Judiciary Committee did not have a quorum to move Barrett's nomination forward to the whole Senate. Nonetheless, Committee Chair Lindsey Graham (R-SC) ignored the quorum rule and held the vote, noting about the Democrats on the Committee: "That was their choice. It will be my choice to vote the nominee out of committee. We're not going to allow them to take over the committee" (Hannon 2020).

With all 12 Republicans on the Committee supporting Barrett's confirmation, the nomination was unanimously (because the Democratic senators had boycotted the vote) advanced to the full Senate (Fandos 2020a; Zhou 2020). Democrats made a variety of procedural motions in an attempt to stop the nomination from coming to a vote. Their efforts failed, and on October 26, Barrett was confirmed to be an Associate Justice of the Supreme Court by a

52–48 vote. All 47 Democrats voted in opposition. They were joined by a single Republican, Susan Collins of Maine (Fandos 2020b).

This overview of the confirmation of Amy Coney Barrett highlights three important aspects of the Supreme Court selection process, each of which we explore more fully in this chapter. First, it illustrates the prominence of the Senate in Supreme Court confirmations. Although the Constitution's charge to the Senate regarding judicial appointments is very short—to provide "advice and consent" to the president—over time, the Senate has institutionalized its role, leading to the contemporary confirmation process (Collins and Ringhand 2016). In the modern era, not only does the Senate get the final say on who sits on the Supreme Court, it does so in a way that is highly visible to the American people. The multiple days of testimony before the Judiciary Committee provide the public with their fullest opportunity to get to know nominees and to see how nominees are treated by members of the Committee. And the public takes advantage of these occasions, with millions of Americans watching gavel-to-gavel coverage of the hearings, and even more catching recaps of the hearings on television, the internet, radio, and in newspapers (Farganis and Wedeking 2014, 100; Joyella 2020).

Second, the events leading to Barrett's confirmation demonstrate the significance of partisanship in the selection of Supreme Court justices. The confirmation process is marked by party-based teamwork, in which senators who share the president's party affiliation work closely to advance a shared agenda, while senators from the opposite party endeavor to stymie the president's appointments (e.g., Epstein and Segal 2005; Lee 2008, 2009). Both Republicans and Democrats use these strategies. Republican teamwork was on full display in 2016 during their boycott of Garland's nomination, and the Democrats worked together in their opposition to Barrett's nomination throughout her confirmation process.

Finally, Barrett's confirmation illustrates the growing diversity of the Court. As noted in the previous chapter, it was not until 1981 that a woman was appointed to the Court and more than a decade longer for Justice Ginsburg to become the Court's second female member. Yet in the 2000s, four women were appointed to the Court, including the Court's first Latina justice, Sonia Sotomayor, and Ketanji Brown Jackson, the Court's first Black female justice. As we show, this growing emphasis on judicial diversity is evident in many ways that, together, reflect evolving senatorial concerns about the roles of women and people of color in American society. This can be seen not only in how senators treat nominees, but also in the types of questions asked and answered at the confirmation hearings.

This chapter proceeds as follows. We begin by discussing how vacancies occur and then explain the president's role in the confirmation process. We next turn to the Senate. In doing so, we highlight the first "modern" Supreme Court confirmation hearing, held in 1939, and explore how the role of the Senate Judiciary Committee in the process has evolved since that time. We then explain how—and why—the senators use the hearings to grill nominees on a host of issues, including their constitutional preferences, positions on the pressing issues of the day, opinions about iconic cases, and personal backgrounds. Next, we show how race and gender have always been relevant to the confirmation hearing process, even when female nominees and nominees of color were themselves absent. We do this by examining the ways race and gender have been discussed at the hearings over time. We also examine how nominees like Barrett and Clarence Thomas, whose appointments bring ideological diversity to the subset of women and people of color serving on the Court, can change how race and gender are discussed during the hearing process. We conclude with a brief discussion of the factors that influence senatorial support or opposition to Supreme Court nominees.

## HOW DO VACANCIES ARISE?

While much has changed about the U.S. Supreme Court over its history, from the number of sitting justices to the location of its courtroom to the diversity of its membership, the basic process of how justices are selected has remained remarkably stable. As outlined in Article II, Section 2 of the U.S. Constitution, the president has the "Power, by and with the Advice and Consent of the Senate, to . . . appoint . . . Judges of the Supreme Court." In other words, the president is tasked with nominating justices, after which the Senate steps in to "consent" to the appointment.

Presidents and senators of both parties have, historically, devoted substantial time and attention to their respective roles in this process. This should come as no surprise, given the combined importance of the Supreme Court's salient role in shaping U.S. legal policy and its justices' longevity in their positions once confirmed. Article III of the Constitution grants Supreme Court justices tenure "during good Behavior", and the justices tend to stick around for many years. Since 1970, justices have served, on average, for more than twenty-five years. With newly appointed justices beginning their tenure on the Court at younger and younger ages, the average length of their service is likely to continue to rise. All of this means that Supreme Court nominations generate significant attention and concern from everyone involved in the process, as well as from large segments of the American public (Nemacheck 2017).

But presidents and senators do not get to appoint Supreme Court justices whenever they want: they must wait for a vacancy. There are four main ways Supreme Court vacancies arise.

First, vacancies can be created through legislation. The size and composition of the federal courts, including the Supreme Court, is not specified in the Constitution, and both have been changed several times throughout our history. As originally structured by Congress in 1789, the Supreme Court had 6 members. In 1801, the lame duck Federalists in Congress responded to Democratic-Republican Thomas Jefferson winning the presidency by reducing the size of the Court to 5. However, once in office, Jefferson restored the number of seats on the Supreme Court back to 6 (Orth 2002). Congress changed the number of Supreme Court justices again in 1807 (to 7), in 1837 (to 9), and in 1863 (to 10).

These changes appear to have been made for a combination of institutional concerns (keeping the number of justices aligned with the number of federal circuits), partisan concerns (giving copartisan presidents additional opportunities to appoint justices), and the pre–Civil War politics of slavery (to first keep and then reduce a proslavery majority on the antebellum Court) (Graber 2007; Presidential Commission on the Supreme Court 2021). In the wake of the Civil War, Congress changed the number of seats on the high Court yet again. Skeptical of President Andrew Johnson, who assumed the presidency after the assassination of President Abraham Lincoln, the Reconstruction-era Congress reduced the number of seats from 10 to 7. It was then restored to 9 in 1869, after the election of Union war hero Ulysses S. Grant (Abraham 2008; Presidential Commission on the Supreme Court 2021; Zeldon 2007). It has remained at 9 ever since, with the last serious effort to change the number of justices coming in 1937, when President Franklin D. Roosevelt unveiled his ultimately unsuccessful "court packing" plan.

The second way a Supreme Court vacancy can occur is through a judicial impeachment. Under Article II of the U.S. Constitution, Supreme Court justices, as well as other federal judges, hold their offices "during good behavior." Article I, Section 2, sets out the process through which federal judges can be impeached (presumably for bad behavior). As with other federal officers (like the president) the removal of a Supreme Court justice through this process requires a simple majority vote in the House for the impeachment and a two-thirds majority vote in the Senate for conviction and removal.

To date, no Supreme Court justice has ever been removed from office through this process. The effort that got the furthest involved staunch Federalist Samuel Chase, who was impeached by the Jeffersonian-Republicans in 1804 in response to his bitterly partisan, anti-Jefferson rhetoric. He was impeached in the House of Representatives along a party line, but the Senate failed to convict him (Perlin 2010; Rehnquist 1992). Chief Justice Earl Warren also was the target of impeachment activists—as a nominee, Clarence Thomas recounted memories of seeing "Impeach Earl Warren" signs along the highways when he was a child (New York Times Archives 1991)—but those efforts did not get very far. Justice Abe Fortas faced a more serious threat of impeachment over allegedly improper financial dealings, but resigned in 1969 before the movement could take root (Neumann 2007). More recently, calls to impeach Justice Brett Kavanaugh following his contentious confirmation hearing failed to gain momentum (Montanaro 2019).

The third way Supreme Court vacancies arise is through the death or retirement of a sitting justice. Over the nation's history, about 45 percent of Supreme Court justices have died in office (Stolzenberg and Lindgren 2010). As highlighted in the opening of this chapter, the most recent vacancy to occur on the Court due to the death of a sitting justice was in 2020 when Justice Ginsburg passed away. This paved the way for President Trump to nominate Amy Coney Barrett as her successor.

The fourth and most common way seats open up on the Court, though, is through retirements, which create about 47 percent of all vacancies (Stolzenberg and Lindgren 2010). Some justices, most recently Justice David Souter, retire while relatively young—Souter retired at age seventy after serving less than two decades on the bench. More commonly, though, justices seem to, or are encouraged to, strategically time their retirements to maximize their time on the bench while minimizing the risk that an ideologically opposed president or senate will fill their seat (Ward 2012). This typically means retiring when they share the partisan affiliation of the incumbent president (Stolzenberg and

Lindgren 2010). The 2021 retirement of Justice Stephen Breyer (appointed by Democrat Bill Clinton) during the first two years of Democrat Joe Biden's first term fits this pattern. So do the retirements of Justice Anthony Kennedy (appointed by Republican Ronald Reagan) during the first two years of Republican Donald Trump's presidency, and Justice Sandra Day O'Connor (also appointed by Reagan) halfway through Republican George W. Bush's second term.

However, justices are not always able to time their retirements to ensure a like-minded successor. Despite somewhat desperate calls for her resignation during President Obama's second term, Ginsburg (appointed by Clinton) did not retire. Her daughter told the press after the justice's death that her mother had expected Democratic candidate Hillary Rodham Clinton to win the 2016 election, and wanted the first female president to name her successor (Bazelon 2020).[1] When Trump won the election instead, Ginsburg reportedly hoped to outlast him, saying just days before her death that her "most fervent wish" is that she "would not be replaced until a new president was installed" (Totenberg 2020). Chief Justice William Rehnquist and Justice Scalia, both appointed by Republican presidents, also both died in office. The seats of each of these justices were filled by presidents from the same party as the president who appointed them, although as discussed above, in Justice Scalia's case that came about only because the Republican-controlled Senate allowed the seat to remain vacant for a record 422 days until it could be filled by President Trump (Abramson 2017).

### HOW ARE VACANCIES FILLED?

Once a vacancy emerges on the Supreme Court, what happens next? In most cases, the initial phase of the appointment process rests entirely with the White House. This does not mean presidents act alone, however. Instead, they frequently seek advice from their closest advisors, such as the U.S. attorney general, White House legal counsel, and others. They also may consult with Senate party leaders, interest groups like the Federalist Society, and even sitting justices (Abraham 2008; Rutkus 2010). Often this process begins before a vacancy even arises, meaning many (if not most) presidents come into the White House with at least some idea of who they will consider nominating to the high Court should the opportunity arise.

This review is quite intensive. Presidents commonly conduct preliminary background checks, and White House lawyers pore over the writing, speeches, and decisions of potential candidates, at times preparing comprehensive reports for presidential review (Collins and Ringhand 2013a). Presidents today also usually personally interview their finalists. These interviews can be consequential. According to numerous reports, Stephen Breyer was passed over for the first Supreme Court vacancy arising under Bill Clinton because of a personal interview gone badly. Breyer had been in a fairly serious bicycle accident several days before the interview and was in the hospital when he was supposed to go to Washington to meet with the president. Despite being in pain and recovering from surgery, Breyer made the trip. He perhaps should not have bothered. Clinton purportedly found him "heartless," and decided to nominate Ruth Bader Ginsburg instead (Mears 2014). Despite this bad luck, history was kind to Breyer: while passed over for this nomination, he did get the nod from Clinton just a year later when the next vacancy arose.

These consultations are eventually formalized into a list of potential names—a *short list*. George W. Bush's staff began working on his short list almost immediately after Bush's election, in anticipation of Chief Justice Rehnquist's retirement. Donald Trump went even further, releasing and publicly discussing during his 2016 presidential campaign the short list of candidates he would consider if given the opportunity to fill the seat being held open by an obliging Senate. When Trump won the 2016 election, he made good on his promise to select a Supreme Court nominee from his list, announcing shortly after his inauguration that Neil Gorsuch was his pick to serve on the high Court. Many of Trump's other short-listed names also were nominated to fill assorted judicial positions that arose over the course of his presidency.

The next step in the process for nominees under serious consideration is to undergo extensive background checks. This includes an investigation into the candidate's background by the Federal Bureau of Investigation and in-depth scrutiny of the candidate's professional work and record by the Department of Justice and other White House officials. As part of this process, the candidate fills out an extensive questionnaire touching on just about every aspect of their personal and professional past. Investigators also conduct interviews, read all of the candidate's judicial decisions and other writings, and dig deep into the candidate's public and private lives (Rutkus 2010). This process helps presidents make their final selections by familiarizing them with the candidate's approach to a variety of issues. It also is designed to reveal any red flags lurking in a candidate's background, especially in regard to things that could damage a nominee later in the process.

## What Is a President Looking For?

After all of this information about potential candidates has been gathered, the president has to make a choice about who to nominate. Presidents have almost boundless discretion in making this choice. Unlike for many other federal offices, the Constitution puts no restrictions on who can sit on the Supreme Court. There are no age, residency, or work experience requirements. Indeed, Supreme Court justices do not even need to be attorneys.

Despite this, there are several things most presidents seem to look for. This includes experience as a judge, a strong judicial record (including an evaluation of how many times their decisions were reversed by higher courts), prior service in government and especially in the executive branch, and the prestige of their educational background and previous professional accomplishments (Epstein, Knight, and Martin 2003; Epstein and Segal 2005; Collins and Ringhand 2013a). Presidents in the past also have been mindful of the American Bar Association's rankings of potential candidates, based on the candidate's perceived integrity, judicial temperament, and professional competence, as "well qualified," "qualified," and "not qualified."[2]

In most cases, these criteria will generate dozens, if not hundreds, of names of individuals who are eminently qualified to take a seat on the high Court. Consequently, presidents cull their lists further by focusing on personal and political priorities. Most obviously, virtually all presidents want to select nominees who will be their ideological allies on the Court.[3] Presidents are usually careful to coach this search for ideological compatibility in terms of a nominee's approach to constitutional interpretation, although some presidents are surprisingly frank about the policy goals they want their nominees to advance.[4] The vast majority of the time, this focus on ideological compatibility results in presidents selecting copartisans to nominate to the Supreme Court. When the president does select a cross-party nominee, such as when Nixon appointed the conservative Democrat Lewis Powell, it often is because the pick is an ideological compatriot even if operating under a different party label (Epstein and Segal 2005, 60). Presidents also evaluate nominees in light of the electoral advantages they might bring to their political party, by, for example, selecting justices likely to uphold congressional copartisans' legislation or nominating candidates championed by factions within the president's party as a way to strengthen and unify the party (Epstein and Segal 2005, 57).

Nominees likewise can enhance the president's own electoral prospects. Today, doing this often means using Supreme Court nominations to cement electoral support among the key demographic groups that make up the president's electoral coalition. Historically, this has included not just race or gender considerations, but also geographical and religious considerations. For example, for many years, the Court had a "Jewish" and a "Catholic" seat, both of which represented important electoral groups various presidents were mindful to attend to. Geographical representation on the Court also has been a meaningful part of the selection process since the founding of the republic and continues to play a role today. Many commentators, for example, approvingly noted that nominee Neil Gorsuch would bring to the Court someone who "understands the West" (McConnell 2017). Similarly, many of those who urged President Biden to select Judge Michelle Childs as his first nominee argued that her South Carolina roots, as well as her public school education, would bring important representational benefits to the Court (Pellish and Swire 2022).

After the nominee has been selected, the final public role of most modern presidents in the process has been to hold a press conference formally announcing their choice and laying out the case for their nominee's confirmation. These presidential addresses usually focus on the candidate's strengths, qualifications, and life experiences. If the nomination is a historic "first," presidents usually tout that fact by highlighting a nominee's race or gender and framing their life stories of as success stories exemplifying the "American dream." For example, when President George H. W. Bush announced his selection of Clarence Thomas, he emphasized Thomas's upbringing in tiny Pinpoint, Georgia, deep in the Jim Crow South (New York Times Archive 1991). When Presidents Reagan and Clinton announced their nominations of O'Connor and Ginsburg, respectively, they both used the opportunity to celebrate their nominees' accomplishments as women entering their professional lives at a time that gave them, as women, less opportunity than that enjoyed by men. President Obama followed this pattern when he announced his nomination of Sonia Sotomayor by explicitly embracing an "only in America" narrative, framing her nomination as a celebration of "the greatness of a country in which such a story is possible" (Obama 2009).

## THE SENATE JUDICIARY COMMITTEE

After the president announces the nominee, the process moves to the U.S. Senate, which holds hearings and debates, and ultimately votes on the fate of Supreme Court nominees. Over the course of the nation's history, the Senate's role has become more formalized. At the country's founding, the Senate as a whole debated and voted on Supreme Court nominations. In relatively short order, in 1816, the Committee on the Judiciary was established and assumed formal responsibility for vetting judicial nominees (Rutkus and Bearden 2009). The Judiciary Committee now handles the early phase of the confirmation process for all Supreme Court and lower federal court nominations. As such, the Judiciary Committee is a coveted Committee assignment for senators (Bullock 1985; Lewis 2014; Miller 2020).

Senators on the Judiciary Committee frequently use their position on this prestigious Committee to raise their profiles among the American public, which can aid their reelection pursuits and future ambitions (Collins and Ringhand 2016; Schoenherr, Lane, and Armaly 2020). During the 2018 Kavanaugh confirmation hearings, a *New York Times* article discussed this as it related to potential 2020 presidential runs for Democratic Judiciary Committee members Senators Cory Booker (D-NJ), Kamala Harris (D-CA), and Amy Klobuchar (D-MN). "There is no time like a stately, nationally televised Supreme Court nomination hearing to grab the attention of the news media and amass valuable footage for future campaign commercials," the *Times* reported (Stolberg 2018). The Judiciary Committee also tends to be made up of senators with an interest in the law, and a large number of Committee members are attorneys (Bullock 1985). More recently, the Committee has become a battleground for highly salient "cultural war" issues, such as abortion and religious freedom, which has attracted senators whose constituents particularly prioritize those issues (Lewis 2014).

Like other congressional committees, the makeup of the Judiciary Committee is based on the partisan divide in the Senate. For instance, in 2022 (117th Congress), the Senate had 50 Democratic members (including two independents who caucused with the Democrats) and 50 Republican members. This translated to a Judiciary Committee made up of 11 Democrats and 11 Republicans, with Democrats heading the Committee since Vice President Kamala Harris, a Democrat who as vice president is also the president of the Senate, casts the deciding vote when the chamber is tied.

The significance of partisanship on the Judiciary Committee cannot be overstated, particularly in the modern era (Basinger and Mak 2012; Boyd, Collins, and Ringhand 2018; Shipan 2008). Same-party senators on the Committee act as a team, coordinating on almost all aspects of confirmations, often in consultation with Senate leadership (e.g., Lee 2008, 2009). This includes the decision whether to support a nominee, what to say in public about nominees, and, most visibly, the questions they ask of nominees at confirmation hearings. Of course, this is not to say that same-party senators always vote the same way—they do not. However, partisanship is one of the single most important factors explaining why senators vote the way they do on Supreme Court nominations (Epstein and Segal 2005; Shipan 2008).

Consider Senate Democrats' approach to the appointment of Amy Coney Barrett by Republican President Trump. Senate Minority Leader Chuck Schumer (D-NY) worked closely with Democrats on and off of the Judiciary Committee to coordinate opposition to the Barrett nomination. This included nearly daily phone calls to Committee members in an effort to focus Democratic confirmation hearing questioning on health care, reproductive rights, and other substantive issues in an effort to paint Barrett as someone willing to overturn the Affordable Care Act and undermine abortion rights. It also involved coordinating to avoid personal attacks on the nominee during the hearings, especially involving Barrett's public Catholic faith, which had been a subject of critical questioning during her confirmation hearing for the lower federal court.

Two years later, the Senate Republicans were similarly coordinated in their response to Democratic President Biden's nomination of Ketanji Brown Jackson. Republican Committee members' tactics included repeated questions on Jackson's judicial record of sentencing child pornography offenders and work as a public defender for Guantánamo Bay detainees. Outside of the hearing room, Republican senators consistently painted Jackson as soft on crime and extreme in her liberal positions. Senator Rick Scott (R-FL), who served as the chair of the National Republican Senatorial Committee, told reporters at a March 2022 leadership press conference that Jackson "seems to be very soft on sexual predators, people that have, you know, harmed our children" (Huey-Burns 2022). Just as had been the case with the Senate Democrats during the Barrett hearing, the Republican senators demonstrated classic party unity during the Jackson hearing.

Between the time a nomination is received in the Senate and the opening of the confirmation hearings, nominees typically make "courtesy calls" to meet with individual senators. This is an especially important function for senators who are not on the Judiciary Committee since it gives them perhaps their only opportunity to get to know nominees on a personal level (Collins and Ringhand 2013a). This period also marks the stage in which nominees fill out a lengthy questionnaire provided by the Judiciary Committee that covers topics including biographical information, financial disclosure statements, public writings and statements, services to the disadvantaged, potential conflicts of interest, and lists of the most significant cases the nominee participated in. Ketanji Brown Jackson's completed questionnaire was thirty-six pages long.

### *The Confirmation Hearings*

The most visible aspect of the modern Supreme Court confirmation process is the question and answer sessions held between the nominees and members of the Judiciary Committee (Collins and Ringhand 2013a, 2019; Watson and Stookey 1987). As prominent as they are today, though, these hearings were not always a part of the Committee's procedure. It was not until 1939 that one of President Franklin Roosevelt's nominees, Felix Frankfurter, first appeared before the Committee to take the type of public, unrestricted questions that today define the confirmation process for many Americans (Collins and Ringhand 2013a; Maltese 1998).

The story of why the Judiciary Committee decided to hold open public hearings in 1939 is, like the diversification of the federal bench described in Chapter 1, a story of how the increased democratization of American politics has changed the Supreme Court confirmation process. It began two years before the Frankfurter nomination, with the confirmation of another Roosevelt nominee, Hugo Black (Collins and Ringhand 2013a, 2016). Prior to his nomination, Black was a Democratic senator from Alabama, and the custom of senatorial courtesy assured him a quick and trouble-free confirmation—he was confirmed just five days after his nomination. However, to ensure this speedy confirmation, the Judiciary Committee debated the nomination in private and apparently ignored allegations of Black's connection to the Ku Klux Klan (KKK), a violent white supremacist organization. A week after Black's confirmation, journalist Ray Sprigle made those allegations public, revealing in the

*Pittsburg-Post Gazette* that Black had purportedly accepted and never revoked a lifetime membership in the KKK.

The story, for which Sprigle won a Pulitzer Prize, was explosive. Senators, the press, and the public questioned why the debate over Black's confirmation took place in secret. Allegations that the senators knew about his connection to the Klan and tried to cover it up shook the nation. Even though he had already received his appointment, Black gave a public radio address to try to tamp down the controversy. In the address, he acknowledged he had been a member of the KKK, but claimed that he no longer considered himself affiliated with the group (New York Times 1937a). Despite Black's address, the damage from his secretive confirmation process was done. Later that year, the ABA petitioned the Senate to hold open, public hearings—a proposal also supported by the press (New York Times 1937b). In response, the Judiciary Committee agreed to hold public hearings on the Court's next nominee to ensure greater public input and scrutiny in the confirmation process (Collins and Ringhand 2016). That nominee was Felix Frankfurter.

Although the Judiciary Committee moved to open hearings after the Black debacle, not all nominees following Frankfurter appeared themselves at the public hearings. It was not until 1955 that all nominees referred to the Judiciary Committee would routinely undergo open and public confirmation hearing questioning (Collins and Ringhand 2013a). The motivation for requiring all nominees to face this type of questioning was twofold (Collins and Ringhand 2016). First, it was an acknowledgement of the Court's growing role in American society, as evidenced by the Warren Court's salient and often controversial decisions in the areas of criminal procedure and civil rights and liberties. Second, it was a response to *Brown v. Board of Education*, decided in 1954. As a result of this landmark—but at the time contentious—decision, senators, the public, and the press wanted to interrogate nominees' perspectives on *Brown*, and what the case represented about the proper role of the Court in the American political system (Collins and Ringhand 2016; Farganis and Wedeking 2014). In short, the Committee answered calls for increasing the democratic accountability of the Supreme Court by subjecting nominees to more direct public scrutiny (Collins and Ringhand 2013a).

Since 1955, the Committee's hearing procedure has remained relatively consistent. The hearings typically begin with a presentation of the nominee by the nominee's home state senators, representatives, or other notable figures. The most recent nominee, Ketanji Brown Jackson, was introduced by retired federal judge Thomas Griffith and University of Pennsylvania law professor Lisa Fairfax. These opening procedures also routinely include a statement by the Committee chair, welcoming the nominee and outlining procedural details for the hearing, and opening statements by the other members of the Committee supporting the nominee or indicating the reasons they may oppose the nomination. Finally, the nominee makes an opening statement, which usually wraps up the first day of the hearings.

The next days are the question and answer sessions that have come to define the hearing process. Although the exact format and length of the hearings differs somewhat from nominee to nominee, in the past few decades hearings tend to proceed as follows. In the first round, each member of the Judiciary Committee is given thirty minutes to question the nominee. The chair of the Committee goes first, followed by the ranking member, who is the most senior member of the minority party on the Committee. The remaining senators question the nominee in order of seniority, alternating between majority and minority party members. After each senator has asked questions in the first round, there is usually a second round of questioning, during which senators are allocated a shorter amount of time for questions. Following this, there may be a third round of questioning, with even less time allocated to each senator. After the nominee questioning has ended, the Committee hears from outside witnesses, both supporting and opposing the nomination (Collins and Ringhand 2013a).

The rigorous questioning that nominees undergo serves several important purposes. First, it represents the primary moment of democratic accountability for potential Supreme Court justices. This occurs through the questions senators ask and the answers senators expect nominees to give. Importantly, senatorial interrogation of nominees closely tracks the salient issues of the day (Collins and Ringhand 2013a). For instance, in 2020, the country was in the middle of a global pandemic, with health care on the minds of most Americans (Saad 2020). Further, there was a pending Supreme Court case about the constitutionality of the Affordable Care Act, which provides health care to millions of individuals. Senators responded to this state of affairs by focusing on these issues at the hearing; specifically, by repeatedly asking Amy Coney Barrett about her views of the Affordable Care Act and the government's role in health care (Rogers 2020).

By asking nominees about the pressing issues of the era in which they were nominated, senators act as surrogates of the American people, channeling their concerns to nominees. And, senators expect nominees to use their answers to demonstrate that they fall within the constitutional mainstream of their era.[5] In recent years, this has meant, for example, embracing a basic constitutional right to privacy, rejecting de jure racial and gender discrimination, and endorsing an individual right to keep and bear arms (Collins and Ringhand 2013a). In this way, the answers nominees give, or do not give, can influence the fate of their nomination in the Senate (Collins and Ringhand 2013a; Farganis and Wedeking 2014).

Table 2.1 reports the most frequently addressed issues at the confirmation hearings, based on the issue categories developed by Collins and Ringhand (2013b) and the Comparative Agendas Project (2022). This table covers more than 42,000 questions and answers given at confirmation hearings from 1939

TABLE 2.1. The Issues Addressed at the Senate Judiciary Committee Hearings of Supreme Court Nominees, 1939–2022

| Issue | Percentage of Statements | Total Statements |
|---|---|---|
| Civil rights | 27.9 | 11,862 |
| Hearing administration | 18.9 | 8,048 |
| Nominee background | 14.5 | 6,186 |
| Judicial philosophy | 12.3 | 5,221 |
| Law, crime, and family | 7.5 | 3,200 |
| Government operations | 6.2 | 2,655 |
| Court administration | 3.1 | 1,321 |
| Labor and employment | 1.3 | 542 |
| Federalism | 1.2 | 511 |
| Other issues | 7.1 | 3,006 |
| Totals | 100 | 42,552 |

Statements represent questions asked and responses at confirmation hearings for senators and nominees. Issue areas representing less than 1 percent of the total column are combined into the "Other issues" category. This table excludes the special session hearings of Clarence Thomas and Brett Kavanaugh dedicated to allegations of sexual misconduct.

to 2022—the entire span of open, public confirmation hearings. The issue areas appear in the first column, the second column indicates the percentage of statements represented by each issue area, and the third column reports the total number of statements in each issue area.

As this table reveals, the most frequently discussed issue at confirmation hearings is civil rights, which accounts for almost one in every three questions and answers. The most common topics in the civil rights category include the right to privacy, freedom of speech and religion, racial discrimination, and gender and sexual orientation discrimination, respectively. As we show in the figures below, race discrimination has long been a part of the hearings, and gender discrimination became a significant part of hearing discourse starting in the 1970s. Thus, although the nominees appearing before the Committee were overwhelmingly white males, especially prior to the very recent past, issues of race and gender have nonetheless made frequent appearances in the senators' questions.

Following discussions of civil rights topics, the next most common issue area is hearing administration. This category captures statements, typically made by senators (and especially the Committee chair), having to do with administrative aspects of the hearings, such as scheduling, the timing of breaks, the order of questioning, submissions to the record, and the like. Questions about nominee background are the third most common area of questioning, constituting about 15 percent of statements. These statements involve the nominee's character, background, education, ethics, and family. About 12 percent of questions and answers relate to a nominee's judicial philosophy, the focus of Chapter 4. Senators frequently interrogate nominees on their judicial philosophies as a way to vet their competence regarding the core task of judging on the Supreme Court—how they would interpret the Constitution. Statements about law, crime, and family, which typically involve issues of criminal procedure, come next, at around 8 percent of all hearing dialogue. The most common questions in this category include those regarding the rights of the criminally accused, such as double jeopardy, search and seizure protections, due process rights, the right to counsel, criminal sentencing, and the like. About 6 percent of questions involve government operations, which most commonly involves questions about the relationships between the Supreme Court, the executive branch, and/ or Congress. Questions about court administration constitute about 3 percent of hearing discourse and typically involve asking nominees their opinions on issues of judicial pay, the size of the Supreme Court, the caseload of the Supreme Court, and other aspects of judicial administration. Labor and employment and federalism constitute about 1 percent of questions each, and often involve questions related to labor unions and employee rights (labor and employment) and the relationship between the federal government and the states (federalism). Issue areas constituting less than 1 percent of overall hearing discussion were combined into the "Other Issues" category, which includes questions and answers regarding topics such as health care, finance, national defense, and international affairs.

### *The Discussion of Race at the Hearings*

Figure 2.1 provides a closer look at attention to the issue of racial discrimination over time. Nominees are arrayed along the y-axis, and the x-axis represents the percentage of civil rights questions that involved discussions of racial and ethnic group discrimination.

As this figure makes clear, discussions of racial discrimination have long been a part of confirmation hearings. Indeed, even though Felix Frankfurter, the first nominee to take questions in an open, public confirmation hearing, was not asked specifically about racial discrimination, issues related to race nonetheless permeated his hearing (Ringhand 2010). Most notably, there was fierce opposition to Frankfurter in some circles because of his Jewish identity and upbringing in Austria. This was on full display when Allen Zoll, a far-right political activist and executive vice-president of the American Federation Against Communism, testified at the hearing against Frankfurter's confirmation, stating:

> There are two reasons why I oppose the appointment of Prof Felix Frankfurter to the Supreme Court of the United States. One is because I believe his record proves him unfitted for the position, irrespective of his race, and the other is because of his race. . . . The Jew has been fostering movements that are subversive to our Government. (Ringhand 2010, 797)

In addition, Frankfurter's hearing was laced with anticommunist, anti-immigration rhetoric. On this front, opponents portrayed Frankfurter as unfit for the Court because he was not a "true" American, but rather a foreign-born national who would sympathize with communists and other subversives and did not see the benefits of American isolationism (Ringhand 2010).

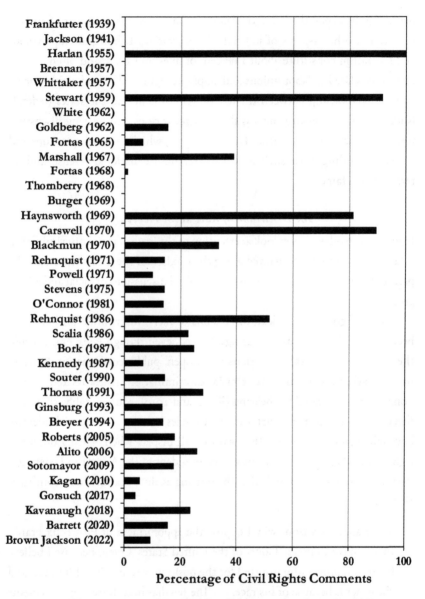

FIGURE 2.1. The Percentage of Civil Rights Comments Involving Racial Discrimination at the Senate Judiciary Committee Confirmation Hearings of Supreme Court Nominees, 1939–2022

Clement Haynsworth's hearing in 1969 initiated an era in which every subsequent nominee faced a goodly number of questions about racial discrimination. Prior to this, less than half of nominees received questions about racial discrimination, although some of those that did received a fairly large number of such queries. This was perhaps most notable at Thurgood Marshall's 1967 hearing, during which the discussion of race took an ominous tone. As noted in Chapter 1, Marshall, the Court's first African American justice, faced explicitly race-based hostility at his hearing (Carter 2021). Southern Democrats accused him of being anti-American and asked if he was "prejudiced against white people."[6] The tone of much of the questioning at his hearing was designed to make him appear ignorant or unfit for service on the high court (Carter 2021; Collins and Ringhand 2013a).

Substantively, race as a legal issue became prominent at the hearings after *Brown v. Board of Education* was decided in 1954. While now firmly entrenched in our constitutional canon, *Brown* was deeply controversial when first decided. The seniority system used in the Senate ensured that Southern Democrats were well represented on the Senate Judiciary Committee for years after *Brown* was decided, and those senators repeatedly used their position on the Committee to express their displeasure with the decision. In the aftermath of *Brown*, in the hearings of John Marshall Harlan (1955) and Potter Stewart (1959), this displeasure came in the form of pointed questions about justices "legislating" from the bench, the possibility that international human rights treaties (requiring racial equality) could "supplant" domestic law, and the need to interpret the Constitution in accordance with the original understanding of its framers (which was presumed to be tolerant of racial discrimination).

The senators' disapproval of *Brown* at these hearings was not subtle. Senator John McClellan (D-AR) told Stewart that he "wholly disagreed" with the *Brown* decision and needed to know Stewart's position on the case before deciding how to cast his confirmation vote.[7] When grilling Stewart about constitutional interpretation, Senator James Eastland (D-MS) told the nominee that, contrary to the Court's opinion in *Brown*, the justices in that case should indeed have "turned the clock back to 1868"[8] and upheld *Plessy v. Ferguson* (1896), the case that established the "separate but equal" doctrine permitting state-sanctioned racial segregation that *Brown* overruled. Recognizing that *Brown* was an extremely controversial issue in 1959, Stewart responded to Eastland's insistent questioning by refusing to take a position on the case, and instead giving the type of waffling response we today more frequently associate with questions about abortion and *Roe v. Wade* (Collins and Ringhand 2013a).

Overt opposition to *Brown* had tapered off by the 1970s. Instead, during the next three decades questions about racial discrimination focused on more contemporary issues. Affirmative action, for example, took center stage at Sonia Sotomayor's hearing in 2009. As a judge on the Second Circuit Court of Appeals, Sotomayor had joined a per curiam (unsigned) panel decision in a case involving the promotion process for firefighters in the City of New Haven, Connecticut. The case, *Ricci v. DeStefano* (2008), was brought by a group of male firefighters who had received top scores on a test the city had administered, intending to use it to make promotion decisions. When few women or people of color scored well on the test, the city commissioned a study to determine whether the test was a valid measure of job performance. When the study determined it was not, the city, citing concerns about its potential liability under Title VII of the Civil Rights Act of 1965, decided against certifying the exam results. The men who had done well on the test, including Frank Ricci and Ben Vargas, sued, claiming the city had discriminated against them in violation of Title VII.

The Second Circuit panel, including Justice Sotomayor, interpreted then existing precedent as allowing public employers acting in good faith to take facially neutral albeit race-conscious actions to avoid liability under Title VII, and dismissed the firefighters' claims. But just weeks before Sotomayor's confirmation hearings began, the Supreme Court, in a 5–4 ruling, overturned the Second Circuit's decision. The decision became a flashpoint at her hearings. Ricci and Vargas both testified at the hearings, detailing how hard they had studied for the test and how betrayed they had felt when the Second Circuit panel rejected their claim in a short, and in their view terse, decision (De Vogue and Cook 2009). Senators opposing Sotomayor's confirmation used the decision to argue that she was unfit for the high Court, and that—like Thurgood Marshall before her—she was biased against white people.[9]

This experience was sadly predictable. As we explore further in Chapter 4, the four nominees in our dataset who are people of color—Thurgood Marshall, Clarence Thomas, Sonia Sotomayor, and Ketanji Brown Jackson—received disproportionately more questions about issues tied to their racial stereotypes. When addressed to Marshall, Sotomayor, and Jackson, these queries often took the form of questioning whether, as members of racial and ethnic minority groups themselves, they could be "neutral' in such cases—a question that seems to assume that a white, male baseline is the presumptively neutral perspective (Johnson 2011; Marrero-Otero 2011). In the case of Thomas, it took the form of concerns from his liberal opponents that he was insufficiently sympathetic to claims of race discrimination, which Thomas experienced as grounded in a stereotype that he, as an African American, would adhere to an "expected orthodoxy" on issues involving race (Lewis 1991).

### *The Discussion of Gender at the Hearings*

Figure 2.2 presents data on the percentage of civil rights comments involving gender and sexual orientation discrimination. As this figure illustrates, discussions of gender discrimination did not arrive at the hearings until the 1970s. This is not to say that there was no mention of gender at early hearings. Rather, early discussions of gender issues at the confirmation hearings looked quite different than today. In the earliest public hearings, if gender was discussed at all, it was usually in the form of thanking the male nominee's wife or daughters, or, in the 1962 hearing of former professional football player Byron White, gushing about how the nominee's "athletic prowess" helped make him a wonderful role model for "male children."[10] Unlike race, then, gender as a *legal* issue arrived much later at the confirmation hearings.

The first mention of gender discrimination at the hearings occurred in 1970, during the confirmation hearing of failed nominee Harold Carswell. Carswell, who was nominated by Richard Nixon, was questioned about a statutory case he had participated in involving employment discrimination against mothers of preschool children. The questioning senator, Birch Bayh (D-IN), expressed concerns about confirming a nominee who "feels that women should not be treated equally with men."[11] Later in the hearing, Senator Marlow Cook (R-KY) returned to the issue, noting as part of his query to Carswell that "you have been accused of being against women, which is an odd sort of thing to be said about men."[12]

The idea of gender discrimination had perhaps become less "odd" by 1971, when questions about the extent to which the equal protection clause of the Fourteenth Amendment prohibited gender discrimination first appeared at William Rehnquist's associate justice hearing. Senators Evan Bayh (D-IN) and Marlow W. Cook (R-KY) closely examined Rehnquist's views on the subject. Rehnquist, citing several cases pending before the Supreme Court, refused to answer their questions, ushering in the stage of the hearings in which the

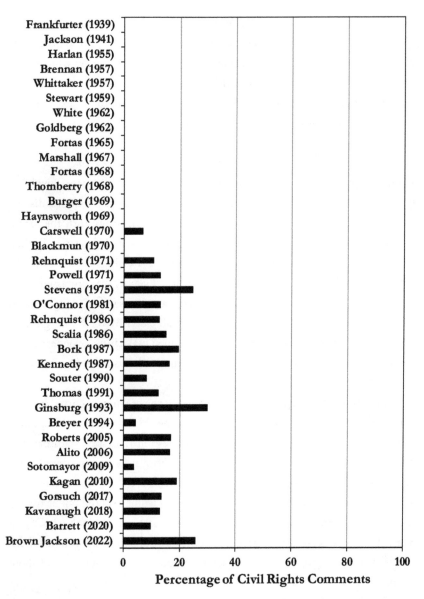

**FIGURE 2.2.** The Percentage of Civil Rights Comments Involving Gender and Sexual Orientation Discrimination at the Senate Judiciary Committee Confirmation Hearings of Supreme Court Nominees, 1939–2022

constitutionality of gender discrimination was considered too controversial of an issue for nominees to discuss.

Two years later, the Supreme Court decided *Roe v. Wade* (1973). *Roe* was not explicitly about gender discrimination and was not decided as an equal protection clause case. Instead, Justice Harry Blackmun famously grounded his majority opinion in the privacy right of a woman with her doctor to make decisions about intimate family matters. Nonetheless, the decision, and the principal of reproductive choice it embodies, have long been tied to issues of gender politics and women's equality. In the decades after it was decided, in fact, *Roe* became one of the most hotly contested Supreme Court decisions ever issued (Collins and Ringhand 2013a).

As Figure 2.3 reveals, none of this happened right away. This figure reports the percentage of civil rights statements about abortion rights at each hearing from 1939 to 2022. The first nominee to testify before the Judiciary Committee after *Roe* was decided was President Gerald Ford's nominee, John Paul Stevens. Stevens, nominated in 1975, was not asked a single question about *Roe*. As Greenhouse and Siegel (2019) have pointed out, in 1975 abortion simply was not the divisive, partisan issue it later became. *Roe*, after all, was a 7–2 decision, with five of the justices voting with the majority (Blackmun, Burger, Brennan, Powell, and Stewart) nominated by Republican presidents. Of the two dissenting justices, one (Rehnquist) was nominated by a Republican president, but the other (White) had been put on the Court by Democratic icon John F. Kennedy.

By 1980, *Roe* had become the constitutional minefield it is today. So it is not a surprise that the case was discussed at length at the hearing of the first female nominee, Sandra Day O'Connor. As noted above, President Reagan nominated O'Connor in 1981, to fill the seat of retiring justice Potter Stewart. Gender was very much in the air at the O'Conner hearing. Unlike when Thurgood Marshall appeared before the Judiciary Committee, senators across the ideological spectrum celebrated O'Connor's ground-breaking nomination, lauding her as a role model and trailblazer.[13] Senator Edward Kennedy (D-MA) questioned her extensively about her own experiences with gender discrimination and the extent to which she believed it posed a problem for other women in the workforce. O'Connor also was asked about abortion, birth control, affirmative action, and whether women should be allowed or required to participate in combat roles in the armed forces (the latter of which seems to have been treated by O'Connor as

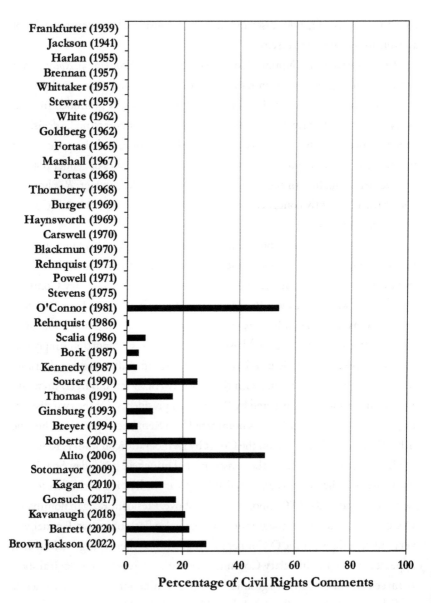

**FIGURE 2.3.** The Percentage of Civil Rights Comments Involving Abortion Rights at the Senate Judiciary Committee Confirmation Hearings of Supreme Court Nominees, 1939–2022

absurd). Nominees following O'Connor have all been asked about their opinions on abortion rights. In fact, since 1990, discussions of abortion rights have averaged about 20 percent of all questions pertaining to civil rights.

As shown in Figure 2.2, issues involving gender and sexual orientation discrimination, including LGBTQ+ equality and the proper interpretation of the equal protection clause, have been standard confirmation fare since the 1980s. Justice Ginsburg's position on abortion was discussed at length at her hearing, as was her work advocating for female veterans. Obama nominee Elena Kagan was queried extensively about her role, in her position as dean of Harvard Law School, in banning military recruiters from Harvard's campus because of the military's "Don't ask, don't tell" position on gay rights.

Justice Amy Coney Barrett's gender also was explicitly addressed at her hearings, most notably by her supporters. Their comments echoed concerns Justice Thomas had raised decades earlier about what happens when women or people of color hold opinions different than that expected of their "group." In Thomas's case, that involved liberal expectations that he, as an African American, should hold certain positions on civil rights issues, and criticism when he did not. In Barrett's case, it involved concerns about Barrett's identity as a conservative woman. The two female Republican senators on the Judiciary Committee, Senators Joni Ernst (R-IA) and Marsha Blackburn (R-TN), took the lead on this issue. Senator Ernst argued that Barrett was being treated harshly by Democratic senators because she did not march "lock step" with the liberal judicial philosophy of Justice Ginsburg, whose seat she would fill. "Diversity of thought," Senator Ernst said, "and an ability to pursue her dreams, is exactly what the women trailblazers of the past fought for."[14] Senator Blackburn went further, accusing Barrett's opponents of stereotyping, mocking, and ridiculing "women on the political right" and believing that Barrett wasn't a "real woman" because, she did not "buy into this agenda of the left."[15]

Issues of gender and sexual orientation discrimination also constituted a large part of Ketanji Brown Jackson's hearing in 2022, making up 26 percent of all civil rights statements, second only to Ruth Bader Ginsburg. Many of these questions came from Republican senators and involved transgender rights, a hot button issue for conservatives. One notable exchange came when Senator Ted Cruz (R-TX) pressed Jackson on her failure to provide a definition of the word "woman" in earlier questioning by Senator Blackburn (R-TN):

SENATOR CRUZ: Right. So yesterday under—under questioning from Senator Blackburn you told her that—that you couldn't define what a woman is, that you are not a biologist. Which—which I think you're the—the only Supreme Court nominee in history who's been unable to answer the question what is a woman.

Let me ask you as a judge, how would you determine if a plaintiff had article three standing to challenge a gender based rule regulation policy without being able to determine what a woman was?

JUDGE JACKSON: So, Senator, I know that I'm a woman. I know that Senator Blackburn is a woman and the woman who I admire most in the world is in the room today, my mother. It sounded as though the question was—

SENATOR CRUZ: —Well, but let—let me ask under the modern leftist sensibilities, if—if I decide right now that—that I'm a woman, then apparently I'm a woman. Does that mean that I would have article three standing to challenge a gender based restriction?

JUDGE JACKSON: Senator, to the extent that you are asking me about who has the ability to bring lawsuits based on gender, those kinds of issues are working their way through the courts and I'm not able to comment on them.

SENATOR CRUZ: Ok. If—if I can change my gender, if I can be a woman, and then an hour later if I decide I'm not a woman anymore I guess I would lose article three standing. Tell me, does that same principle apply to other protected characteristics? For example, I'm—I'm an Hispanic man. Could—could I decide I was an Asian man?[16]

Clearly, the battles about gender, power, and politics continue at the Supreme Court confirmation hearings.

## THE FINAL STEPS: SENATE DEBATE AND VOTE

Following the confirmation hearings, the Senate Judiciary Committee votes on whether, and how, to advance the nomination to the full Senate. Most nominations are reported out of the Judiciary Committee favorably, indicating that a majority of the Committee support confirmation. Nominations can also be reported negatively, indicating that a majority of the Committee opposes confirmation; reported without recommendation, signaling that many members of the Committee have reservations about the nomination; or not reported out at all, which does not occur in the modern era and would result in the nomination dying in committee (Collins and Ringhand 2013a; Rutkus 2010).

Once a nomination is reported out of the Judiciary Committee, it goes to the full Senate for debate and a vote. During Senate debate, senators are allocated a set amount of time to speak in favor of, or against, a nomination. Frequent topics of discussion include a nominee's judicial philosophy, qualifications for office, positions on salient issues, and statements made at the confirmation hearings. Although this stage of the confirmation process is referred to as a "debate," in actuality, there is little debating going on as senators have generally made up their minds whether to support or oppose the nominee. As such, senators tend to use their speaking time to highlight to their constituents their position on the nomination (Collins and Ringhand 2013a, 2016; Schoenherr, Lane, and Armaly 2020).

Before 2017, opponents of a Supreme Court nominee could in theory prevent a vote on the nomination by refusing to invoke cloture of a debate—in other words, by "filibustering" it. The filibuster is a Senate rule, first adopted in 1917, which allows the Senate to end debate on an issue with a supermajority vote. Contrary to its use in the modern era, the rule was originally designed to make sure debate could be ended, not to empower a minority of senators to continue it indefinitely: before 1917, a single senator could refuse to end debate by holding the floor, thus tying up Senate business indefinitely. The two-thirds cloture rule adopted in 1917 (changed to three-fifths in 1975) ensured that this no longer happens. Over time, however, the filibuster became used more frequently by opponents of legislation as a mechanism to prevent passage of bills they did not like, even when the legislation enjoyed majority support and would have passed with a straight up-or-down vote on the merits. The 1975 rule change also allowed other Senate business to continue during the filibuster, thereby ending the need to physically hold the floor, and making use of the filibuster more routine. As Chafetz has observed, these changes meant in effect that by the 1990s it was accurate to describe the filibuster as "nothing more than a sixty-vote requirement for the passage of most business through the Senate" (2017, 109).

The filibuster was rarely used against Supreme Court nominees, however. Floor votes on several nominees, including Clarence Thomas and Samuel Alito, were allowed to go forward even though they did not have sufficient support to survive a filibuster if one had been imposed.[17] During the bitter battles over lower court nominees that took place during the administrations of George W. Bush and Barack Obama, a bipartisan group of senators (the so-called Gang of 14) successfully reached an agreement to prevent the filibustering of Supreme Court nominees (Chafetz 2017, 101). After the Republicans' year-long blockade of Obama nominee Merrick Garland, however, even that agreement broke down. When President Trump took office and nominated Neil Gorsuch to fill the long-empty seat, Democrats filibustered the nomination, only to have the Republican majority respond by eliminating the filibuster for Supreme Court nominees and thereby enabling a straight up-or-down vote on Gorsuch's nomination (Chafetz 2017, 109).

## CONCLUSION

The purpose of this chapter was twofold. First, we provided an overview of the nomination and confirmation process, from how seats open up on the Court to the full vote in the Senate. In doing so, we focused in particular on the role of the Senate Judiciary Committee, noting that the hearings before the Committee are the most visible part of the confirmation process, providing millions of Americans with the opportunity to get to know nominees, form opinions about their fitness for the high Court, and see how nominees are treated by senators. We also provided an introduction to some of the ways that race and gender have been present at the hearings, even when female nominees and nominees of color have themselves been absent. As we saw, race in particular has been a mainstay of confirmation discourse since the first "modern" hearing held in 1939. How these issues are discussed, however, has changed over time, as the senators and nominees respond to the changing concerns and preferences of the American public.

In the chapters that follow, we build on this foundation, by examining the hearing experience of female nominees and nominees of color. In doing so, we develop our theoretical expectations for why and how the gender and race of nominees may change the nature of the hearings, and we test those expectations using data on all of the public confirmation hearings held before the Senate Judiciary Committee since 1939. As that discussion demonstrates, there is good reason to be concerned that woman and people of color may be treated differently by the Committee than white men, who have been—and continue to be—overrepresented on both the Supreme Court and in the Senate. By looking

at the types of questions senators ask nominees, how frequently senators interrupt nominees, the words used by senators in interacting with nominees, and
other aspects of the hearings, the remainder of this book investigates if there is
a bias with respect to how female and person of color Supreme Court nominees
are treated during their most high-profile appearance before both the Senate
and the American public.

# THREE

## THEORIZING BIAS IN THE CONFIRMATION HEARINGS

During her Supreme Court confirmation hearings in 2009, Sonia Sotomayor was asked a series of questions by Senator Lindsey Graham (R-SC) about her time serving on the U.S. Court of Appeals for the Second Circuit. Graham's lengthy interrogation focused very specifically on the way Sotomayor engaged in oral arguments while sitting on that federal appellate court. His concern was not about the content of the questions she asked the attorneys or how her questions affected the way she decided cases. Instead, Graham wanted to talk about Sotomayor's questioning *style* and *temperament*:

> SENATOR GRAHAM: One thing that stood out about your record is that when you look at the almanac of the Federal judiciary, lawyers anonymously rate judges in terms of temperament.
>
> And here's what they said about you: "she's a terror on the bench"; "she's temperamental, excitable"; "she seems angry"; "she's overly aggressive, not very judicial"; "she does not have a very good temperament"; "she abuses lawyers"; "she really lacks judicial temperament"; "she believes in an out-of-control—she behaves in an out-of-control manner"; "she makes inappropriate outbursts"; "she is nasty to lawyers"; "she will attack lawyers for making an argument she does not like"; "she can be a bit of a bully."

When you look at the evaluation of the judges on the Second Circuit, you stand out like a sore thumb in terms of your temperament. What is your answer to these criticisms?

JUDGE SOTOMAYOR: I do ask tough questions at oral argument.

SENATOR GRAHAM: Are you the only one that asks tough questions in oral argument?

JUDGE SOTOMAYOR: No. No, not at all. I can only explain what I'm doing, which is, when I ask lawyers tough questions, it's to give them an opportunity to explain their positions on both sides and to persuade me that they're right. I do know that in the Second Circuit, because we only give litigants 10 minutes of oral argument each, that the processes in the Second Circuit are different than in most other circuits across the country, and that some lawyers do find that our court—which is not just me, but our court generally—is described as a "hot bench". It's a term of art lawyers use. It means that they're peppered with questions. Lots of lawyers who are unfamiliar with the process in the Second Circuit find that tough bench difficult and challenging.

SENATOR GRAHAM: If I may interject, Judge, they find you difficult and challenging more than your colleagues. And the only reason I mention this is that it stands out when you—you know, there are many positive things about you, and these hearings are—are—are designed to talk—talk about the good and the bad. And I—I never liked appearing before a judge that I thought was a bully. It's hard enough being a lawyer, having your client there to begin with, without the judge just beating you up for no good reason. Do you think you have a temperament problem?

JUDGE SOTOMAYOR: No, sir. . . .[1]

As this sharp exchange between Senator Graham and Sotomayor makes clear, Graham's point was to question Sotomayor's judicial temperament. On its face, concerns about a nominee's temperament may seem entirely innocuous and reasonable. After all, judicial temperament—defined by the American Bar Association as having "compassion, decisiveness, open-mindedness, courtesy, patience, freedom from bias and commitment to equal justice under the law" (American Bar Association 2020, 3)—is considered by many to be an important qualification for service in the federal judiciary. But was there something much less innocuous—such as gender or ethnicity bias—underlying Senator Graham's questions?

For decades, scholars have studied how powerholding, dominant group members in society, like Graham, frequently (and sometimes implicitly) attach stereotypes and negative bias to numerical minority group members around them. This bias can then affect what behavior is deemed to be acceptable and evaluated positively for one's group. For a female Latina judge, like Sotomayor, this means that stereotypical masculine behavior on the bench, like tough questioning, may be viewed negatively and perceived as a threat (Lugo-Lugo and Bloodsworth-Lugo 2017). So what might be seen as positive traits in someone else—perhaps framed as an "aggressive" or "pointed" questioner—are seen in Sotomayor's case as evidence that she is "nasty," a "bully," and lacks the necessary judicial temperament to serve on the Supreme Court.

There are additional reasons to be skeptical of Senator Graham's exchange with Sotomayor. Instead of discussing potential concerns about Sotomayor's judging style through the use of empirical evidence like the American Bar Association's rating of her (which gave Sotomayor the highest rating available—"well qualified") or on-the-record statements from lawyers, litigants, or fellow judges, Graham used quotes from the *Almanac of the Federal Judiciary*. The very reliance on the *Almanac* as a source of credible evidence about a judge is suspect since lawyers' comments about judges appearing in the *Almanac* are anonymous, voluntary, and self-reported. As we have learned from research in other contexts, like "Rate My Professor" online teaching evaluations, voluntary self-reporting forums are "overwhelmingly populated by those who have strong feelings on the matter-at-hand, and typically strong negative feelings generate more voluntary self-reporting than positive feelings" (Katrompas and Metsis 2021, 536). What is more, these sorts of voluntary and anonymous evaluations are very often subject to (again negative) race, ethnicity, and gender bias (Basow, Codos, and Martin 2013; Bayishi, Madera, and Hebl 2010). Graham's *Almanac*-based evidence was questionable in another regard too: Graham selectively culled only the most negative comments about Sotomayor appearing in the volume (Kar 2009). Omitted positive comments on then Judge Sotomayor included things like "She's on the ball at oral argument. She really listens to responses." "She's brilliant," "She's usually right on target." and "She really is a good questioner. You have got to be prepared with her" (Kar 2009).[2]

Two years after her successful appointment to the Supreme Court, Justice Sotomayor reflected on her confirmation hearing exchange with Senator Graham and how gender interacts with people's perceptions about judges like her. "There are expectations about how women and men should behave," she told a group of law students two years after her nomination. "I am probably a bit more aggressive, but to hear people describe me as brash, and rude, the language used suggests a difference in expectations about what's OK for people's behavior" (Ward 2011). In other words, in Sotomayor's mind, other judges who behave in exactly the same way she does while on the bench, but who happen to be men, would not and have not been subject to the same negatively toned attacks she faced at her hearing. In speaking about the different gender expectations judges face, Sotomayor may have had one of her then colleagues on the Supreme Court—Justice Antonin Scalia—in mind. Like Sotomayor, Scalia was known for his "biting and aggressive questioning" during his thirty years on the Supreme Court (Mauro 2013). Sotomayor herself would call Scalia's oral argument style "sometimes even combative" (Sotomayor 2017, 1609). But unlike Sotomayor, Scalia's behavior did not lead to any high-profile and evaluative questioning about whether he had a judicial temperament problem and in fact likely contributed to his reputation as "brilliant."

In this chapter, we lay the theoretical groundwork explaining why Graham's questions, and much of the questioning faced by nominees who are not white men, may well have been driven at least in part by bias toward women and people of color. We talk about when and why negative bias, whether conscious or unconscious, is most likely to emerge in society broadly as well as specifically during Supreme Court confirmation hearings. In doing so, we examine ideas about group membership and status hierarchies among groups. As we will see, dominant in-group members (like white men) tend to rely very heavily on stereotypes as shortcuts to view and assess those who are members of other, lower status out-groups like women and people of color. This is particularly true when in-group members hold powerful societal positions.

The relevance of this theory to members of the Senator Judiciary Committee is apparent, given the high prestige and power held by senators serving on the Committee as well as the long dominance of white men in the U.S. Senate. As a result, we expect to see women and nominees of color face more obstacles during their confirmation hearings than do other nominees. This chapter also talks about how politics—which are always present in the interactions between nominees and senators—are likely to affect and sometimes mitigate the ways in which gender and racial biases manifest during a nominee's hearing.

## ROOM FOR BIAS

Women and people of color continue to face bias in American society. Explicit bias—"conscious and controllable" attitudes (Tinkler 2012)—has long been a problem in our communities, with women and people of color facing institutional and policy-related obstacles, often enshrined in law, affecting the right to vote, serve on juries, gain employment, use public and private services, and so much more. Explicit biases have been visible during Supreme Court confirmation hearings. Think back to Felix Frankfurter's hearing in 1939, where witnesses repeatedly argued the nominee was unfit to sit on the Court because of his status as an immigrant and Jew (Ringhand 2010). This wasn't subtle. One witness at the hearing testified in opposition to Frankfurter by noting that "if you are going to put an alien on the Supreme Court Bench of the United States it will show others in foreign countries that they can come over here and do the same thing."[3] Explicit bias like this may be less common today, but as Clarke (2018) argues, we should not argue "that explicit bias is in the past" (586). And, indeed, future chapters will highlight other confirmation hearing examples where explicit race, ethnicity, and gender biases did seem to motivate questions posed toward female nominees and nominees of color.

Nonetheless, much of the scholarly work in this area has shifted from explicit bias to implicit bias—attitudes that are "activated automatically without cognitive effort or even awareness" (Tinkler 2012). Implicit biases in our public and private interactions remain an ongoing concern in American society. Rarely a day goes by without a major news story covering how unconscious biases effect the daily lives of many Americans. Think back to April 2018 when two Black men reported that they were waiting in a Philadelphia Starbucks for a friend and had asked to use the restroom (McCleary and Vera 2018). A coffee shop employee told the men the restrooms were only for paying customers and asked them to leave. When they failed to do so, the employee called the police. The police arrived and eventually arrested the two men. Within days, Starbucks CEO Kevin Johnson issued a strong statement calling the incident "reprehensible" and "disheartening," apologizing to the two men, noting that the company's "practices and training led to a bad outcome," and acknowledging that the employee's "basis for the call to the Philadelphia Police Department was wrong" (CNN Staff 2018). Starbucks's response following this incident seemed to indicate that it recognized the implicit racial bias behind what occurred—in other words, that had the two people waiting in the coffee shop been white men or women, the employee would not have called the police.

Similar stories abound in the justice and political systems in the United States. Within the criminal justice system, for example, police regularly face accusations of racially imbalanced use of force, arrests, and traffic stops, among other actions (e.g., Browning et al. 1994; Weitzer and Tuch 1999; Wright and Headley 2020). And in politics, female candidates for office receive scathing critiques and discussion about their clothing, marital status, motherhood, and temperament for office that male candidates rarely, if ever, must endure (e.g., Heith 2001; Stabile et al. 2019; Van der Pas and Aaldering 2020). The framing of then Judge Sotomayor's robust questioning at oral arguments as overly aggressive bullying is not, in this context, at all surprising. Her experience was not an anomaly, but part of a larger pattern lived each day by women and people of color in our society.

A rich body of interdisciplinary work helps explain how readily these types of biases can affect senators' behavior toward nominees during the Supreme Court confirmation hearing process (e.g., Arvey 1979; Biernat and Kobrynowicz 1997; Cuddy, Fiske, and Glick 2008; Davison and Burke 2000; Eagly and Karau 2002). In what follows, we see how hierarchical societal groups form, how people within those groups interact with each other (both in and out of their own group), and how biased behavior can then emerge. This happens when, due to a lack of knowledge about members of other groups, those in dominant groups, especially when they hold significant amounts of power, rely on negative group stereotypes to view and assess outsiders.

## GROUP FORMATION AND HIERARCHIES

Social grouping involves "two or more individuals who share a common social identification of themselves or . . . perceive themselves to be members of the same social category" (Turner 1982, 15). This grouping of people together is driven by the desire to be included with others (Brewer 2001) and helps to provide "individual and societal needs for order, structure, simplification, [and] predictability" (Hogg and Abrams 1988, 18). Group membership also is key in shaping a person's identity, behavior, and life experiences. "People's concepts of who they are, of what sort of people they are, and how they relate to others (whether members of the same group—*ingroup*—or of different groups—*outgroup*) is largely determined by the groups to which they feel they belong" (Hogg and Abrams 1988, 2).

Social identity theory, which dates back to the 1970s, has been widely influential in the cross-disciplinary study of human group formation and behavior. The theory suggests that social groups are just as much about who they *exclude* as who they *include*. While group assimilation is driven partly by inclusion motivations, people also have "an opposing need for *differentiation* that is satisfied by distinguishing the self from others" (Brewer 2001, 21). Indeed, when we categorize others around us into groups, it tends to be done "overwhelmingly with reference to *self*" where people either "perceive others as members of the same category as self (ingroup members) or as members of a different category to self (outgroup members)" (Hogg and Abrams 1988, 21).

With this sorting of self and others into in-groups and out-groups comes the initiation, "typically spontaneously," of an evaluative bias where "people categorized as ingroup members are evaluated more favorably than outgroup members" (Johnson et al. 2006, 240). As a result of their categorization, in-group members enjoy in-group positivity, which comes with more and better rewards, more positive evaluations, more admiration and trust, and stronger "qualitative recall of their behaviors" (Johnson et al. 2006, 240).

There also is an inherent hierarchical dimension to social identity theory: "It maintains that *society comprises social categories which stand in power and status relations to one another*" (Hogg and Abrams 1988, 14, emphasis in original). In many ways, the dominant in-group "has the material power to promulgate its own version of the nature of society, the groups within it and their relationships" (Hogg and Abrams 1988, 27). For in-group members, the "orientation is simply 'us' versus 'not us'" (Brewer 2001, 23) and focused on protecting the in-group's perceived superiority (Brown and Capozza 2006). Once a social hierarchy like this is established, it is difficult to dismantle. As Magee and Galinsky (2008) note, "a number of organizational and psychological processes conspire to create different degrees of opportunity to acquire and maintain power and status for individuals and groups at different levels of hierarchies" (23).

This grouping and differentiation extends to race and gender, among other categories. Majorities, usually white men, constitute an in-group, while numerical minority and less powerful members of society, usually women and members of racial and ethnic minority groups, constitute out-groups. Gender and race can function, in effect, as status cues within social hierarchies, signaling to in-group, majority group members that minority group members are of a different status than are members of the majority group (Christensen, Szmer, and Stritch 2012; Eagly, Makhijani, and Klonsky 1992; Foschi 2000; Inesi and Cable 2015; Moyer and Haire 2015). Prejudice toward these perceived lower status groups can, and often does, result (Sears et al. 2000, 24).

## STEREOTYPING OF OUT-GROUP MEMBERS

As has become clear from our discussion so far, members of the in-group—the majority group—value their differences from out-group members and also know less about the out-group than they do about fellow members of the in-group (Davison and Burke 2000, 231). Consequently, in-group members are likely to view out-group members "as more similar to and more interchangeable with one another" (Dovidio et al. 1992, 170)—in short, as stereotypes. As defined by Magee and Smith (2013), stereotypes "are high-level constructs, generalized descriptions of the ways in which categories of people are believed to think and act *across* situations" (168). Stereotypes are also "beliefs that all members of a particular group have the same qualities" (Hogg and Abrams 1988, 65). Stereotypes can be both descriptive ("how most people in the group supposedly behave, what they allegedly prefer, and where their competence supposedly lies") and prescriptive ("how certain groups *should* think, feel, and behave") (Fiske 1993, 623).

In the absence of knowledge about and first-hand experience working with out-group members, group stereotypes inform the in-group's understanding of out-group members (Davison and Burke 2000). Out-group members are then judged consistently with the stereotypical, homogeneous group expectation (Biernat and Kobrynowicz 1997). These out-group expectations are hard to overcome, since stereotypes are "rigid and resistant to education" (Hogg and Abrams 1988, 66–67).

Research indicates that lower-status groups like women and people of color face negative stereotypes related to experience and competency to complete tasks (Karakowsky, McBey, and Miller 2004, 414). These perceived differences and the difficulties they create may be particularly salient for intersectional individuals—those whose identities intersect with multiple out-groups. Women of color, for example, can face stereotyping challenges not based simply on either race or gender, but on the interplay of both via gendered racism (Cassese 2019; Collins and Moyer 2008; Crenshaw 1989; Essed 1991; Rosette et al. 2016). We examine the connection between stereotypes, competency, and expertise in much more detail in Chapter 4, but, for now, we note that numerous studies find that group stereotypes are important to understanding bias and discrimination toward out-group members (Arvey 1979; Christensen, Szmer, and Stritch 2012; Davison and Burke 2000; Dovidio and Gaertner 2000; Fiske and Taylor 2013; Quillian 2006).

Fiske (1993, 623) notes that "category-based or stereotypic responses contrast with fully individuated, attribute-by-attribute consideration of another person." Unlike with out-group members, when in-group members assess and evaluate one another, they enjoy the more favorable individualized, attribute-specific consideration imagined by Fiske (Davison and Burke 2000). In-group members are also more likely to be trusted (Collins, Dumas, and Moyer 2017) and "viewed as distinctive and positive on subjectively important dimensions" (Fiske and Taylor 2013, 441). In other words, in-group membership comes with benefits that extend from higher status and more resources to favoritism and an appreciation of one's individual strengths.

## POWER HOLDERS

Implicit bias may be most likely to manifest among those in-group members who hold power. In this context, power is "the capacity to influence other people; it emerges from control over valuable resources and the ability to administer rewards and punishments" (Galinsky et al. 2006, 1068). Power is present when there is "asymmetric control over valued resources" and "desired outcomes" (Magee and Smith 2013, 159). These definitions of power may not extend to all in-group members, but they are certainly applicable for a subset of in-group members like organizational leaders and political elites, among others.

Where there are powerful people, there are also those who lack power, and the two are interrelated. "As the balance of control tips to the more powerful," Smith and Magee (2015, 152) note, "the balance of dependence tips to the less powerful, whose outcomes are more influenced by (i.e., dependent on) the decisions and actions of the powerful." This power imbalance has the effect of putting the less powerful at a disadvantage in many ways, including to moti-vate them to "attend to their high-power counterparts because their counter-parts can influence their outcomes" (Magee and Smith 2013, 160). The core motivation of in-group power holders is holding on to and even growing their power. Powerful people are often "predominantly concerned with their own desires and well-being" (Galinsky et al. 2006, 1068). Those with power often secure resources for themselves and others in the in-group, which further builds their power. In other words, "power begets more power" (Magee and Galinsky 2008, 371).

While holding on to and growing their own power, power holders are not likely to worry about the needs of out-group members and may even perceive them to be threats (Kinder and Sears 1981; Sears et al. 2000; Smith 2020). Power holders do a poor job of showing empathy toward and taking and understand-ing the perspective of others from different walks of life (Galinsky et al. 2006; Magee and Galinsky 2008; Smith and Magee 2015). There appear to be mul-tiple reasons explaining why power holders struggle with perspective taking, including the numerous demands on their time and their "lack of motivation to even attend to what their counterparts are thinking and feeling because their counterparts have little influence on their outcomes" (Magee and Smith 2013, 161). These limitations also result in high-powered in-group members being im-pervious to persuasion efforts coming from individuals with lower power and status (Magee and Galinsky 2008). This is a sobering reality given the degree of control over outcomes held by those in power.

Perspective-taking has been found to reduce reliance on stereotypes (Magee and Galinsky 2008; Batson et al. 1997; Galinsky and Moskowitz 2000), but since power holders are less likely to see or appreciate the perspec-tives of others, they are at higher risk of relying on stereotypes in ways that are even more concrete and concentrated than is the case for in-group members generally (Magee and Smith 2013). Power holders tend to struggle to recall key details and individuating features about their subordinates except when doing so was central to the power holders' goals (Magee and Galinsky 2008; Over-beck and Park 2006). Stereotypes offer power holders, who are overburdened, distracted, have limited cognitive space and/or are not dependent on those of lower status for their success, shortcuts in their relations with out-group members (Fiske 1993; Galinsky et al. 2006). As Fiske (1993, 621) succinctly put it, the powerful among us use stereotypes "because they do not need to pay attention, they cannot easily pay attention, and they may not be personally motivated to pay attention."

## SUPREME COURT CONFIRMATION
## HEARING IMPLICATIONS

If the Supreme Court confirmation process is subject to the type of out-group bias discussed above, the hearings are likely to be where it is most visible. Accounts from some nominees themselves suggest that this happens. We saw this in the opening pages of this chapter, with Justice Sonia Sotomayor's discussion about how people have varying expectations for the behavior of women and men. Justice Clarence Thomas also famously spoke about bias at his confirmation hearing, particularly in relation to the allegations of sexual harassment brought by Anita Hill (Morrison 1992). In starkly racialized language, Thomas referred to his experience before the Senate Judiciary Committee as a "high-tech lynching for uppity blacks" (United States Senate 1991, 157). Commentators on Supreme Court confirmation hearings have made similar observations over the years (Collins and Ringhand 2013a, 169–70; Kenney 2014, 230).

By coupling out-group theory with the bias literature and applying both to the Supreme Court's confirmation hearings process, we can begin to see how the hearings may play out differently for in- and out-group nominees. These theories, as well as the experimental and observational studies underlying them, give us reason to believe that members of the Senate Judiciary Committee may be more likely to view female and person of color nominees as inherently "different" from in-group white and male nominees. Our discussion in Chapter 2 informs, in two key ways, why it is that out-group theory applies so well to our study of potential bias in the behavior of the Committee's senators. First, there has been both historical and contemporary dominance of male and white senators on the Senate Judiciary Committee. It was not until the 114th Congress—i.e., 2015—that the Committee had more than three women or people of color simultaneously serving on it. Because of this relative lack of gender and racial diversity among the Committee's members, male and white Supreme Court nominees appearing before the Committee for hearings are likely to be in most senators' gender and racial in-groups. Second, membership in the U.S. Senate in general, and specifically on the Senate Judiciary Committee, is a prestigious and powerful position in American society. Senators are quintessential power holders with the capacity to influence people, asymmetrically control valuable resources and outcomes, and administer rewards per our above definitions.

For in-group nominees—here men and white nominees—several benefits are likely to flow from their shared group membership with the senators asking questions during the Committee's hearings. Recall that in-group members tend to view other in-groupers positively and are motivated in their behavior to protect their group's perceived power and superior status in society. This in-group positivity bias brings with it favorable evaluation, trust, admiration, and better recall about them, among other things. We would expect this to lead to in-group nominees receiving questions and treatment from senators during their hearings that reflect this positive outlook and give the nominee the benefit of the doubt. Similarly, in-group members are more likely to be judged based on their individual record—for our nominees, this means things like their experiences, background, and prior judicial behavior—rather than senators' stereotypes about their group.

In contrast, female and nonwhite nominees appearing before the Committee generally belong to the racial and gender out-group relative to the majority of senators serving on the Committee. Just as shared in-group status is likely to facilitate a smoother confirmation hearing for some, out-group status will throw up obstacles for others. One notable theme of our above discussion of bias toward out-group members is that in-group members, especially when sitting in positions of power, tend to rely heavily on group stereotypes when evaluating out-group members. This is especially true when there isn't a strong, pre-existing relationship between the two. Power holders like senators also struggle to show empathy toward and understand the differing perspectives of others who are not like them. Applied to the confirmation hearing context, the use of group stereotypes means that out-group nominees are likely to be judged consistently with an in-group senator's assumptions about how women or people of color behave or think. Since in-group perceptions of out-group members are often quite negative—a topic we return to in more detail in Chapter 4—this is likely to lead to a more negative confirmation experience for those nominees. Importantly, where in-group senators lean on out-group stereotypes for evaluating out-group (but not in-group) nominees, it also means those out-group nominees do not benefit from being judged based on their personal records, strengths, and attributes in the same ways in-group nominees do.

Given the robustness of this theoretical research, we expect differences to emerge in how in-group and out-group nominees are treated by senators during their hearings. But we recognize that in many cases, especially in the modern era, the questioning senators may either not be aware that they are treating in-group nominees differently from out-group nominees or may be savvy enough to avoid overtly biased behavior. As a result, instead of exclusively engaging in explicitly biased treatment, we would expect skeptical senators' questioning time during a nominee's hearing to be infected with more implicit bias, and we have designed our measurements to account for this. In the chapters that follow, we will see notable areas where it appears that race, gender, and ethnicity biases do in fact emerge during Supreme Court confirmation hearings.

### Intersection of Out-Group Bias with Politics

Politics matters too. The Senate and its Judiciary Committee are political bodies run by politically motivated senators. It should come as no surprise, therefore, that so much about what occurs within the Senate Judiciary Committee—including when and how out-group bias operates—is infused with political dynamics. By "political dynamics," we mean the partisan and political goals that drive senators' behavior in the Senate chamber.

The scholarship we rely on in this book recognizes and accounts for the role partisanship and politics play in how and when different types of biases are most likely to take hold. Out-group stereotyping and discriminatory behavior can sometimes be avoided by people who hold goals that will be better achieved through avoiding negative stereotyping of out-group members (Kawakami et al. 2000). Whether out-group stereotyping takes place also can be conditional on the presence of an attitude-behavior link among in-group members (Davison and Burke 2000). As Sinclair and Kunda (2000, 1330) put it, "People's use of stereotypes in a given interpersonal situation may depend on the motives they bring to that situation."

This research recognizes that preferences, goals, and personal motivations affect the circumstances under which bias directed toward out-group members will actually take place. When an out-group member shares an in-group person's values, ideals, and policy priorities, the in-group member may be able to control stereotypes and biased perceptions of out-group members. This can, in turn, inhibit stereotyping activation or lessen the negative impact of stereotypes (Kawakami et al. 2000; Sears et al. 2000). By contrast, when the preferences between an in-group actor and the out-group member being evaluated do not align, stereotypes are more likely to be adopted and acted upon. And, indeed, the effects of these stereotypes may be negatively magnified, leading to much higher levels of discriminatory behavior toward out-group members. These dichotomous predictions for the presence of stereotyping behavior of out-group members are, once again, further enhanced when in-group members sit in positions of power. The powerful will attend closely to the individual characteristics of out-group members that are useful to their goals but largely disregard and default to stereotyping for all other out-group members (Magee and Galinsky 2008).

Previous research finds a strong connection between political attitudes and preferences and the magnitude of activated out-group stereotypes. At the U.S. Supreme Court, justices are less likely to vote for legal positions favored by women attorneys than those favored by male attorneys, but there is about a 10 percent higher likelihood of support for the female lawyer's position if it is consistent with the justice's ideology (Szmer, Sarver, and Kaheny 2010). For Senate candidates, there is a strong link between political preferences and perceptions of women (Koch 2000) and people of color (Sigelman et al. 1995).

In the context of Supreme Court confirmation hearings, therefore, we expect that partisan congruence between the questioning senator and the nominee will serve an important conditioning role on the presence and level of out-group bias. The modern Senate is highly polarized along party lines (Lee 2008), and committee membership reflects the partisan composition of the full Senate (Epstein and Segal 2005). Senate parties act as "teams," with coordination on important issues like presidential agenda items and procedural control (Lee 2009). Importantly, ideological proximity and policy agreement are not the only reasons that Senate partisans support one another; rather, some members will work with their party "because they understand the value of team play" (Lee 2009, 47). It would be "quite surprising if Democrats were not more likely to support Democratic presidents than were Republicans, and vice versa" (Segal 1987, 1001). Unsurprisingly, this is exactly what the evidence indicates for the Senate's confirmation process: nearly all senators of the same party as the president support his Supreme Court nominees but significantly fewer opposition party senators do so (Epstein and Segal 2005; Farganis and Wedeking 2014).

How might this "partisan climate" in the Senate's deliberations about Supreme Court nominees (Epstein and Segal 2005) differentially affect in-group

and out-group nominees? Recall that out-group evaluation bias toward Supreme Court nominees often stems from a lack of (or inattentiveness to) specific
information about and trust in the predictability of an out-group nominee's
future behavior and decisions. And at the same time, the presence of power is
said to increase a person's "goal-directed activity" (Galinsky et al. 2006, 1068),
with senators' goals aligning nicely with their political parties. In the case of
out-group nominees (and their appointing president) who share the questioning senator's party, much of this uncertainty or distrust will, inevitably, be lessened. In other words, shared party provides a set of common expectations for
the senator and nominee that may help avoid the strong activation of out-group
biases. Those with great power, like senators, can be very focused when interacting with people "who possess characteristics that would be useful for the
power-holder" (Magee and Galinsky 2008, 371). By contrast, when the nominee
hails from the opposite party as the senator, stereotypes are likely to be magnified. In these cases, there is no shared set of expectations to stand in the way of
gender and racial stereotyping leading to biased behavior. And because partisan
divisions are piled on top of out-group status stereotyping, senators are likely to
be particularly wary of the competence of these nominees.

What does this mean for how senators will behave during Supreme Court
confirmation hearings? Democratic senators are likely to have a set of common
expectations for and trust in the nominees of Democratic presidents, and Republican senators are likely to have a set of common expectations for and trust
in the nominees of Republican presidents (e.g., Cottrill and Peretti 2013). Their
shared party affiliation is likely to help avoid the strong activation of biases and
discrimination among copartisans. When that shared affiliation is absent, however, stereotypes are more likely to be magnified because there is no shared set of
expectations to stand in the way of gender and racial stereotyping (Boyd, Collins,
and Ringhand 2018). And because partisan divisions are piled on top of minority
status stereotyping, senators are likely to be particularly wary of these nominees.
We discuss this intersection of bias and partisanship in each of the remaining
chapters and explain its magnifying or mitigating effects, as appropriate.

## CONCLUSION

This chapter has introduced our theory on what can cause the emergence of explicit and implicit bias toward some but not others in society. We have seen that

group formation in society, combined with power hierarchies and the reliance on negative stereotyping rather than individual information to evaluate people, creates space for biased behavior. The targets of that bias tend to be out-group members, who are members of nondominant societal groups and hold lower levels of power. While in-group and out-group membership can be based on a variety of societal grouping characteristics, gender, race, and ethnicity group bias can be seen in multiple settings, from Starbucks to police departments to law firms to the U.S. Senate.

As we have discussed, the risk of biased behavior is particularly potent in the Supreme Court confirmation hearings, when powerful, typically white, male senators face off against increasingly diverse nominees. Sometimes those nominees share senators' group membership and may benefit from intragroup favoritism and individualized evaluation. Other times, however, nominees enter their hearings as true out-group members, with all of the disadvantages that attach to that status.

With this theoretical context established, we now turn to in-depth empirical analyses of the specific contexts during the Supreme Court confirmation hearings where biased behavior from in-group senators toward women and people of color nominees may occur. In Chapter 4, we assess whether nominees, based on their gender, race, and ethnicity, face distinct levels of subject-matter stereotyping and skepticism toward their competency to serve on the Court. In Chapter 5, we turn to an examination of the proclivity of Judiciary Committee senators to interrupt nominees to see if these interruptions—which can be intrusive efforts to exercise control over a conversation—occur at different rates depending on the nominee's group membership. Then, in Chapter 6, we analyze the language senators use to question nominees to see whether fellow in-group nominees receive more positive tone from senators, and fewer words associated with doubt, than female nominees and nominees of color.

# FOUR

## PROFESSIONAL COMPETENCE AND EXPERTISE

*Women in law, even today, are not entering a bias-free profession. . . .*
*Men of the bench and bar generally held what the French call an idee fixe,*
*the unyielding conviction that women and lawyering, no less judging, do*
*not mix.*

—JUSTICE RUTH BADER GINSBURG (2007)

Long-standing traditions and stereotypes suggest that the legal profession, and, in particular, judging on the highest Court in the country, are jobs best suited to white males. As Justice Ginsburg's words reflect, female nominees to the Supreme Court, even today, can face an uphill battle in convincing senators of their fitness to serve as a justice. The same can surely be said for nominees of color. These nominees face multiple hurdles on their way to confirmation. In addition to having to rebut casual assumptions that women and person of color judges lack some sort of stereotyped aptitude to serve in the legal profession, they also confront aggressive questioning about their ability to be impartial in exactly the areas of law where they have real or perceived strengths: gender and race.

The 1967 confirmation hearing of Thurgood Marshall, the first African American appointed to the Supreme Court, highlighted just how this can play out, in questioning from Senator James Eastland (D-MS), the chairman of the Senate Judiciary Committee:

THE CHAIRMAN. In deciding cases will you make a selection between constitutional principle based on your own sense of right and wrong?

JUDGE MARSHALL. Well, my own sense of right and wrong is the Constitution itself.

THE CHAIRMAN. In other words, what you say is that you would follow the real meaning of the Constitution of the United States as you see it?

JUDGE MARSHALL. As I interpret it as an individual, after careful study of the briefs and argument and the consultation with the other members of the Court in conference.

THE CHAIRMAN. Will you decide cases on the basis of asking yourself the question, "is this a fair proposition?"

JUDGE MARSHALL. Not my own—I would—let me put it this way, Senator. I would hope that my own ideas of fairness are based entirely on the Constitution, and I would not under any circumstances find—where the Constitution says this and my "personal feelings" say that, I would go with the Constitution. I am obliged to.

THE CHAIRMAN. You would go with this.

JUDGE MARSHALL. Sir

THE CHAIRMAN. You would go with what you said is this, the Constitution.

JUDGE MARSHALL. The Constitution, absolutely.

THE CHAIRMAN. Now, you have been in a lot of institutions in the Southern States.

JUDGE MARSHALL. Yes, sir.

THE CHAIRMAN. Are you prejudiced against white people in the South?

JUDGE MARSHALL. Not at all. I was brought up what I would say way up South in Baltimore, Md. And I worked for white people all my life until I got in college. And from there most of my practice, of course, was in the South, and I don't know, with the possible exception of one person that I was against in the South, that I have any feeling about them.

THE CHAIRMAN. Now, if you are approved, you will give people in that area of the country and the States in that area of the country the same fair and square treatment that you give people in other areas of the country?

JUDGE MARSHALL. No question whatsoever.[1]

In this exchange, Marshall, a celebrated attorney in the civil rights movement, was having his objectivity questioned. Eastland attacked Marshall's ability to be

impartial in civil rights cases and required Marshall to repeatedly rebut the accusation he would show favoritism to Black parties and would be racially biased
against white people.

Ruth Bader Ginsburg's perceptions of how gender bias infiltrated the
bench and bar and Thurgood Marshall's Senate Judiciary Committee experience illustrate the barriers that female nominees and nominees of color face
during their Judiciary Committee hearings. This problem is well documented
in other areas. Implicit and explicit biases among interviewers impose obstacles for female and person of color candidates that do not exist for their similarly situated white, male counterparts. Even when the female or person of
color candidate ultimately gets the job or promotion she seeks, achieving that
goal can first require overcoming a "presumption of incompetence" that at-
taches, via group stereotypes, to women and people of color. Similarly, women
and people of color are often stereotyped as issue experts in areas relating to
race and gender. These subject matter stereotypes can shape the evaluation
and selection process for candidates and affect perceptions of candidates' fitness to take on leadership positions. These competency and subject matter stereotypes and biases can contaminate the process even for female and person
of color candidates who are objectively as or more qualified than their white,
male competitors.

The U.S. Supreme Court's selection process provides an ideal arena for
further assessing and documenting the obstacles that successful women and
people of color may face as they go through the nomination process—or "job
interview,"[2] as Senator Al Franken (D-MN) referred to it during Gorsuch's
hearing—for the legal profession's most prestigious job. In this chapter we do
just that. We detail the theory of competence and subject matter stereotypes
for women and people of color, including reviewing the relevant political and
legal context settings where prior research finds evidence of these stereotypes in
action. We then apply the theory to the Supreme Court confirmation hearing
context and discuss how partisanship may condition the effects of out-group
bias. Using our data on confirmation hearings from 1939 to 2022, we analyze
the presence of competence and subject matter stereotypes. The results indicate
that women nominees and nominees of color do, at times, have to "work twice
as hard" (Biernat and Kobrynowicz 1997, 546) as other nominees to prove their
fitness to serve on the Court.

## COMPETENCE AND SUBJECT MATTER STEREOTYPES

As we describe in Chapter 3, out-group stereotyping is prevalent. Those in power—the in-group—lack reliable information about and experience with out-group members. As a result, they can resort to the use of biased group stereotypes when evaluating those who are not in power. During Supreme Court confirmation hearings, our out-groups of focus—female and people of color nominees—are likely to face two types of stereotypes: that they are less professionally competent, and that they are unable to remain impartial when deciding cases related to their perceived subject matter areas of strength.

Out-group theory predicts that biases and stereotypes can have a significant negative impact on perceptions of an individual's professional competence— that is, their "ability to do well on a task judged to be valuable" in the field of interest (Foschi 2000, 22). Competence-related stereotypes in the workplace are important since being stereotyped as incompetent likely results in an individual's job performance and experience being "evaluated less positively than equivalent work" by in-group members (Magee and Galinsky 2008, 34). Because of gender stereotypes, "evaluators assume women lack the masculine competencies necessary to succeed" at jobs, especially in leadership or management (Schneider et al. 2010, 369). Racial stereotypes yield similar results. The effect is a "presumption of incompetence" for women and people of color (Arvey 1979; Biernat and Kobrynowicz 1997; Cuddy, Fiske, and Glick 2008; Davison and Burke 2000; Eagly and Karau 2002; Nelson et al. 2019). This presumption of incompetence can remain even when out-group applicants' relevant application records and previous job performance are, objectively speaking, equivalent or even stronger than those belonging to in-group (male, white) applicants (Eagly, Makhijani, and Klonsky 1992; Firth 1982; Inesi and Cable 2015; Lott 1985). As Heilman and Haynes (2005, 905) put it, "sometimes even indisputably successful outcomes are not enough to overcome the impact of stereotypes."

Out-group theory also anticipates the occurrence of gender and racial stereotyping of tasks, beliefs, and expertise. Here's how this type of stereotyping operates: tasks and issues stereotyped as masculine (white) produce higher perceptions of expertise for men (whites) and women (people of color) stereotyped tasks and issues result in higher perceived expertise for women (people of color) (Karakowsky and Siegel 1999). While the exact areas of expertise attributed to genders and races can depend on the arena of focus, common attributions include expertise in leadership, military, crime, and economy (American white men); in abortion, sex-related employment discrimination, civil rights, poverty, and education (American women); and in affirmative action, crime, poverty, and racial discrimination (Black Americans) (see, e.g., Holman, Merolla, and Zechmeister 2011; Huddy and Terkildsen 1993a; 1993b; Lawless 2004; McDermott 1998; Peffley, Hurwitz, and Sniderman 1997; Schneider and Bos 2011). Research also indicates that men and white individuals both are more likely to adhere strongly to gender and race role beliefs, respectively, and engage in consistent, negative stereotyping on these dimensions (Karakowsky, McBey, and Miller 2004; Schneider and Bos 2011; Shah 2015).

When present, gender or racial stereotyping of expertise or beliefs can lead to additional inferences about the person's "issue positions, policy competencies, ideological leanings, and character traits" (Koch 2000, 414). This stereotype inferencing is most likely to occur when "the stereotypes have specific behavioral implications" (Karl and Ryan 2016, 260). Expertise stereotyped as belonging to in-group members (men and whites) is typically more valued in hiring processes, particularly those involving leadership positions. Out-group members interviewing or being evaluated in positions traditionally held by in-group members may also face additional emphasis on the out-group's stereotyped expertise because of a perceived threat to the in-group's interests (Goldman 2017, 721). Applied to race, Hajnal (2007, 3) notes that "many Whites fear that a Black leader will favor the Black community over the White community." In other words, coming from a place of fear for the in-group's values and standing, in-group members may seek to ensure that the out-group employee or candidate will behave impartially in her position and not engage in gender or racial favoritism.

As a result of this competency bias and expertise stereotyping, low-status out-group members will need to display more evidence of their ability for the task at hand (Biernat and Fuegen 2001). At the same time, they will be allowed less latitude than in-group members in the face of evidence of ability or experience insufficiencies (Biernat and Kobrynowicz 1997). To overcome this imbalanced assessment, lower-status interviewees and employees must "jump through more hoops" (Biernat and Kobrynowicz 1997, 546) to prove their professional aptitude for the position or task. This use of double standards in the evaluation of out-group candidates is a "subtle exclusionary practice" (Foschi 2000, 27).

Experimental and observational studies confirm the strong presence of this type of bias and stereotyping against women and people of color in a variety of employment settings. Women and people of color regularly face a perceived lack of fit for higher-level leadership and managerial positions (Heilman 2001; Smith et al. 2019). The likelihood of women being devalued is particularly high when they occupy male-dominated roles or are evaluated by men (Eagly, Makhijani, and Klonsky 1992; Inesi and Cable 2015; Heilman and Haynes 2005). Quillian's (2006) review of race discrimination studies similarly demonstrated that "subordinate groups have predominately negative stereotypic attributions when evaluated by dominant group members" (320).

## COMPETENCE AND EXPERTISE STEREOTYPES
## IN POLITICAL AND LEGAL CONTEXTS

Political and legal elites seem to be as vulnerable to competence bias and stereotyping threats as are others, both from the public and from other professional elites. For example, evidence indicates that the public perceives female political candidates to have lower competence than male candidates, particularly when accounting for opposition candidates' quality and gender (Branton et al. 2018).[3] State legislators rate their Black colleagues' legislative effectiveness much lower than that of white legislators (Haynie 2002), even after controlling for relevant experience, bill introductions, committee membership, partisanship, and seniority factors. Female cabinet secretary-designates are likewise less likely to be granted insider status during their Senate confirmation hearings than their male counterparts with similar career paths (Borrelli 1997).

Women and Black politicians also face numerous issue area stereotypes that can affect their success in winning elections and retaining public support. For women, stereotypical masculine strengths, like military and economics, are generally viewed as "more important for higher levels and types of office than competence in typical areas of female policy strength" (Huddy and Terkildsen 1993b, 504–5). Holman, Merolla, and Zechmeister (2011, 174) argue that these "belief- and trait-based gender stereotypes" are "one part of the uphill battle that female political figures face." Lawless (2004) sees evidence of this in action with survey respondents' preferences for presidential gender during times of war. For race, there are strong stereotypes that white politicians have policy breadth across important issues but that Black politicians have more narrow strengths related to race and poverty issues (Shah 2015; Sigelman et al. 1995; Williams 1990). These stereotypes about a Black candidate's expertise affect the likelihood of voting for that candidate (McDermott 1998; Shah 2015).

Legal elites face similar hurdles. Research on lawyers and law firms reveals that "the perception of difference, sex stereotyping, and treating women as a category rather than individually, provide serious obstacles" to female lawyers' advancement in the legal profession (Epstein et al. 1995, 304). A national survey of U.S. attorneys revealed vast gulfs in perceptions of competency between white male attorneys and other attorneys (Epner 2006). Surveyed women of color attorneys, in particular, noted that "they had to disprove preconceived negative notions about their legal skills when they joined" their law firm, and convince skeptical senior colleagues that they belonged (Epner 2006, 24).

For attorneys interacting with judges and other courtroom staff, women and person of color lawyers face higher levels of demeaning and discriminatory behavior than their counterparts (Collins, Dumas, and Moyer 2017). Male judges are much more likely to hold negative stereotypes about female lawyers than are female judges, with surveyed male judges more likely than female judges to agree with statements such as "Female attorneys lack the competence of their male colleagues," "Men are more credible than women," and "A woman who is outspoken or strongly adversarial is obnoxious" (Martin, Reynolds, and Keith 2002, 693). At the U.S. Supreme Court, Szmer, Sarver, and Kaheny (2010) reveal that Supreme Court justices were nearly 9 percent less likely to vote in favor of legal positions favored by women attorneys than those favored by male attorneys. The effects of these stereotypes may play some role in explaining why women and people of color still lag behind white men in upper management employment and compensation, including in the legal field. In 2017, while over 45 percent of law firm associates were women, just 23 percent were partners. Similarly, for people of color, 2017 associate figures were 23 percent, but were only around 8 percent for partners (National Association for Legal Career Professionals 2018).

Turning to perceptions and evaluations of judges, work by Nelson (2015) indicates that citizens perceive female judges to be "lacking in legal knowledge" relative to male judges. Sen (2014) finds that female and person of color federal district court nominees were more likely to receive lower ratings from the American Bar Association than white and male nominees. This was the case even after controlling for key factors like party affiliation, education, and experience. As Sen notes, "We cannot rule out the possibility of implicit bias against these sorts of nominees" (63). Studies provide evidence that female and person of color state judges receive lower judicial performance evaluations than their male and white colleagues (Gill, Lazos, and Waters 2011) and that some Black male and white female state supreme court justices are less likely than their colleagues to receive opinion writing assignments (Christensen, Szmer, and Stritch 2012). Finally, experimental work indicates that judicial decisions were perceived as more authoritative when labeled as authored by "Anthony Kennedy" than by "Sandra Day O'Connor" (Boddery, Moyer, and Yates 2019).

Together, this evidence seems to suggest that some legal and political elites make biased evaluations of female and person of color lawyers, judges, and candidates. Within the legal system and judiciary, much of this lingering bias seems rooted in stereotyping of the legal profession as a white male's field of work, with the common perception being that "women and people of color do not belong in prestigious legal occupations, like that of attorney or judge" (Moyer et al. 2021, 456; see also Clark 2004; Fix and Johnson 2017; Gill, Kagan, and Marouf 2019).[4]

## SUPREME COURT CONFIRMATION HEARING APPLICATION

By coupling out-group theory with the bias in hiring literature and applying both to the Supreme Court's confirmation hearings process, we can begin to develop expectations regarding how the hearings may play out differently for in- and out-group nominees. These theories, as well as the experimental and observational studies underlying them, give us good reason to believe that the "hiring" senators are likely to view female and person of color nominees as inherently "different" and less well suited to be judges than in-group white and male nominees.

If such bias is present at the hearings, it is likely to emerge implicitly rather than explicitly. In many cases, the questioning senators may not even be aware that they are treating in-group nominees differently from out-group nominees. As such, we might expect skeptical senators to use their questioning time to require out-group nominees to more elaborately prove that they have the professional competence or impartiality required to sit on the high Court.

### *Theorizing Supreme Court Professional Competence Bias*

Since all nominees to the Supreme Court are likely to be among the most talented and experienced lawyers of their generations, professional competence at the Supreme Court selection level cannot be captured simply by looking at a nominee's educational pedigree or job experience. Consequently, we would expect perceptions of competence at Supreme Court confirmation hearings to be tied to something with more nuance: a nominee's ability, in the eyes of the questioning senator, to get the Constitution "right" by using the "correct" method of constitutional interpretation. As Senator Orrin Hatch (R-UT) stated at the Sotomayor hearing, "A judicial nominee's qualifications include not only legal experience but, more importantly, judicial philosophy."[5] Examples of judicial philosophy-related questions include those about constitutional interpretation, original intent, "living constitutionalism," stare decisis, judicial activism, and the use of empathy. If the definition of professional competence is "the ability to do well on a task judged to be valuable" in the field of interest (e.g., Foschi 2000, 22), then the core professional competence of a Supreme Court justice is to correctly interpret the U.S. Constitution. To do otherwise is to fail at the essential task required of the job.

The senators and nominees are quite clear on this point. When Senator Strom Thurmond (R-SC) wanted to make Thurgood Marshall look unfit to sit on the high Court, he launched an elaborate attack on Marshall's ability to correctly understand and interpret the original understanding of the Fourteenth Amendment.[6] Likewise, during his opening statement during Ketanji Brown Jackson's hearing, Senator Cornyn (R-TX) noted that it was "imperative" that the senators explore Jackson's judicial philosophy. Cornyn continued:

> I was a bit troubled when you—that you have not so far provided us with much clarity on that matter. Someone as accomplished as you are who spent years engaging and thinking about our Constitution and laws has surely formed a judicial philosophy.[7]

Senator Chuck Schumer (D-NY) similarly opened the Alito hearing by describing a nominee's "most important qualification" as his "judicial philosophy,"[8] and Senator Jeff Sessions (R-AL) skeptically informed Sonia Sotomayor in his opening statement at her hearing that the senators would "inquire into how your philosophy, which allows subjectivity in the courtroom, affects your decision-making."[9] Justice Alito, testifying before the Committee in 2006, captured the sentiment succinctly, stating simply that "the job of a Supreme Court Justice [is] to interpret the Constitution."[10]

There is unquestionably deep disagreement about what the "correct" method of constitutional interpretation is, and senators are likely to form their preferences on the matter in ways that advance their underlying policy goals (Post and Siegel 2006). Nonetheless, in the context of the confirmation hearings, questioning nominees about their judicial philosophies is a tool senators use to explore how, as future justices, nominees would execute that core task. When senators perceive a nominee as using the wrong interpretive methods, the senators will also view the nominee as unqualified to sit on the Supreme Court.

Applied here, the theory predicts that in-group nominees will enjoy much more of a presumption of mainstream, professional competence, while similarly situated female and person of color nominees may enjoy no such presumption. Rather, stereotypes and negative perceptions of out-group nominees will lead them to be perceived as less willing or able to behave in a similarly professional manner. We would thus expect questioning senators to express this skepticism by requiring person of color and female nominees to demonstrate their professional competence (or reveal their lack thereof) by spending more of their confirmation hearing time answering questions about their judicial philosophies. In-group nominees therefore should expect to receive a lower proportion of questions in the areas of judicial philosophy than out-group nominees, even when accounting for the influence of partisanship.

### *Theorizing Supreme Court Subject Matter Bias*

In addition to stereotypes about professional competence, we also expect subject matter stereotypes to affect questioning practices toward in- and out-group nominees during their confirmation hearings. As we detail above, expertise in tasks and subject matters is often stereotyped based on gender and race. Just as this theory applies to the resulting perceptions and evaluations of politicians, lawyers, and judges, it also is likely to have implications for how nominees are treated during their confirmation hearings.

Some gender and race stereotyped issues do not emerge with high frequency at the Supreme Court, or at nominees' confirmation hearings, including areas like military, education, or the economy (Collins and Ringhand 2013a; Ringhand and Collins 2011). However, the nature of Supreme Court decision making means that some subjects stereotyped as out-group strengths are ripe for controversy and questioning during confirmation hearings. For female nominees, these stereotyped strengths include issues like abortion and gender discrimination. Huddy and Terkildsen (1993a, 132) observe similar stereotypes for female political candidates: "Women were seen as most competent to deal with women's issues, tough and ambitious women even more so." For people of color, stereotyped strengths line up with race-connected issues like race discrimination, but they also involve negative stereotypes on issues like crime (Peffley, Hurwitz, and Sniderman 1997). Once again, issue competency stereotypes from studies of politicians are informative, with Schneider and Bos (2011) reporting high issue competency stereotypes for Black politicians in race relations, affirmative action, and equal rights. Conversely, Peffley, Hurwitz, and Sniderman (1997) find that white respondents have negative views of Black Americans on areas like crime and welfare policy.

The underlying implications of the theory of issue area stereotypes are particularly salient in the confirmation hearing context. Namely, "minority groups are often perceived as highly threatening to the dominant group's interests" (Goldman 2017, 736), and this type of stereotyping is most likely to occur where there are specific links to potential future behavior (Karl and Ryan 2016). As such, women and person of color nominees are likely to be inequitably pushed to provide evidence of their ability to avoid favoritism toward other out-group members and interests in their Supreme Court decision making. Recall the example from Justice Thurgood Marshall's confirmation hearing that began this chapter where Marshall was vigorously pushed to defend his ability to remain fair and impartial toward white interests in race cases.

As noted elsewhere in this book, Justice Sonia Sotomayor faced a similar line of questioning from multiple senators in response to her "wise Latina" comments. On this topic, Senator Kyl (R-AZ) grilled Sotomayor for several minutes on her commitment to remain impartial and not favor women and minority interests in her decisions. In one portion of this questioning, Kyl said:

> You made the statement that is now relatively famous: 'I would hope that a wise Latina woman with the richness of her experiences would more often than not reach a better conclusion.' . . . But you didn't in your speech say that this is not good, we need to set this aside. Instead, you seemed to be celebrating it. The clear inference is it is a good thing that this is happening. . . . Not only are you not saying anything negative about that, but you seem to

embrace that difference in concluding that you will make better decisions. That is the basis of concern that a lot of people have.[11]

Whether talking about Marshall, Sotomayor, or some other nominee to the Court, the out-group status of these nominees appears to lead senators to view them, implicitly or explicitly, as less able to behave impartially as a justice when resolving cases related to their group's stereotyped strengths. The senators may thus try to expose this tendency or require the nominee to work hard to dispel it by interrogating the nominee more deeply in these areas in their allotted time for questions. Equally qualified in-group nominees, in contrast, would not be likely to receive nearly as many questions about these issue areas since in-group senators will have more confidence in the impartiality of in-group nominees on these issues.

## THE CONDITIONING EFFECT OF
## POLITICS ON OUT-GROUP BIAS

As detailed in Chapter 3, there is good reason to believe that partisan congruence between the questioning senator and the nominee conditions the presence and magnitude of out-group bias during Supreme Court confirmation hearings. Recall that out-group evaluation bias toward Supreme Court nominees often stems from a lack of specific information about and trust in the predictability of an out-group nominee's future behavior and decisions. In the case of out-group nominees (and their appointing president) who share the questioning senator's party, much of this uncertainty or distrust will inevitably be lessened. In other words, shared party provides a set of common expectations for the senator and nominee that may help avoid the strong activation of out-group biases. By contrast, when the nominee hails from the opposite party as the senator, stereotypes are likely to be magnified. In these cases, there is no shared set of expectations to stand in the way of gender and racial stereotyping leading to biased behavior. And because partisan divisions are piled on top of out-group status stereotyping, senators are likely to be particularly wary of the competence and perceived subject matter strengths of these nominees. As a result, we expect to see a higher volume of questions relating to judicial philosophy and subject matter strengths asked of opposite party, out-group nominees.

Based on the above discussion, our resulting formalized hypotheses are:

HYPOTHESIS 4.1: Female Supreme Court nominees not from the senators' political party will receive a higher proportion of judicial philosophy questions from male senators than will other nominees.

HYPOTHESIS 4.2: Person of color Supreme Court nominees not from the senators' political party will receive a higher proportion of judicial philosophy questions from white senators than will other nominees.

HYPOTHESIS 4.3: Female Supreme Court nominees not from the senators' political party will receive a higher proportion of abortion and gender discrimination questions from male senators than will other nominees.

HYPOTHESIS 4.4: Person of color Supreme Court nominees not from the senators' political party will receive a higher proportion of race discrimination and crime questions from white senators than will other nominees.

## DATA AND METHODS

We test our hypotheses using the data described in the Introduction. This dataset contains information on the subject matter of every statement made at every open, transcribed Supreme Court confirmation hearing held before the Senate Judiciary Committee from 1939 to 2022.[12] Because we are interested in the relative amount of attention senators devote to questioning nominees in particular issue areas, the unit of analysis used throughout this chapter is the senator-nominee pair. This means that there is one observation for every senator who questioned a nominee at his or her confirmation hearing (e.g., one observation for Senator Sessions during the Sotomayor hearing and one observation for Sessions during the Kagan hearing).[13] This allows us to examine the extent to which each senator featured a particular topic in his or her questioning of the nominee.

Our empirical analyses are tailored to reflect out-group theory's focus on the status of *both* the senator and the nominee, and the dominance of white men on the Senate Judiciary Committee over time (e.g., Boyd, Collins, and Ringhand 2018). We limit our analyses in this chapter to male senators' questions (for gender-related analyses) and white senators' questions (for person of color–related analyses) during Supreme Court confirmation hearings.[14] Thus, the gender models allow us to examine whether male senators treat female nominees differently than male senators treat male nominees, and the racial models allow us to investigate whether white senators treat nominees of color differently than white senators treat white nominees.[15] We present a descriptive analysis of the questioning behavior of the limited number of female senators and senators of color in the book's concluding chapter.

Our first dependent variable represents the proportion of senatorial questions devoted to explorations of the nominees' judicial philosophies. Questions about judicial philosophy include those that involve a nominee's judicial philosophy and constitutional interpretation as a concept, but do not include questions about constitutional interpretation that arise in the context of a specific issue area or are related to particular constitutional outcomes or cases. Thus, questions about judicial philosophy focus on the primary task of a Supreme Court justice—how to interpret the Constitution. Overall, 12 percent of questions asked by senators involve querying nominees about their judicial philosophies. This makes this the second most common substantive topic of questioning at the hearings, after civil rights.

We employ four dependent variables to test the subject matter hypotheses. To examine gender differences, we use the proportion of senatorial questions devoted to pressing nominees about abortion and gender discrimination. To examine racial discrepancies, we use the proportion of senators' questioning devoted to racial discrimination and crime. We chose to focus on these issue areas for two reasons. First, they have been identified in previous literature as areas where women and people of color are expected to have views that may differ from white males (e.g., Boyd 2016; Boyd, Epstein, and Martin 2010; Harris and Sen 2019; Huddy and Terkildsen 1993a; Schneider and Bos 2011; Steffensmeier and Britt 2001; Welch, Combs, and Gruhl 1988; Wheelock, Stroshine, and O'Hear 2019). Second, these issue areas are frequently discussed at confirmation hearings, with racial discrimination, gender discrimination, and abortion rights constituting three of the top five most frequently discussed civil rights topics (e.g., Collins and Ringhand 2013a; Ringhand and Collins 2011), and crime representing the fifth most commonly addressed issue area overall. In contrast, other issues that women and people of color are frequently stereotyped as being different from their white, male counterparts, such as the economy and the military, are rarely discussed at Supreme Court confirmation hearings (Collins and Ringhand 2013a, 88–96).

To test our hypotheses, we set up a series of variables that allow us to capture the gender, race, and party affiliation of the questioning senator and the nominee. *Female* is scored 1 for questions asked by male senators to female nominees (Ginsburg, Kagan, O'Connor, Sotomayor, and Jackson) and 0 for questions asked by male senators to male nominees, based on information in Epstein et al. (2022) and United States Senate (2022a). *Male* is coded in the opposite way (1 for male senator–male nominee questions; 0 for male senator–female nominee questions). *Nominee of Color* is scored 1 for questions asked by white senators to nominees of color (Marshall, Sotomayor, Thomas, and Jackson) and 0 for questions asked by white senators to white nominees (Epstein et al. 2022; United States Senate 2022b). *White* is coded in the opposite way (1 for white senator–white nominee questions; 0 for white senator–nominee of color questions). *Same Party* is scored 1 if the senator questioning the nominee shares the partisan affiliation of the president who appointed the nominee and 0 if the senator and nominee have opposing party affiliations (Carroll et al. 2015; Epstein et al. 2022). *Different Party* is coded in the opposite way.[16]

Based on these constituent variables, the modeling below focuses primarily on the four possible combinations for a nominee's out-group status and party affiliation (for a similar modeling technique see Boyd, Collins, and Ringhand 2018). Doing so allows us to better understand the conditionality present between these statuses and how they compare to one another when it comes to the proportion of questions asked in a given issue area. For nominee gender, the four resulting combinations are: (1) *Female, Same Party*, (2) *Male, Different Party*, (3) *Male, Same Party*, and (4) *Female, Different Party*. Every senator-nominee pair within the data belongs to one (and only one) of these groups. For nominee race, the four similarly designed groupings are: (1) *Nominee of Color, Same Party*, (2) *White, Different Party*, (3) *White, Same Party*, and (4) *Nominee of Color, Different Party*.

Because our theory is focused on examining how out-group nominees from the opposite party of the questioning senator are differently treated, the *Female, Different Party* variable serves as the baseline in our statistical models that examine gender differences. Based on our hypotheses, we expect that the *Female, Same Party* variable will be negatively signed, indicating that female nominees receive a smaller proportion of questions in the issue areas under analysis from same-party senators, compared to female, different-party nominees. We expect the *Male, Different Party* variable will be negatively signed, revealing that male nominees receive a smaller proportion of questions regarding these issue areas from different-party senators, compared to female, different-party nominees.

The *Male, Different Party* variable is arguably the most important variable in our models because it specifically allows us to examine gender differences, while holding the nominee's different-party status constant. In other words, it tells us how senators who are already primed to be skeptical of a nominee (because of their different-party status) exacerbate this skepticism because of a nominee's gender. Lastly, we expect that the *Male, Same Party* variable will be negatively signed, indicating that male nominees receive a smaller proportion of questions in these areas from same-party senators, compared to different-party senators questioning female nominees. Our expectations for the variables pertaining the race and party of the nominee and senator also follow this logic.

We include three additional variables in the models to account for other factors that might affect the proportion of questions asked by senators about these issue areas. First, we control for each nominee's qualifications, which is intended to capture senators' views of each nominee's professional preparation for the Supreme Court. *Nominee Qualifications* is based on the assessment of a nominee's professional credentials for the Court that appeared in newspaper editorials in four leading newspapers: *Chicago Tribune*, *Los Angeles Times*, *New York Times*, and *Washington Post* (Cameron, Cover, and Segal 1990). This variable ranges from 0 to 1, with higher values indicating more qualified nominees, and was obtained from Epstein et al. (2022).[17] We expect this variable will be negatively signed, indicating that senators ask nominees perceived to be more professionally qualified for the Court a smaller proportion of questions about these issue areas.

Second, we include a variable that indicates whether or not the nominee had prior judicial experience. *Nominee Judge* is coded 1 if the nominee served as a judge on a state or federal court and 0 otherwise, based on information in Epstein et al. (2022). We expect senators to ask nominees with judicial experience a higher proportion of questions regarding their perspectives on these issue areas since these individuals have established track records that are accessible to senators. As a result, senators can base their questions in these issue areas on the nominees' judicial opinions from the lower courts on which they served (e.g., Batta et al. 2012; Williams and Baum 2006). Accordingly, we expect this variable to be positively signed.[18]

Finally, we include a *Senator Reelection Year* variable that captures whether the senator questioning the nominee was up for reelection during the year of the hearing, based on information in United States Senate (2022c). This variable is coded 1 if the senator was up for reelection and 0 otherwise. Because senators can use the questions they ask at the hearings to promote their reelection prospects, we expect them to ask more questions in these issue areas than senators who are not up for reelection. This is because senators can use these questions to demonstrate to their constituents that they take their position on the Judiciary Committee seriously and are willing to rigorously engage nominees on matters relevant to their fitness for the bench and in important issue areas (Collins and Ringhand 2016; Schoenherr, Lane, and Armaly 2020). Accordingly, we expect this variable will be positively signed.[19]

Because our dependent variables are proportions that cannot take on negative values and cannot exceed 1, we employ fractional logit models.[20] Since nominees appear in the data more than once, we use robust standard errors, clustered on nominee. Although the fractional logit model is somewhat sophisticated, readers do not need a background in statistical modeling to understand our results. This is the case because we graphically present our statistical results in an easy to understand manner, instead of presenting them in the more conventional table form. For those interested, the appendix to this chapter contains the traditional regression coefficient tables.

## EMPIRICAL RESULTS

### Judicial Philosophy

Before presenting the results from our statistical models, we provide descriptive analyses of the gender and racial dynamics of issue area questioning at the hearings. Figure 4.1 reports the proportion of judicial philosophy questions from senators from 1939 to 2022. The top figure focuses on senators' judicial philosophy questions, broken down by gender and partisanship, and the bottom figure reports this information with respect to nominee race and partisanship.

These figures provide preliminary support for our gender hypothesis, although the differences with respect to race are less pronounced. The top figure indicates that 17 percent of questions asked of female, different-party nominees involve judicial philosophy, compared to 10 percent for female, same-party nominees; 13 percent for male, same-party nominees; and 14 percent for male, different-party nominees. Thus, it is evident that senators more frequently challenge the competence of female nominees to interpret the Constitution relative

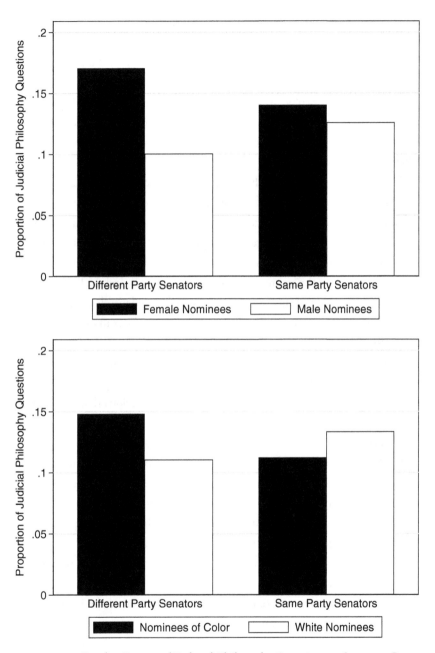

FIGURE 4.1. Gender, Race, and Judicial Philosophy Questions at Supreme Court Confirmation Hearings, 1939–2022

to male nominees, and this is particularly the case if the senators are from the opposite party of the president who appointed the nominees.

Turning now to the bottom figure that focuses on race, the expected differences are present, but much more modest. That is, 15 percent of questions asked of nominees of color from the opposite party of the questioning senator involve judicial philosophy, compared to 11 percent for same-party nominees of color; 13 percent for white, same-party nominees; and 11 percent for white, different-party nominees.

Figure 4.2 contains the results of our fractional logit models that examine influences on the proportion of judicial philosophy questions. The top graph focuses on gender differences and the bottom graph on racial differences. These graphs show the predicted change in the proportion of judicial philosophy questions corresponding to a one-unit increase in each of the independent variables. The circles represent the estimates of the marginal effects, and the lines coming off the circles are 90 percent confident intervals. The independent variables are statistically significant at the 0.05 (one-tailed) level if the confidence intervals do not cross the solid line at zero.

The top graph, focusing on gender disparities, provides support for our key hypothesis. Female nominees being questioned by different-party senators are asked 8 percentage points more judicial philosophy questions than male nominees being questioned by different-party senators, as revealed by the marginal effect of the *Male, Different Party* variable. In other words, preemptively skeptical (different-party) senators grill female nominees much harder than they do similarly situated male nominees about the nominee's ability to competently perform the core professional task of constitutional interpretation. Because an average of 12 percent of all questions involve a nominee's judicial philosophy, this is a very large substantive effect, indicating that female, different-party nominees receive substantially more judicial philosophy questions than male, different-party nominees.

Interestingly, same-party senators are not responding to the increased judicial philosophy questioning from different-party senators by generating a corresponding increase of their own friendly questioning in this area. This type of "tit for tat" ritual is readily observable in other contexts in the hearings (Collins and Ringhand 2013a), but Figure 4.2 shows that it is not happening here. Same-party senators do not respond to the increased skeptical questioning of different-party senators in this area by providing their same-party female

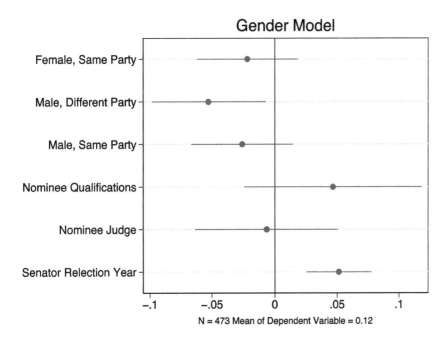

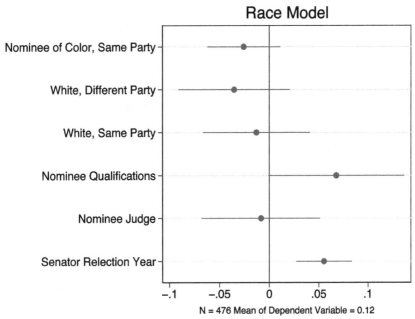

FIGURE 4.2. Influences on the Judicial Philosophy Questioning of Supreme Court Nominees, 1939–2022

nominees with increased opportunities to rebut that skepticism under friendly questioning.[21]

Stereotypes regarding female nominees' professional competence, reflected through questioning about judicial philosophy, thus may harm female nominees in three distinct ways. First, female nominees are subjected to more rigorous questioning in this area by different-party senators who may see such questioning as revealing a perceived weakness. Second, their male counterparts enjoy the privilege of not being subjected to a similar rigorous questioning by different-party senators, and therefore do not have their professional competence publicly challenged in the same way. Third, female nominees are not provided compensatory opportunities by same-party senators to demonstrate their professional competence through a corresponding increase in friendly questioning in this area from same-party senators.

Turning now to the control variables, the model does not indicate that more-qualified nominees, or nominees with previous judicial experience, receive a higher proportion of questions regarding their judicial philosophies. It does, however, indicate that senators up for reelection ask 5 percentage points more judicial philosophy questions than Judiciary Committee members who are not running for reelection. This suggest that senators may leverage these questions to show their constituents that they take their role on the Committee very seriously, and to generate favorable media coverage that may aid their reelections (e.g., Collins and Ringhand 2016; Schoenherr, Lane, and Armaly 2020).

The bottom graph in Figure 4.2 reports the results of the model that explores whether white senators ask nominees of color a higher proportion of questions regarding their judicial philosophies. Unlike the model that explores gender differences, this model fails to reveal racial differences, conditioned or unconditioned on shared party affiliation, on this measure. This is indicated by the fact that the confidence intervals for the nominee race and partisanship variables all cross the solid line at zero. Although unexpected, we can offer one possible explanation for this nonresult. As noted above, our research design anticipates senators' unwillingness to use the hearing process to explicitly and directly call out nominees of color for their perceived lack of professional competence. We therefore use questioning about judicial philosophy as a vehicle through which this senatorial skepticism about the competence of nominees of color will be manifested. It may be the case, however, that senators do not require any such proxy in regard to nominees who are people of color because the purported professional incompetence of these nominees is being discussed directly and explicitly, as seemed to be the case with respect to nominees Marshall and Sotomayor, both of whom had their competence for the Court questioned more directly by senators, as discussed previously.

### *Subject Matter Stereotypes*

We now turn to examining the extent to which bias appears at the confirmation hearings through questioning nominees on subject matters about which senators are likely to perceive female nominees and nominees of color as having expertise or beliefs potentially threatening to the dominant groups' interests. Figure 4.3 reports the proportion of abortion rights and gender discrimination questions senators asked nominees, broken down by gender and partisanship. Abortion rights queries appear in the upper graph and gender discrimination inquiries appear in the bottom graph.

Both figures provide strong, though preliminary, support for our theoretical expectations. Starting with the top graph, 4.9 percent of the questions senators ask female, different-party nominees involve abortion rights, compared to 4.5 percent for female, same-party nominees; 2.1 percent for male, different-party nominees; and 1.6 percent for male, same-party nominees. Thus, senators much more frequently query female nominees about their positions on abortion rights, and this is particularly true if they do not share the partisan affiliation of the female nominee.

The bottom graph reveals a similar picture with respect to gender discrimination questions. Senators devote 3.9 percent of their questions to interrogating female, different-party nominees on gender discrimination, compared to 2.8 percent for female, same-party nominees; 2.6 percent for male, different-party nominees; and 1.8 percent for male, same-party nominees. This indicates that female nominees receive more abortion rights and gender discrimination questioning than do male nominees, regardless of whether they share the partisanship of the questioning senator.

Figure 4.4 depicts the frequency of senatorial questioning on two areas that senators may perceive the expertise or beliefs of nominees of color to be threatening to white interests—racial discrimination and crime. The results regarding racial discrimination questions are quite striking for nominees of color, irrespective of whether they share the party affiliation of the questioning senator.

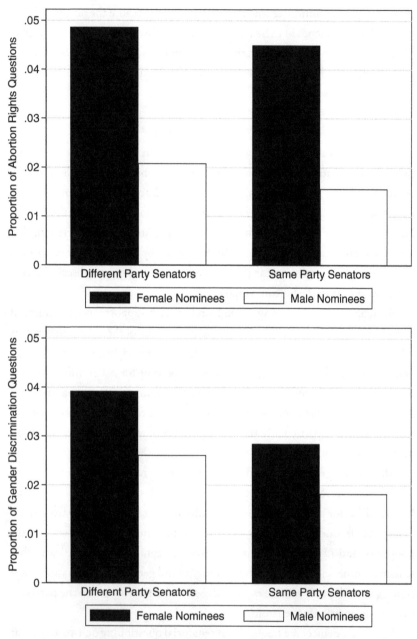

**FIGURE 4.3.** Gender and Abortion Rights and Gender Discrimination Questions at Supreme Court Confirmation Hearings, 1939–2022

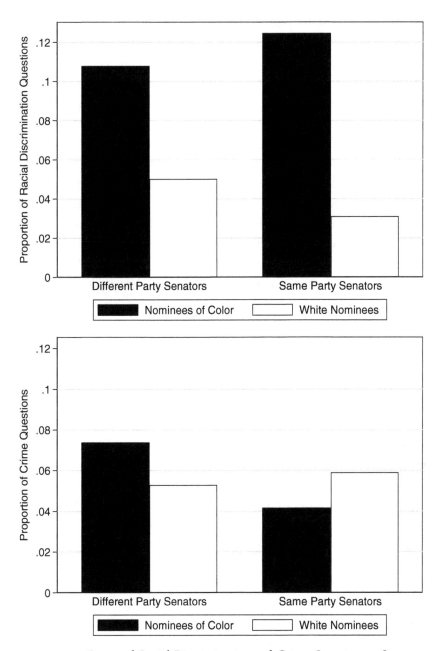

**FIGURE 4.4.** Race and Racial Discrimination and Crime Questions at Supreme Court Confirmation Hearings, 1939–2022

Indeed, 13 percent of the questions asked by same-party senators involve racial discrimination, and this number is 11 percent for different-party senators. In contrast, for white nominees, different-party senators devote 5 percent of their questioning to racial discrimination and same-party senators ask only 3 percent of questions in this area. This suggests that it is a nominee's race that is driving senators' attention to racial discrimination questions, not shared (or opposing) party status.

The results with respect to questions about crime plotted in Figure 4.4 are more nuanced with respect to nominee race. Recall we anticipated that different-party nominees of color would receive the highest volume of crime questions. This is indeed what this figure reveals, with different-party senators devoting 7 percent of their questioning of nominees of color to crime. This is in sharp distinction from same-party nominees of color, who are asked the fewest percentage of crime questions, at 4 percent. It is also a larger volume of crime questions than that received by white nominees, who are queried about crime in 5 percent of different-party senatorial remarks, and 6 percent of same-party senatorial questions. This suggests that the combined effect of a nominee's race and their partisan status is likely driving the volume of questions about crime. In other words, it appears different-party senators are eager to interrogate nominees of color about crime, while same-party senators do not choose to draw attention to this area in their questioning.

Figure 4.5 contains the results of our fractional logit models that examine influences on the proportion of abortion rights and gender discrimination questions. The top graph focuses on abortion rights queries, and the bottom graph highlights gender discrimination questions. As before, the circles represent the marginal effect of a one unit change in each independent variable. These effects are statistically significant if the confidence intervals do not cross the solid line at zero.

Beginning with influences on abortion rights questioning, the results reveal that gender distinctions do exist, conditioned on the partisanship of the nominee and the questioning senator. That is, although female, different-party nominees do not receive more abortion rights questions than female, same-party nominees, senators do question female nominees from the opposing party on abortion rights more so than male nominees. Compared to male, same-party nominees, female, different-party nominees receive about 3 percentage points more questions regarding their views on abortion rights, and they get about 2

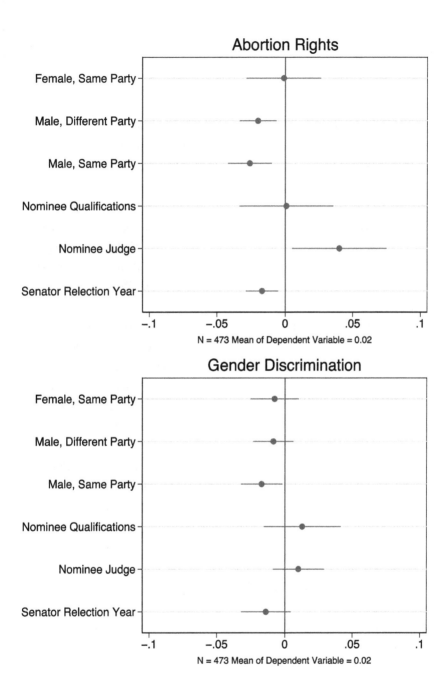

**FIGURE 4.5.** Influences on the Abortion Rights and Gender Discrimination Questioning of Supreme Court Nominees, 1939–2022

percentage points more abortion questions compared to male, different-party nominees. This supports our hypotheses that male senators may perceive that female, different-party nominees might hold views on reproductive rights that may threaten their own. As a result, they engage female, different-party nominees in more rigorous questioning of those views as compared to male nominees. Further, because on average about 2 percent of all senatorial questioning involves abortion rights, these are large effects, indicating that female, different-party nominees receive more than twice as many abortion rights questions as male nominees. The results also indicate that nominees with previous judicial experience receive much more questioning about reproductive rights—about 4 percentage points more—than nominees who were not judges. This suggests that senators may be questioning these nominees about their previous judicial decisions involving reproductive rights (Batta et al. 2012; Williams and Baum 2006).

The bottom graph reports our results regarding questions about gender discrimination. Female, different-party nominees receive about 2 percentage points more gender discrimination questions than male, same-party nominees. However, there are not differences in the volume of gender discrimination questioning among female, different-party nominees and female, same-party nominees, nor male, different-party nominees. This indicates that, compared to male, same-party nominees, senators are likely more skeptical of female nominees from the opposing political party, and therefore engage those nominees in more questioning of their views on matters of gender discrimination.

Finally, Figure 4.6 reports the results of our models examining racial discrimination and crime questions. The top graph reveals qualified support for our expectations with respect to racial discrimination questions. Compared to white, same-party nominees, nominees of color from the opposite party of the questioning senator receive about 3 percentage points more questions about their views on racial discrimination. This is again a substantially large effect since the average percentage of racial discrimination questions is 4 percent. It corroborates our belief that white senators on the Judiciary Committee may be uncomfortable with the views of nominees of color regarding racial discrimination. As a result, they ask these nominees more questions about those views relative to the white, same-party nominees. However, the results do not support any other distinctions based on the race and partisanship of other nominee types.

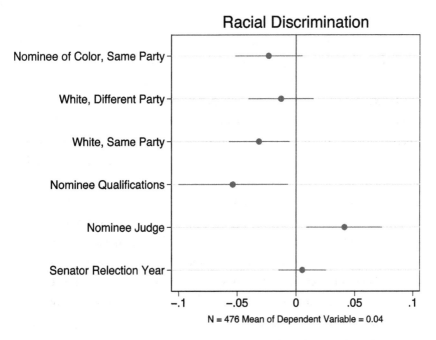

N = 476 Mean of Dependent Variable = 0.04

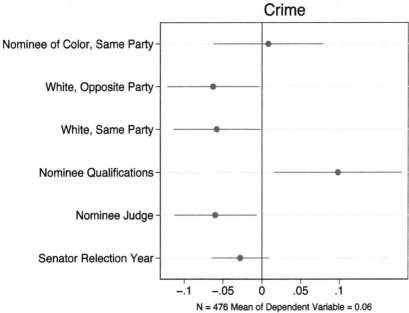

N = 476 Mean of Dependent Variable = 0.06

**FIGURE 4.6.** Influences on the Racial Discrimination and Crime Questioning of Supreme Court Nominees, 1939–2022

The model does, however, reveal that two of our control variables do influence racial discrimination questioning. Nominees that are more qualified receive fewer questions regarding racial discrimination than less qualified individuals. This suggests that senators may be more comfortable with the race discrimination views of more qualified nominees, asking them fewer questions about this issue area. Conversely, senators ask nominees with previous judicial experience about 4 percentage points more racial discrimination questions. As noted above, they are likely doing so to address these nominees' previous judicial decisions on racial discrimination.

The bottom graph provides support for racial distinctions regarding questioning nominees about crime. Here, different-party nominees of color receive about 6 percentage points more questions about their opinions on crime than both same- and different-party white nominees. Because the average nominee receives about 6 percent of questions about crime, these are very large effects, indicating that different-party nominees of color are queried twice as often as white nominees about crime. As with our other findings regarding gender and racial discrepancies, this is indicative of the possibility that white senators have some trepidation with respect to the views of different-party nominees of color relative to white nominees and grill those nominees on their perspectives on crime and the Court's criminal law precedents. We also find that more-qualified nominees are asked a higher volume of questions on crime, while nominees with previous judicial experience are asked fewer questions about criminal law than those without such experience.

## CONCLUSIONS

The experience of actress and dancer Ginger Rogers is often used to illustrate the additional burdens that some professionals face relative to their "costars." As Ellison and Smith (2013, 61) put it: "While the movies of Fred Astaire and Ginger Rogers display the artistry of a fabulous couple dancing fully in sync, Rogers' role presented an added and formidable challenge. She is required to anticipate, balance, and reverse in a mirror image, maintaining all the while an air of floating grace and effortless fluidity." In other words, as is frequently said, she had to do everything he did, but backwards and in heels. This analogy applies well to the Judiciary Committee's hearings. Our inquiry indicates that this imbalance exists for women and people of color during their confirmation hearings, with these nominees, at least at times, having to work much harder than other nominees to prove their fitness to serve on the Supreme Court. Justice Ginsburg, it seems, was correct. Women and nominees of color face an idée fixe ('fixed idea') when trying to break into positions of power in the judicial system, including service on the Supreme Court. The long-standing practices of white men serving as Supreme Court justices, along with the accompanying gendered and racialized stereotypes about competence and subject matter strengths, place an undue onus on female nominees and nominees of color as they traverse the confirmation hearing process.

This extends to both questions related to nominee competence to serve on the Supreme Court and gendered and racial stereotypes as to subject matter competence and a nominee's ability to maintain impartiality.

First, we find that, as predicted by out-group theory and prior studies of gender bias in hiring, male senators grill female, different-party nominees on their judicial philosophies—questions representing the core professional skill expected of U.S. Supreme Court justices—more so than they press male, different-party nominees. Because this questioning comes from different-party—and presumably skeptical—senators, it indicates that gender is likely the motivating factor here, since different-party senators do not press male nominees to defend their competence with the same vigor. We do not, however, find evidence that nominees of color face similarly high levels of judicial philosophy questions relative to white nominees.

Second, our results provide evidence that, as predicted by theory, in-group senators engage in gender and racial stereotyping of tasks, beliefs, and expertise relevant to serving on the Supreme Court. Our findings reveal that both female nominees and nominees of color face more extensive questioning than certain types of other nominees in areas falling within their perceived strengths—for women, abortion and gender discrimination, and for nominees of color, racial discrimination and crime.

This chapter thus confirms that female nominees and nominees of color, despite being among the most accomplished lawyers of their respective generations, are subjected to a different type of confirmation process than are male and white nominees. And as we will see in the next chapter, the differences women and people of color face during their confirmation hearings do not stop with the subject matters addressed in the senators' questions.

**APPENDIX TABLE 4.1.** Influences on the Judicial Philosophy Questioning of Supreme Court Nominees, 1939–2022

| | Gender Model | Race Model |
|---|---|---|
| Female, Same Party | -0.205 | |
| | (0.229) | |
| Male, Different Party | -0.496* | |
| | (0.273) | |
| Male, Same Party | -0.244 | |
| | (0.234) | |
| Nominee of Color, Same Party | | -0.239 |
| | | (0.204) |
| White, Different Party | | -0.328 |
| | | (0.316) |
| White, Same Party | | -0.120 |
| | | (0.304) |
| Nominee Qualifications | 0.438 | 0.631* |
| | (0.395) | (0.381) |
| Nominee Judge | -0.061 | -0.078 |
| | (0.324) | (0.335) |
| Senator Reelection Year | 0.483* | 0.515* |
| | (0.160) | (0.176) |
| Constant | -2.044* | -2.274* |
| | (0.451 | (0.501) |
| AIC | 0.612 | 0.614 |
| N | 473 | 476 |

* $p < 0.05$ (one-tailed). The dependent variable is the proportion of a senator's statements that involved judicial philosophy questions. Entries are fractional logit regression coefficients. Numbers in parentheses are robust standard errors, clustered on nominee.

**APPENDIX TABLE 4.2.** Influences on the Abortion Rights and Gender Discrimination Questioning of Supreme Court Nominees, 1939–2022

| | Abortion Rights | Gender Discrimination |
|---|---|---|
| Female, Same Party | -0.044 | -0.316 |
| | (0.712) | (0.470) |
| Male, Different Party | -0.848* | -0.355 |
| | (0.447) | (0.379) |
| Male, Same Party | -1.104* | -0.714* |
| | (0.531) | (0.384) |
| Nominee Qualifications | 0.038 | 0.539 |
| | (0.893) | (0.688) |
| Nominee Judge | 1.706* | 0.420 |
| | (0.768) | (0.471) |
| Senator Reelection Year | -0.724* | -0.585 |
| | (0.292) | (0.445) |
| Constant | -4.512* | -3.979* |
| | (1.343) | (0.790) |
| AIC | 0.210 | 0.218 |
| N | 473 | 473 |

* $p < 0.05$ (one-tailed). The dependent variable is the proportion of a senator's statements that involved abortion rights and gender discrimination questions. Entries are fractional logit regression coefficients. Numbers in parentheses are robust standard errors, clustered on nominee.

**APPENDIX TABLE 4.3.** Influences on the Racial Discrimination and Crime Questioning of Supreme Court Nominees, 1939–2022

| | Racial Discrimination | Crime |
|---|---|---|
| Nominee of Color, Same Party | -0.579 | 0.141 |
| | (0.411) | (0.734) |
| White, Different Party | -0.321 | -1.083* |
| | (0.436) | (0.587) |
| White, Same Party | -0.785* | -1.002* |
| | (0.402) | (0.572) |
| Nominee Qualifications | -1.340* | 1.693* |
| | (0.719) | (0.904) |
| Nominee Judge | 1.028* | -1.034* |
| | (0.390) | (0.472) |
| Senator Reelection Year | 0.131 | -0.481 |
| | (0.306) | (0.363) |
| Constant | -2.562* | -2.415* |
| | (0.768) | (0.890) |
| AIC | 0.305 | 0.402 |
| N | 476 | 476 |

* $p < 0.05$ (one-tailed). The dependent variable is the proportion of a senator's statements that involved racial discrimination and crime questions. Entries are fractional logit regression coefficients. Numbers in parentheses are robust standard errors, clustered on nominee.

# FIVE

## INTERRUPTIONS

During the Senate Judiciary Committee confirmation hearings for U.S. Supreme Court nominee Elena Kagan in 2010, an interesting exchange took place between Kagan and Senator Coburn, the Republican from Oklahoma. In his questioning, Coburn pushed Kagan on her views on the role of foreign law in Supreme Court decision making. The subject matter of the inquiry was not particularly notable, but the exchange nonetheless is striking for anyone familiar with the gender and power dynamics of conversational styles:

SENATOR COBURN. Do you have a comment about what I've said?

MS. KAGAN. Well, I suppose a few comments, Senator Coburn. Let me take on just a couple of the particulars, and then maybe make a more general comment. You said, as Solicitor General, I advocated the use of—of foreign law in some circumstances. I do just want to make clear that what I said in those—those questions—

SENATOR COBURN. Here's your quote exactly.

MS. KAGAN —[continuing]. Was—was that, because there are justices on the Supreme Court who believe in the use of foreign law in some circumstances, that I would think it was appropriate, as an advocate, to argue from foreign law or to cite foreign law in any circumstance—

SENATOR COBURN. Well, but that isn't what you said here.

MS. KAGAN. Well, I think, Senator Coburn, with all respect, that if you look at the question and you look at the answer, I was speaking in my role as an advocate, saying that the primary consideration of an advocate is to count to five and to try to do the best the advocate can to ensure that the position that the advocate has taken will prevail.

SENATOR COBURN. But it's not your position, because some other justices are using foreign law, you have the authority to do that as well.

MS. KAGAN. As an advocate, to the extent that I think that foreign law arguments will help the government's case, then I will use those foreign law arguments, is what I—

SENATOR COBURN. All right. Let me read something to you. As is obvious, I'm not a lawyer. OK. It's pretty obvious. But Article 3, Section 2 says this: "The judicial power shall extend to all cases in law and equity arising under this Constitution, the laws of the United States, and the treaties made."[1]

Senator Coburn's apprehension about the use of foreign law in U.S. courts is vividly displayed during this question and answer segment, in part because of the way that Coburn repeatedly found ways to dominate the discussion. During the course of this short exchange, Coburn interrupted Kagan three times (noted by the "—" at the end of a speaker's turn). Through the use of interruptions, Coburn was able to continually seize the conversational floor and assert power over how the exchange would proceed and Kagan's opportunity to answer.

In this particular line of questioning, Senator Coburn, a male, interrupted Kagan, a female nominee, multiple times. Senator Coburn's repeated interruptions of nominee Kagan is just one of many examples of similar interruptions of female and person of color nominees' statements during Supreme Court confirmation hearings. While male and white nominees also are interrupted during their confirmation hearings, scholars have demonstrated for years that women and people of color are much more likely to experience interruptions than are white men (Anderson and Leaper 1998; Hancock and Rubin 2014; Leman and Ikoko 2010; Snyder 2014). Politicians, lawyers, and Supreme Court justices are not immune from these interruption patterns. It would be no surprise, then, if Supreme Court confirmation hearings before the Judiciary Committee yield similar inequities in interruption patterns.

The potential presence of gender and racial bias via interruption patterns during Supreme Court confirmation hearings is important. Speech interruptions are often intrusive attempts to exercise conversational control (Johnson 1994) that place the interrupter in a "dominant position, relative to the speaker" (Karpowitz, Mendelberg, and Mattioli 2015, 161). This can be true even when the interrupter intends to help or support the original speaker through the interruption (Mendelberg, Karpowitz, and Oliphant 2014, 20). Interruptions can thus have a silencing effect on women and people of color (Mendelberg, Karpowitz, and Oliphant 2014, 21) and reinforce sex- and race-based stereotypes of leaders and others in professional settings (Feldman and Gill 2019). Further, senatorial interruptions at confirmation hearings demonstrate disrespect for nominees and can serve to paint the interrupted nominees in a negative light.

In this chapter, we explore confirmation hearing exchanges like that between Senator Coburn and nominee Kagan to examine the broader interruption patterns in the exchanges between Supreme Court nominees and members of the Senate Judiciary Committee. We begin by explaining why studying interruptions matters and why there is good reason to believe that female nominees and nominees of color are likely to be more frequently interrupted at confirmation hearings, especially by different-party senators. Next, we present a separate case for positive interruptions and posit that senators will more frequently interrupt their female and people of color copartisans in the belief that doing so will help their performances at the confirmation hearings. To examine these possibilities, we utilize an original database that contains information on all interruptions from 1939 to 2022. Our results indicate that there are important gender and racial dynamics to interruptions at confirmation hearings. Notably, senators more frequently interrupt out-group nominees, something that can have a silencing effect on the women and people of color testifying before the Judiciary Committee.

## INTERRUPTIONS AS CONTROL AND DOMINANCE

Speaking provides a meaningful opportunity to "establish authority and status as a valuable member of the group" (Mendelberg, Karpowitz, and Oliphant 2014, 20). The right of a speaker to have a full, unimpeded turn to talk during a conversation is considered by many to be critical to respectful discourse (Goldberg 1990, 884). In multiperson speaking settings, the strong norm is that of taking turns, where "for some limited period one person alone holds the floor and acts primarily as speaker and the other person acts primarily as listener" (Beattie 1982, 93). Speech exchange systems and turn taking exist across types of speech—from casual conversation to formal debate to high ceremony (Zimmerman and West 1975). Across contexts, turn taking "is made necessary by the cognitive limitations of human beings" since people struggle to "talk and listen simultaneously" (Beattie 1982, 93). When speakers alternate between turns in a smooth and unencumbered way, this "signifies liking, affiliation, and sensitivity to the interactive needs of others" (Bresnahan and Cai 1996, 172).

Interruptions—the act of "talking before the speaker's turn is finished and perhaps prevent him or her from completing the thought" (Smith-Lovin and Brody 1989, 425)—break the conversational turn-taking rule. Interruptions can be used "to control the topic of conversation" (Aries 1996, 79), "disorganize the speech and ideas of the interrupted" (Smith-Lovin and Brody 1989, 425), and "stop a speaker from continuing what he/she is doing" (Ekström 2009, 388). Some interruptions go so far as to bid to "take the floor in a negative or hostile manner," raise objections, or fully change the topic of conversation (Leman and Ikoko 2010, 64).

Scholars agree that many interruptions are closely linked with dominance, control, power, and status (e.g., Goldberg 1990; Johnson 1994; Karpowitz, Mendelberg, and Mattioli 2015; Smith-Lovin and Brody 1989)—common themes examined throughout this book. As Goldberg put it:

> Whether successful or not, it is the imputation of volitional intent—intent to disrupt, to take over the turnspace occupied by another, and to generally interfere with the projected form, content, and/or "ownership" of what is said—which leads to the assumption that interruptions are interactional strategies for exerting and overtly displaying power or control over both the discourse and its participants. (1990, 884, internal citations omitted)

In other words, interruptions are "a power play" (Mendelberg, Karpowitz, and Oliphant 2014). As a result, interruptions are an effective method for seizing and building "the power of the interrupter by placing him or her in a dominant position, relative to the speaker" (Karpowitz, Mendelberg, and Mattioli 2015). Similarly, interruption efforts are deemed to be excellent and sensitive measures of conversational control and dominance (Smith-Lovin and Brody 1989).

The effects of interruptions during conversations can be wide-ranging and ultimately modify, in meaningful ways, what gets discussed and what decision making results. As Black, Johnson, and Wedeking (2012, 19) argue in the context of studying interruptions during Supreme Court oral arguments:

> By interrupting the current speaker, another member of a group discussion can change the entire dynamic of a decision-making process.... While communication is generally meant to convey specific information in a group decision-making process, interruptions are meant to alter the topic or overall dynamic of the conversation. Doing so may, in turn, alter the group's ultimate decisions.

Black, Johnson, and Wedeking suggest that during Supreme Court oral arguments, interruptions powerfully serve to prevent speaking justices from signaling their preferences and intentions and coordinating with colleagues. It is not difficult to imagine similar effects on or consequences emanating from interruptions of confirmation hearing nominees. After all, confirmation hearing interruptions may stall nominees' efforts to defend their judicial philosophy, justify prior controversial comments or opinions, or develop credibility and rapport while answering senators' questions, to name just a few possibilities. In short, interruptions at the hearings may be harmful to nominees.

## GENDER, RACE, AND INTERRUPTIONS

While interruptions happen in all types of speech contexts and speaker pairings, there is strong potential for interruption patterns during confirmation hearings to be linked to race, ethnicity, and gender. As Chapter 3 theorizes, bias (often implicit) toward women and people of color means that they are often assumed to be of a different, lower status than those in majority groups. At the same time, majority groups hold status and power and take steps to retain (and grow) their power and derogate those deemed to be their subordinates (Christensen, Szmer, and Stritch 2012; Magee and Galinsky 2008). The combination of bias and status and power advantages in society among men and racial majorities can result in these powerful groups inferring that "they are entitled to take the conversational floor" (Anderson and Leaper 1998, 226). This can manifest through more frequent interruptions of the speech of women and people of color.

When female and person of color speakers experience a disproportionate number of interruptions in a public forum, the implications can be grave. Majority groups seeking to maintain power and status and foster inequality can use interruptions. Interruptions "clearly allow the powerful, high-status speakers more access to important interpersonal resources (the 'floor') at the expense of their lower-status partners" (Smith-Lovin and Brody 1989, 425). Interruptions can also have a "negative, silencing effect on lower-status groups, since those groups' authority is fragile and disagreements they may direct at high-status members tend to be countered with aggressive reactions or backlash" (Mendelberg, Karpowitz, and Oliphant 2014, 21). Inequities in who is interrupted thus may further entrench the power and voice of majority classes and signal weakness among those who lack power.

Scholarly research finds strong evidence that gender disparities in groups are an important factor in predicting interruptions. Numerous studies find that female speakers are often much more likely to experience interruptions than male speakers (Anderson and Leaper 1999; Hancock and Rubin 2014; Snyder 2014). Leman and Ikoko (2010) find that person of color speakers receive more negative interruptions than those belonging to the racial in-group.

The empirical results are also strong in political and legal contexts.[2] In her study of the conversation between senators and witnesses during David Souter's 1990 Senate Judiciary Committee hearings, Mattei (1998) demonstrates that senators interrupted female witnesses far more often than they did male witnesses. Indeed, of the forty-one interruptions by senators observed in the study, 82 percent were of female witnesses. At the U.S. Supreme Court, recent studies examine the interruption phenomenon and find striking gendered effects. Feldman and Gill (2019) and Jacobi and Schweers (2017) find that female justices on the Court are interrupted more frequently by fellow justices than are their male colleagues. Similarly, research examining Supreme Court oral arguments during the early days of the COVID-19 pandemic, in which the Court heard arguments telephonically, found evidence that female justices were cut off by Chief Justice Roberts more frequently than their male colleagues (Jacobi, Johnson, Ringsmuth, and Sag 2021; Litman 2020). And Patton and Smith (2017) find that female lawyers are, for most issue areas, interrupted more than male lawyers during oral arguments.

Evidence also indicates the presence of similar interruption pattern disparities in legal settings beyond the Supreme Court. Bogoch's (1999) study of

Israeli district courts found that women lawyers—both prosecutors and defense attorneys—were interrupted during their examination of witnesses with greater frequency than male lawyers serving in similar roles. As another stark example of differences in interruptions, an anonymous female lawyer practicing in the U.S. federal courts reported: "During deposition, opposing counsel rudely cut off [my] questioning and kept talking and yelling louder over my objections. . . . [He] told me to 'back off, honey!'" (Cortina et al. 2002, 263). Notably, race and ethnicity in the context of interruptions have received much less scholarly attention than gender, particularly in legal and political settings.

This also is likely to play out in similar ways with interruptive behavior toward Supreme Court nominees during their Senate confirmation hearings. Members of the Judiciary Committee may be more likely to interrupt female nominees and nominees of color than white, male nominees because they see, consciously or not, the former nominees as unfamiliar out-group members who may not share their core values. Further, by interrupting a nominee, a senator can attempt to paint the nominee as less than forthcoming, in the sense that interruptions at confirmation hearings often signal that the senator is unhappy with the nominee's answer to the senator's question.

An example from the hearings helps to demonstrate the power of interruptions to senators. During the confirmation hearings for Clarence Thomas in 1991, Senator Dennis DeConcini (D-AZ) pushed the nominee on his work as the chairman of the Equal Employment Opportunity Commission from 1982 to 1990 and what appeared to be a lack of effort by the agency to reach out to the Hispanic community about pursuing discrimination charges.

> SENATOR DECONCINI. Did you go and meet with the Council of La Raza, the GI Forum, or any of the other national or local Hispanic groups, to see what they would suggest you do, or to ask for their counsel and suggestions and advice?
>
> JUDGE THOMAS. Senator, I can't name, again, sitting here, all of the groups that I have met with, but one of our Commissioners in particular was very, very active, and he and I spent a great deal of time together, because he would go, and he would report back on what the perceptions of the problems were and approaches that we could take. Again, he and I were there the entirety of my tenure, with the exception of a few months. And a second Commissioner who was also Hispanic, he and I worked very

closely together to begin to address some of these problems. And I am sure
both of them were very active and very involved, and I think they would
both tell you that I always—

SENATOR DECONCINI. Judge, I appreciate that, but it doesn't answer my
question. What did you do?[3]

As we can see during this exchange, Senator DeConcini was trying to make a
very specific point. By cutting off Thomas's answer, DeConcini was able to simultaneously control the conversation and convey his unhappiness with Thomas's response.

Just as we have seen in other confirmation hearing contexts throughout this
book, inequities in interruptions based on nominee race and gender may emerge
in combination with partisanship dynamics between senators and nominees.
With interruptions, Smith-Lovin and Brody (1989) argue that "friends" interrupt less frequently than others. Other research indicates that individuals who
do not know each other well are more likely "to rely on characteristics such
as sex to define status/power relationships" and have higher interruption levels
(James and Clarke 1993, 261). Johnson, Black, and Wedeking (2009, 350) also
find that "justices who take opposite ideological positions more frequently interrupt each other." Jacobi and Schweers (2017, 1488) confirm the presence of
an interactive effect between justice gender and ideology in the likelihood of
interruptions, finding that "interruptions occur most frequently when gender
and ideology are both different" and that the "strongest effect is of conservative
men interrupting liberal women."

As discussed in Chapter 3, the highly partisan modern Senate and its committees encourage party-based teamwork (Epstein and Segal 2007; Lee 2008,
2009). How might this "partisan climate" in the Senate's deliberations over Supreme Court nominees affect interruptive behavior toward female nominees and
nominees of color (compared to male and white nominees) during the confirmation hearings? We expect that shared party will lessen the gendered and racial
effects of most interruptive behavior. Regardless of race or gender, senators will
be more likely to view same-party nominees as "friends" than those appointed
by an different-party president. Because of the shared party, there will be much
less need for assertiveness or aggressiveness in questioning since there is unlikely
to be attempts to sink the nomination. This should, in turn, reduce the likelihood of intrusive-intentioned interruptions based on gender or race. By contrast,

different-party nominees may face heightened stereotypes and hostility. They are seen as "different," without the mitigating salve of a shared party identity, and questioning senators are incentivized by partisan loyalties to behave assertively. These different-party, female and person of color nominees are thus likely to receive a higher rate of interruptions than their same- party counterparts.

To see this minority status effect combined with a partisanship effect, we turn to an exchange from the confirmation hearing of Justice Sonia Sotomayor. In this example, Senator Orrin Hatch (R-UT) is questioning Sotomayor about Second Amendment–related precedent. The line of questioning is not especially hostile, but Hatch's interruption of Sotomayor allows him to effectively wield his power over the nominee and the conversation's direction.

SENATOR HATCH. Now, I want to begin here today by looking at your cases in an area that is very important to many of us, and that is the Second Amendment, the right to keep and bear arms, and your conclusion that the right is not fundamental.

Now, in the 2004 case entitled *United States* v. *Sanchez-Villar*, you handled the Second Amendment issue in a short footnote. You cited the Second Circuit's decision in *United States* v. *Toner* for the proposition of the right to possess a gun is not a fundamental right.

Toner in turn relied on the Supreme Court's decision in *United States* v. *Miller*. Last year, in the *District of Columbia* v. *Heller*, the Supreme Court examined *Miller* and concluded that, "The case did not even purport to be a thorough examination of the Second Amendment," and that *Miller* provided "no explanation of the content of the right."

You are familiar with that.

JUDGE SOTOMAYOR. I am, sir.

SENATOR HATCH. Okay. So let me ask you, doesn't the Supreme Court's treatment of *Miller* at least cast doubts on whether relying on *Miller*, as the Second Circuit has done for this proposition, is proper?

JUDGE SOTOMAYOR. The issue—

SENATOR HATCH. Remember, I am saying at least cast doubts.

JUDGE SOTOMAYOR [continuing]. Well, that is what I believe Justice Scalia implied in his footnote 23, but he acknowledged that the issue of whether the right, as understood in Supreme Court jurisprudence, was fundamental. It's not that I considered it unfundamental, but that the

Supreme Court didn't consider it fundamental so as to be incorporated against the states.[4]

This exchange between Senator Hatch and Sotomayor illustrates what could be a combined effect on interruptions patters of the nominee's race/gender and a lack of shared partisanship between the nominee and senator. The fact that Hatch quickly interrupted Sotomayor to remind her of the essence of his question was disruptive to Sotomayor's attempt to answer the senator's question. Would Hatch have done this to a male nominee or a copartisan? Possibly, but our theory suggests this type of interruptive behavior is more likely to be targeted at female nominees and nominees of color who do not share the party affiliation of the questioning senator.

An exchange from Ketanji Brown Jackson's hearing offers another example. Here, Senator Lindsey Graham (R-SC) questions Jackson about her service as a public defender for detainees at Guantánamo Bay and her positions on national security issues:

SENATOR GRAHAM. Of the five men we released from Gitmo as part of a prisoner swap for Sergeant Bergdahl. Here's what—here's where they're at. Mohammed Faizal was appointed deputy minister of defense, Noor was appointed acting minister of Borders and Tribal Affairs, Rosicky was appointed as acting intelligence director, Zakir, again, acting Minister of Information Culture Defense, Omar was appointed as the new governor of the southeastern province of Khost.

These were five people that we had in our control. They're now helping the Taliban run the country. Would you say that our system in terms of releasing people needs to be looked at?

JUDGE JACKSON. Senator, what I'd say is that that's not a job for the courts in this way, that—

SENATOR GRAHAM. As an American does that bother you?

JUDGE JACKSON. Well, obviously Senator, any repeated criminal behavior or repeated attacks acts of war, bother me, yes, in America—

SENATOR GRAHAM. Well, it bothers me. While I will not hold it against you, nor should I, the fact that you represent Gitmo detainees, I think it's time to look at this system, new folks. When 31 percent of people are going back to fight to kill Americans and now running the Taliban government, we have gone wrong somewhere. Are we still at war?

JUDGE JACKSON. So the AMUF, the authorization for military force, is still in effect. Congress has authorized the use of force against people in—in this way.

SENATOR GRAHAM But do you personally believe that al Qaeda, ISIS type groups are still at war with us?

JUDGE JACKSON. I think, yes—I mean I think we—

SENATOR GRAHAM: So we're still in a state of war with certain elements of radical Islam to this very day?[5]

Just as was the case with Hatch's interruption of Sotomayor, Graham's repeated interruptions of Jackson allow the senator to dominate the direction of the exchange and disrupt the nominee's ability to finish her points in a way that we expect is repeated in other female and person of color nominees' experiences before the Senate Judiciary Committee.

This discussion and these examples lead to the following hypotheses on interruption patterns, each of which we test below:

HYPOTHESIS 5.1: Female, different-party nominees will be interrupted more than other nominees.

HYPOTHESIS 5.2: Person of color, different-party nominees will be interrupted more than other nominees.

## A SEPARATE CASE FOR POSITIVE INTERRUPTIONS

Not every interruption is "a miniature battle for ascendency" (Meltzer et al. 1971, 392) with an intention to intrude on the speaker's points. Rather, some interruptions are much more supportive and positive in nature. These types of interruptions include, for example, attempts to build rapport and collaboration, assist the speaker, support and engage with the speaker's points, provide cues about mutual understanding, or express simple uncertainty (Bresnahan and Cai 1996; Chowdhury, Danieli, and Riccardi 2015; Feldman and Gill 2019; Hilton 2016; Leman, Ahmen, and Ozarow 2005; Truong 2013).

However, even when an interruption is intended to help or support the original speaker in some way, the act can still have chilling effects on speakers and communicate the presence of status hierarchies. As Feldman and Gill (2019, 175) argue, "the effects of interruptions are not always in line with their intended purposes. Interruptions that are intended to establish rapport can have a disruptive effect" and cause the interrupted speaker to stop talking altogether. As a result, observers of even the most positively intentioned interruptions may view the interrupter as the more dominant, confident, or powerful participant in the conversation (and, by contrast, the interrupted party as weaker and less confident) (Mendelberg, Karpowitz, and Oliphant 2014; Wolfartsberger 2011).

"Friendly" interruptions like this may be more frequently present for women and person of color speakers than for white and male speakers. We think that implicit biases against women and person of color speakers may again play a notable role in explaining the patterns in supportive interruptions. Interrupters may perceive women and minority speakers to be weaker and in need of help during their conversation. Or, instead, interrupters may be concerned that other parties perceive these original speakers to be weaker and more likely to have their ideas and arguments subject to attack from opponents. Supportive interrupters, in effect, may be attempting to preemptively defend the interrupted party from less friendly outside sources.

Given our above observations about the highly partisan nature of confirmation hearings and the emphasis on party-based teamwork, supportive interruptions may be particularly likely to emerge during the hearings from senators who share party affiliations with the nominee. Because of the widely held perceptions that women nominees and nominees of color are weaker than other nominees, partisan allies may go out of their way to behave supportively and attempt to bolster the performance of these nominees. Positive interruptions provide a pathway for so-inclined senators to do just that. Numerous examples exist in the confirmation hearing transcripts of senators interrupting women and nominees of color to finish their statements, summarize their words, or positively bolster their record—all with an apparent intention to aid and support the nominee.

Another example, from Clarence Thomas's hearing, shows how positive interruptions are often used. During a tense line of questioning between Senator Patrick Leahy (D-VT) and Thomas about Thomas's views of natural law principles, Senator Strom Thurmond (R-SC) interrupted Thomas so as to chastise his colleague Leahy and ensure that Thomas retained the speaking floor to proceed. The exchange played out like this:

JUDGE THOMAS. Let me explain what I was trying to say. What I was trying to say—

SENATOR LEAHY. You cannot answer that specific question?

JUDGE THOMAS. What I am trying to say, so I am not misunderstood, Senator—

SENATOR THURMOND. Mr. Chairman, he has a right to explain his position.[6]

Senator Thurmond's interruption of Thomas is a "friendly" interruption since Thurmond's intention seems to have been to ensure that his partisan ally, Thomas, had a chance to talk in his, and not Leahy's, preferred way. However, the interruption happened after Thomas had already begun his answer to Leahy in his own words and in his own way. If the nominee were Scalia or Kennedy—a white, male nominee—Thurmond might not have interjected in the same way.

An additional example, this one from Ruth Bader Ginsburg's confirmation hearing, shows how positive interruptions sometimes function to summarize a nominee's words and record in an overwhelmingly supportive fashion. Here, Senator DeConcini was questioning Ginsburg on her advocacy for and leadership on societal changes like the Equal Rights Amendment:

JUDGE GINSBURG. Senator DeConcini, first let me clarify what I meant by a dead-end street. I meant that blacks couldn't vote. We know what the history of the white primaries and literacy tests were. Women became galvanized in the 1970s. I think we are going to see more and more political activity for advancement of women's stature. Some of the results of that activity are visible in this room. I don't think it has stopped.

That doesn't mean that I am not an advocate of a statement in our fundamental instrument of government that equality of rights shall not be denied or abridged on account of sex. I am and I—

SENATOR DECONCINI. Well, Judge, I would classify you as a leader. And I am not going to put words in your mouth, but that is how I interpret what you have told us. My observation of what you have told me here is that, certainly in the area of gender discrimination, you lead. You don't follow. That is what you have done, though on occasion, on many occasions, you have concurred with other judges, but you certainly have been a leader there. That is really what I wanted to know.[7]

As the exchange shows, during the course of her careful answer, DeConcini interrupted Ginsburg to summarize her words in a positive and glowing fashion—that

Ginsburg is a leader in this area of law and advocacy. Doing so was surely seen by the senator as being helpful to the nominee. At the same time, however, DeConcini's interruption had the effect of putting words in Ginsburg's mouth, despite the senator's statement that he did not intend to do that very thing.

Our discussion and these two examples from Thomas's and Ginsburg's hearings, respectively, lead to the following hypotheses on positive interruption patterns for nominees more generally:

> HYPOTHESIS 5.3: Female, same-party nominees will receive more positive interruptions than other nominees.
>
> HYPOTHESIS 5.4: Person of color, same-party nominees will receive more positive interruptions than other nominees.

## DATA AND METHODOLOGY

To examine our hypotheses, we use the data introduced in the Introduction, which contain information on the extent to which senators interrupted Supreme Court nominees from 1939 to 2022. Interruptions are identified in the confirmation hearing transcripts as long dashes that end a statement, as exemplified below:

> MS. KAGAN: I guess I would like to go back to—I'll just give you one case, just to make sure that—
> SENATOR KYL: Well, can I just keep moving on?[8]

Because not all interruptions are created equal (e.g., Anderson and Leaper 1998; Feldman and Gill 2019; Friedrich 1972; Truong 2013), we focus here on intrusive and positive interruptions to test our hypotheses.

Intrusive interruptions are those in which the interrupting speaker successfully takes over the conversational floor causing the original speaker to stop talking as a result of the interrupter's incursion (Anderson and Leaper 1998). Senator Kyl's interruption of Kagan above exemplifies this. In this exchange, Kyl prevented Kagan from giving the example she intended to provide and instead compelled her to move onto another topic. In contrast, back-channel interruptions are short signs of active listening (Anderson and Leaper 1998). These brief utterances typically demonstrate enthusiasm, agreement, or rapport, and do not attempt to take over the speaking turn from the original speaker. In our data, senators interrupted nominees in 13 percent of their opportunities to do so, and 92 percent of these interruptions are categorized as intrusive. We use these intrusive interruptions to explore Hypotheses 5.1 and 5.2.

To test Hypothesis 5.3 and 5.4, we also distinguish between positive and negative interruptions. Positive interruptions signal support for the speaker, often by expressing solidarity with the speaker by finishing the speaker's thought (Leman, Ahmed, and Ozarow 2005; Mendelberg, Karpowitz, and Oliphant 2014). An interruption is coded as positive "if it expressed agreement with the speaker, if it made an effectively positive request for elaboration ('that's a great idea; how do you think we should do it'), or if it completed the speaker's thought (often repeating several of the speaker's words, then continuing to a normal transition place)" (Smith-Lovin and Brody 1989, 428).[9] A positive interruption is demonstrated in the following exchange:

> MS. KAGAN. Senator Feinstein, I do think that the continuing holding of *Roe* and *Doe v. Bolton* is that women's lives and women's health have to be protected in abortion regulation. Now, the *Gonzalez* case said that with respect to a particular procedure, that the statute Congress passed, which passed a statute without a health exception and with only a life exception, was appropriate because of the large degree of medical uncertainty involved—
>
> SENATOR FEINSTEIN. Because of the procedure.
>
> MS. KAGAN. Because of the procedure. But with respect to abortion generally, putting that procedure aside, I think that the continuing holdings of the Court are that the woman's life and that the woman's health must be protected in any abortion regulation.[10]

Conversely, negative interruptions are attempts to take over the conversational floor in a hostile or negative manner (Karpowitz, Mendelberg, and Mattioli 2015; Leman, Ahmed, and Ozarow 2005; Mendelberg, Karpowitz, and Oliphant 2014). An interruption is coded as negative "if it expressed disagreement with the speaker, raised an objection to the speaker's idea, or introduced a complete change of topic (disregarding the speaker's utterance entirely)" (Smith-Lovin and Brody 1989, 428). In our data, 35 percent of senatorial interruptions of nominees are coded as positive.

To examine whether female nominees and nominees of color are interrupted more often than their white, male counterparts, we use the modeling strategy employed in Chapter 4. The unit of analysis is the senator-nominee pair, meaning there is one observation for every senator who questioned a nominee at their confirmation hearing. The first dependent variable, which tests Hypotheses 5.1 and 5.2, is the proportion of statements made by each senator that involved intrusively interrupting the nominee. We focus on intrusive interruptions, instead of all interruptions, since intrusive interruptions correspond more closely with our theoretical expectations.[11] The second dependent variable, which tests Hypotheses 5.3 and 5.4, is the proportion of statements made by each senator that involved positively interrupting the nominee. Because these dependent variables are proportions that cannot take on negative values, we use fractional logit models, with robust standard errors clustered on the nominee (Papke and Wooldridge 1996). As before, we estimate separate models for female nominees and nominees of color and limit our examinations with respect to gender to male senators on the Judiciary Committee, and our analysis of racial differences to white senators.

In the female nominee model, *Female, Same Party* is scored 1 for female nominees who share the partisan affiliation of the questioning senator, and 0 otherwise. *Male, Different Party* is scored 1 for male nominees who are the opposite party of the questioning senator, and 0 otherwise. *Male, Same Party* is scored 1 for male nominees who are copartisans of the questioning senator, and 0 otherwise. Because the baseline category is female nominees from the opposite party of the questioning senator, we expect these variables will be negatively signed in the intrusive interruption models. This indicates that female, same-party; male, different-party; and male, same-party nominees are intrusively interrupted less often than female, different-party nominees. In the positive interruption model, we use *Female, Same Party* as the baseline category, and include the *Female, Different Party* variable in the model, since this provides the most direct test of Hypothesis 5.3. We anticipate that the *Female, Different Party*; *Male, Different Party*; and *Male, Same Party* variables will be negatively signed, indicating that female, same-party nominees receive more positive interruptions than these other types of nominees.

This same coding strategy is applied to the person of color–focused model, resulting in the inclusion of three variables, with minority, different-party nominees serving as the baseline in the intrusive interruptions model: *Nominee of Color, Same Party*; *White, Different Party*; and *White, Same Party*. In this model, we expect these variables will be negatively signed, indicating that different-party nominees of color receive more intrusive interruptions. In the positive interruptions model, we use *Nominee of Color, Same Party* as the baseline and anticipate that the variables capturing the three other nominee types will be negatively signed, indicating that senators positively interrupt nominees of color that are their copartisans more often than other categories of nominees.

We include the control variables from the previous chapter. We believe that senators will give greater deference to more qualified nominees and nominees with previous judicial experience, interrupting such nominees less frequently (Boyd, Collins, and Ringhand 2018). Accordingly, we expect the *Nominee Qualifications* and *Nominee Judge* variables will be negatively signed. We anticipate that senators up for reelection will seek to use the hearings to garner media attention that might enhance their reelection prospects (Collins and Ringhand 2016; Schoenherr, Lane, and Armaly 2020). One way to do this is to control the conversational floor, which can be accomplished by more frequently interrupting nominees. Accordingly, we expect the *Senator Reelection Year* variable will be positively signed.

## EMPIRICAL RESULTS

### *Intrusive Interruptions*

Prior to presenting the results of our statistical models, it is useful to examine the underlying dynamics of interruptions at confirmation hearings. Figure 5.1 reports intrusive interruptions from 1939 to 2022. The top figure indicates the proportion of senators' statements that are intrusive interruptions, broken down by gender and partisanship, and the bottom figure reports this information with respect to nominee race and partisanship.

These figures provide strong, though preliminary, support for our hypotheses. Looking first at the gender figure, it is evident that senators intrusively interrupt female nominees more often than they interrupt male nominees. Overall, senators intrusively interrupt female nominees in 8.4 percent of their statements, compared to 4.7 percent for male nominees, thus providing clear evidence of gender bias at the hearings. But, it is also clear that copartisanship mitigates this bias. Senators interrupt female, different-party nominees in 12 percent of their statements, compared to 6 percent for male, different-party nominees; 6 percent for female, same-party nominees; and 3 percent for male, same-party nominees. In other words, while same-party and different-party

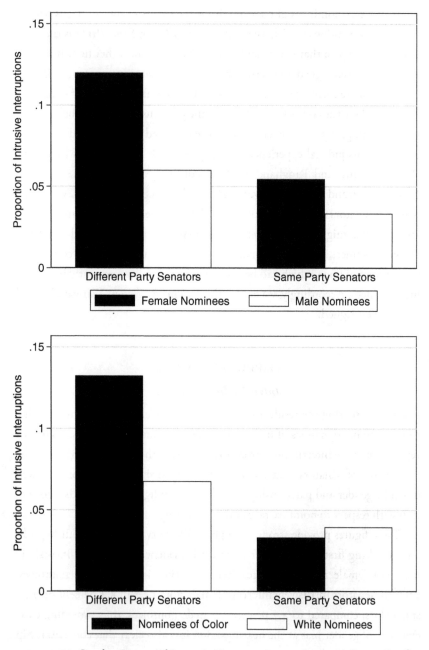

**FIGURE 5.1.** Gender, Race, and Intrusive Interruptions at Supreme Court Confirmation Hearings, 1939–2022

senators interrupt female nominees more than male nominees, different-party senators intrusively interrupt female nominees much more than male nominees.

The bottom graph in Figure 5.1 reveals similar dynamics with respect to race. Overall, senators intrusively interrupt nominees of color in 7.8 percent of their statements, compared to 5.3 percent for white nominees. Although this aggregate figure suggests that race plays a somewhat smaller role than gender, when copartisanship is considered, the findings are much more revealing. Different-party senators intrusively interrupt nominees of color in 13 percent of their comments, compared to 7 percent for white, different-party nominees; 4 percent for white, same-party nominees; and 3 percent for same-party nominees of color. This indicates that different-party senators are particularly likely to intrusively interrupt person of color nominees, while same-party senators intrusively interrupt nominees of color slightly less frequently than they interrupt white nominees.

Turning now to our full statistical results, Figure 5.2 graphically depicts the results from our fractional logit model of intrusive interruptions. The graphs report the predicted change in the proportion of intrusive interruptions that correspond to a one-unit change in each of the independent variables. The circles represent the point estimates of the marginal effects, and the lines coming off the circles are 90 percent confidence intervals. The marginal effects are significant at the 95 percent (one-tailed) level or lower if the confidence intervals do not cross the zero line.

Beginning with the gender model in the upper graph, we find strong support for Hypothesis 5.1. After controlling for other factors, female, different-party nominees are intrusively interrupted about 4 percentage points more than female, same-party nominees; about 4 percentage points more than male, different-party nominees; and about 7 percentage points more than male, same-party nominees. Given that senators intrusively interrupt nominees in an average of 6 percent of their statements, these are relatively large substantive differences. They reveal, for example, that female, different-party nominees are interrupted more than twice as often as male, same-party nominees. Thus, male senators on the Judiciary Committee show a clear bias against female, different-party nominees in terms of intrusively interrupting their statements at the hearings. This bias is particularly strong in comparison to male, same-party nominees, who senators interrupt much less frequently. Though we find clear

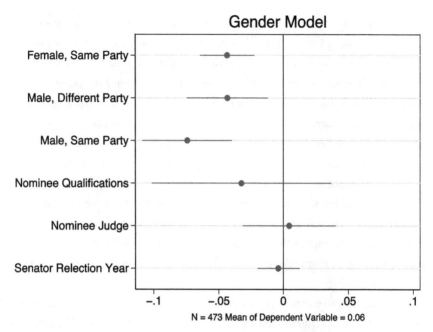

Gender Model

N = 473 Mean of Dependent Variable = 0.06

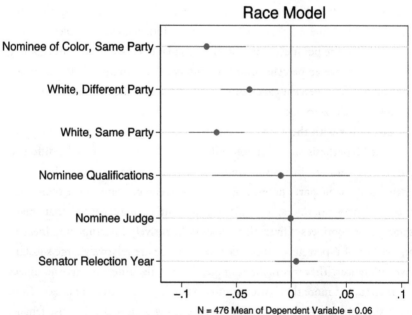

Race Model

N = 476 Mean of Dependent Variable = 0.06

FIGURE 5.2. Influences on the Intrusive Interruptions of Supreme Court Nominees, 1939–2022

evidence of gender bias against female nominees, the control variables do not shape the extent to which male senators intrusively interrupt nominees.

The bottom graph in Figure 5.2 reports our results for intrusive interruptions of nominees based on race and ethnicity. Again, we find strong evidence of bias against person of color nominees as expected in Hypothesis 5.2. Different-party nominees of color are intrusively interrupted about 4 percentage points more frequently than white, different-party nominees; about 7 percentage points more than white, same-party nominees; and about 8 percentage points more than same-party nominees of color. Thus, these results indicate that senators more frequently take over the conversational floor from nominees of color, especially if they were appointed by a president of the opposite party as the senator. This provides senators the opportunity to challenge the nominees' statements in a very public setting, casting doubts as to their fitness for the Court. And, as with the results based on gender, these are very large substantive effects since senators, on average, intrusively interrupt nominees in 6 percent of their chances to do so.

### *Positive Interruptions*

We now turn to examining the extent to which senators positively interrupt nominees in an effort to show support for the nominee. Figure 5.3 depicts positive interruptions from 1939 to 2022. The top graph reports the proportion of senators' statements that are positive interruptions, broken down by gender and partisanship, and the bottom figure provides this information with respect to nominee race and partisanship.

Looking first at the gender and positive interruptions depicted in the top graph, it is evident that senators positively interrupt female nominees much more frequently than male nominees. Overall, senators positively interrupt female nominees in 4.5 percent of their statements, compared to less than 2 percent for male nominees. This indicates that senators more frequently take steps to aid female nominees than male nominees in their testimony by expressing agreement, positively requesting elaboration, or agreeing with the nominees' thoughts through an interruption. Interestingly, partisanship does not play as major a conditioning role as it does with respect to intrusive interruptions. For example, different-party senators positively interrupt female nominees in 4.4 percent of their statements, compared to 4.7 percent for female, same-party nominees. Different-party senators positively interrupt male nominees in

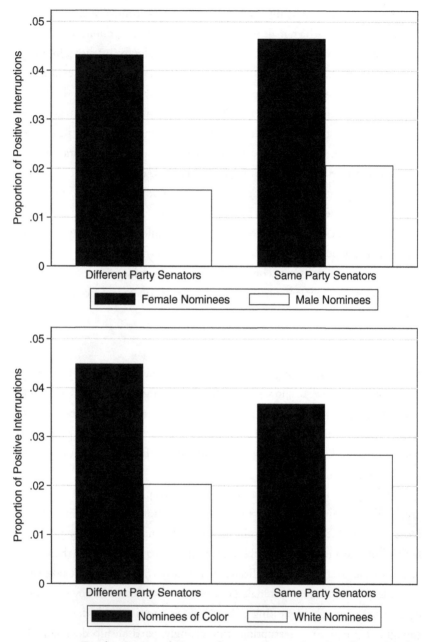

**FIGURE 5.3.** Gender, Race, and Positive Interruptions at Supreme Court Confirmation Hearings, 1939–2022

1.6 percent of their statements, compared to 2.1 percent for male, same-party nominees. Consequently, it appears that gender is the primary factor driving positive interruptions, with partisanship playing a more minimal role.

The bottom graph in Figure 5.3 reports the differences between nominees of color and white nominees in terms of the extent to which they are positively interrupted. Overall, person of color nominees are interrupted in 4 percent of their statements, compared to 2.3 percent for white nominees. Different-party senators positively interrupt nominees of color in 4.5 percent of their statements, compared to 3.8 percent for same-party senators. Different-party senators interrupt white nominees in 2 percent of their statements, compared to 2.6 percent for same-party senators. This indicates that senators tend to interrupt nominees of color in more "supportive" ways than white nominees. It also suggests that shared partisanship plays a limited role, similar to the results with respect to gender.

To examine these differences more rigorously, Figure 5.4 reports the marginal effects from the fractional logit model. The graphs indicate the predicted change in the proportion of positive interruptions corresponding to a one-unit change in each of the independent variables. The marginal effects are significant at the 95 percent (one-tailed) level or lower if the confidence intervals do not cross the zero line.

Beginning with the gender model of positive interruptions in the upper graph, we find that, as expected, female, same-party nominees are positively interrupted more frequently than two other nominee types. That is, senators positively interrupt female, same-party nominees 2.8 percentage points more often than male, different-party nominees and 2.2 percentage points more often than male, same-party nominees. And, because senators positively interrupt nominees in 2 percent of their opportunities to do so, these are substantively large effects, more than doubling the frequency of a nominee being positively interrupted. However, there is no difference in the extent to which same party and different-party senators interrupt female nominees. Thus, these findings indicate that senators are more willing to interrupt female copartisans in an effort to aid them in their testimony compared to male nominees.

The bottom graph in Figure 5.4 reports the results from the model that examines race and positive interruptions. This figure fails to provide support for our expectations since none of the nominee type variables achieve statistical significance at conventional levels. Thus, although there are some differences in

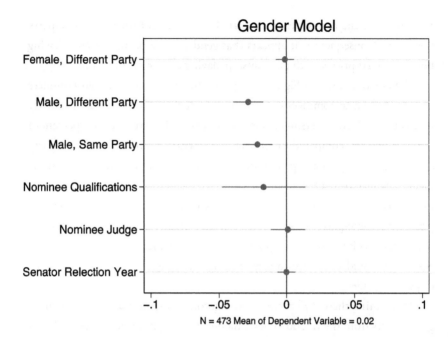

Gender Model

N = 473 Mean of Dependent Variable = 0.02

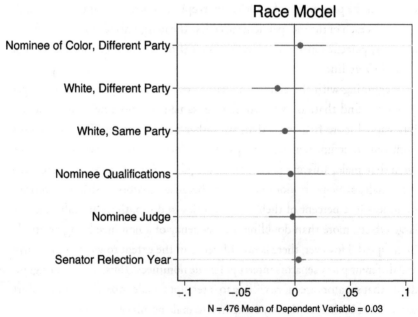

Race Model

N = 476 Mean of Dependent Variable = 0.03

FIGURE 5.4. Influences on the Positive Interruptions of Supreme Court Nominees, 1939–2022

the volume of positive interruptions in the descriptive data, these fail to hold up in a statistical model that includes control variables.

## CONCLUSION

This chapter began with an exchange between Senator Coburn and Elena Kagan during Kagan's 2010 confirmation hearing. Over the course of mere minutes of questioning, Senator Coburn interrupted the nominee three times. In doing so, the senator exerted power over the conversation. The chapter went on to explore whether this type of exchange happens equally frequently to all nominees or whether women and people of color are interrupted more often.

As we have observed in other aspects of our study of race and gender during Supreme Court confirmation hearings, our results again indicate that female nominees and nominees of color have a different confirmation experience than their white, male counterparts. This is particularly true with regard to intrusive interruptions, in which female nominees and nominees of color from the opposite party of the questioning senator are interrupted more frequently than any other type of nominee. Because these types of interruptions involve attempts to take over the conversational floor from nominees, they also portray the interrupted nominee in a negative manner.

We also examined the gender and racial dynamics of positive interruptions at the hearings—those interruptions intended to aid the nominee by showing agreement with the speaker. We found that female, same-party nominees also receive more positive interruptions than male nominees. Although senators engaging in positive interruptions may intend to help nominees, the action of the interruption can nonetheless have negative consequences for nominees since they can disrupt nominees' ability to express their opinions. In doing so, these positive interruptions signal to onlookers the presence of status hierarchies. So while they may be intended to be helpful, positive interruptions provide additional evidence that senators engage in behaviors that demonstrate bias, however well intended, against the nominee.

Interruptions cause real harm, both in and out of the Senate Judiciary Committee hearing room. They build power and place a speaker in a dominant position in a conversation and can "set the tone for dialogue elsewhere" (Feldman and Gill 2019, 174). Senators who frequently interrupt female and person of color nominees may behave similarly in other committee hearings and on the floor of the Senate, and other national, state, and local politicians may adopt comparable practices in their legislative and public-facing work.

Interruptions also, of course, have a silencing effect on those who are inter-rupted. As we have shown in this chapter, female nominees and nominees of color are disproportionately interrupted relative to white, male nominees. These interruptions prevent nominees from answering senators' questions, finishing their thoughts, and demonstrating their competence in the issue area of the in-quiry. They are prevented, in other words, from speaking for themselves.[12] We are left to wonder "what if" these female and person of color nominees had the opportunity to continue speaking without the interruption. Would the nomi-nee have uttered a famous quote or laid the groundwork for a powerful legacy in some other way? Would she have provided the artful legal analysis necessary to convince fence-leaning senators of her judicial fitness? We will never know, because she was interrupted, and the full potential of her speech was lost to us.

Gender, Race, Party, and Intrusive Interruptions at Supreme Court Confirmation Hearings, 1939–2022

| | Gender Model | Race Model |
|---|---|---|
| Female, Same Party | -0.850* | |
| | (0.207) | |
| Male, Different Party | -0.847* | |
| | (0.374) | |
| Male, Same Party | -1.451* | |
| | (0.367) | |
| Nominee of Color, Same Party | | -1.455* |
| | | (0.364) |
| White, Different Party | | -0.715* |
| | | (0.330) |
| White, Same Party | | -1.284* |
| | | (0.288) |
| Nominee Qualifications | -0.636 | -0.176 |
| | (0.800) | (0.713) |
| Nominee Judge | 0.087 | -0.009 |
| | (0.427) | (0.560) |
| Senator Reelection Year | -0.077 | 0.085 |
| | (0.193) | (0.218) |
| Constant | -1.496 | -1.774* |
| | (0.929) | (0.865) |
| AIC | 0.353 | 0.362 |
| N | 473 | 476 |

* $p < 0.05$ (one-tailed). The dependent variable is the proportion of a senator's statements that involved intrusively interrupting the nominee. Entries are fractional logit regression coefficients. Numbers in parentheses are robust standard errors, clustered on nominee.

**APPENDIX TABLE 5.2.** Gender, Race, Party, and Positive Interruptions at Supreme Court Confirmation Hearings, 1939–2022

| | Gender Model | Race Model |
|---|---|---|
| Female, Different Party | -0.048 | |
| | (0.175) | |
| Male, Different Party | -1.217* | |
| | (0.279) | |
| Male, Same Party | -0.922* | |
| | (0.303) | |
| Nominee of Color, Different Party | | 0.216 |
| | | (0.570) |
| White, Different Party | | -0.615 |
| | | (0.560) |
| White, Same Party | | -0.350 |
| | | (0.540) |
| Nominee Qualifications | -0.730 | -0.150 |
| | (0.772) | (0.744) |
| Nominee Judge | 0.044 | -0.076 |
| | (0.328) | (0.522) |
| Senator Reelection Year | -0.005 | 0.137 |
| | (0.173) | (0.158) |
| Constant | -2.427* | -3.099* |
| | (0.731) | (0.989) |
| AIC | 0.207 | 0.220 |
| N | 473 | 476 |

* $p < 0.05$ (one-tailed). The dependent variable is the proportion of a senator's statements that involved positively interrupting the nominee. Entries are fractional logit regression coefficients. Numbers in parentheses are robust standard errors, clustered on nominee.

# SIX

## LANGUAGE CHOICES

Words matter, including during Senate Judiciary Committee confirmation hearings. "Language and talk are central to social life" (Hollander and Abelson 2014, 181). Language is also "an important element in the creation and negotiation of social structures, institutions, and relationships" (Bogoch 1999, 331). But the words senators choose to use when talking to and about Supreme Court nominees during the confirmation hearings can vary considerably. Consider, for example, the following statements made by senators during the confirmation hearings of Elena Kagan and John Roberts. Both statements were made by senators from a party different from that of the nominating president, and both are expressing concern about a position taken by the nominee. But they have little else in common. In the first statement, Senator Jeff Sessions (R-AL) harshly criticized Kagan's testimony:

> SENATOR SESSIONS [TO KAGAN]: Well, I would just say, while my time is running down, I am just a little taken aback by the tone of your remarks because it is unconnected to reality. I know what happened at Harvard. I know you were an outspoken leader against the military policy. I know you acted without legal authority to reverse Harvard's policy and deny the military equal access to campus until you were threatened by the U.S. Government of loss of Federal funds. This is what happened.[1]

In the second statement, Senator Chuck Schumer (D-NY) offers more muted concern about Roberts' evasiveness in answering certain questions.

> SENATOR SCHUMER [TO ROBERTS]: You know, you have always said you cannot talk about decided cases because people might think there is some bias, but you introduced an argument I have heard you make to me privately, but I don't know if you made it here publicly, which is you don't want to try and, quote, get my vote by changing your position, and there shouldn't be a bartering process at these hearings. I would like to say to you that I don't think there should be either, and I don't think anyone does. I am not asking you, I don't think any member of this Committee, from Mr. Coburn all the way to the other end, is asking you to try and tailor your answers to what you think we want to hear. That would be unfair to you and unfair to us.[2]

These examples illustrate how much variation there is in senatorial questioning of nominees, even when accounting for partisan disagreement. Sessions combatively implies that Kagan is being deceitful or delusional, saying that her words were "unconnected to reality." He then claims that he (unlike her) knows what actually happened before laying out his version of the facts. In contrast, Schumer expresses his concern with Roberts' nonresponsiveness much more respectfully. Schumer even endorses Roberts' general hearing strategy, noting his agreement that Roberts should not "tailor" his answers to what he thinks the senators want to hear.

Whether knowingly done or not, these senators' language choices—the harsh attack on Kagan's honesty versus the gentle probing of Roberts' strategy—send a powerful message far beyond the content of the questions: one of these nominees is more welcome before the Committee than the other. Are these examples representative of a larger pattern of how race and gender intersect with partisanship to create different hearing experiences for female nominees and nominees of color? Scholarly evidence abounds to indicate that the answer may be yes.

Language is "an important element, often the most important element, in the way we present ourselves to others in everyday life" (Bogoch 1999, 330). Word choices convey not only message content but are also significant "because they point to a speaker's feelings and to the situations in which they find themselves" (Hart 2001; 44). In the context of intergroup relations, where societal in-groups communicate with out-group members, "linguistic elements . . . can be powerful forces of inequality" (Hollander and Abelson 2014, 188). Indeed, language choices offer in-group speakers a salient opportunity to exercise their group-based preferences and express their values. This means that in-group positivity and bias toward out-group members, in the form of skepticism and negativity about them, are likely to emerge in the words that in-group speakers choose when interacting with out-group members like women and people of color.

We begin this chapter by introducing the theory of when and why language choice differences can emerge in intergroup conversational settings. We then examine the words used by senators on the Judiciary Committee to see if women and person of color nominees to the Supreme Court face more language skepticism and negativity from questioning senators than do white and male nominees. Relative to in-group nominees, we expect that in-group senators will use less positively and more negatively-toned language when speaking to out-group nominees. Similarly, we anticipate that these senators will use more differentiation words (words like "hasn't" or "but") to draw out distinctions or uncertainty about the nominee when questioning female nominees and nominees of color, again relative to in-group nominees. In each of these situations (tone and differentiation words), we expect that bias in word choice will be particularly potent among different-party senators. To empirically investigate this, we employ computer-assisted text analysis of our original database containing the text of all senatorial statements to Supreme Court nominees testifying before the Judiciary Committee from 1939 to 2022. Our results indicate support for our language difference expectations. Female nominees and nominees of color do, once again, face a more negative, less favorable hearing environment than do white male nominees, particularly when being questioned by different-party senators.

## BIAS AND LANGUAGE CHOICES

A speaker's words, in and of themselves, can convey content and information to an audience (Hogg and Abrams 1988, 195). At Supreme Court confirmation hearings, this informational value of senators' words is meaningful, but their words' literal meanings are not the only thing being communicated (Black et al. 2011; Pennebaker, Mehl, and Niederhoffer 2003). In nearly all conversational settings, there is no one way to conduct a conversation. Instead, speakers have discretion and "may choose from a variety of ways of expressing a single idea" (Hollander and Abelson 2014, 186).

A speaker's language choices—including what to communicate, what words to use, and how to carry out the communication—tell us a great deal about the speaker and their environment. Speech provides social markers that indicate "the speakers' personality, social status, age, mood, [and] social group membership" (Hogg and Abrams 1988, 195). Similarly, words provide insights into a speaker's feelings, goals, strategies, and biases (Black et al. 2011; Bogoch 1999; Collins and Eshbaugh-Soha 2020; Hart 2011; Rubini and Kruglanski 1997) and the ways people "work toward interactional goals through talk" (Hollander and Abelson 2014, 190). Speech choices convey information not just about the speaker but also about the speaker's attitudes toward the receiver(s) of the speech, including whether the speaker views the recipient as an equal, in the conversation or society at large. Notably, while not all of the "linguistic features we use are conscious and strategic choices," they nonetheless are informative (Boguch 1999, 330).

Language choices are closely tied to the out-group bias theory we examined in detail in Chapter 4, because language provides a means of carrying out a key step undergirding the theory: "categorizing people into social groups and for creating stereotypes attached to those groups" (Hollander and Abelson 2014, 181). Speakers' word choices convey how they feel about and what they believe about their own group and that of other groups (Harwood 2018). Communication style "reflects upon group membership" (Reid and Ng 1999, 122). For in-groupers in particular, linguistic strategies offer a powerful tool for furthering intragroup strategies and ideals. Language helps "in establishing and maintaining power asymmetries" (Besnier 1990, 436), maintaining control (Mattei 1998, 442), exercising dominance, and fostering inequality between the in-group and the out-group (Hollander and Abelson 2014, 190). Rein and Ng (1999) go so far as to say that "language should not be seen solely as a passive conduit of power but as an active coplayer in the exercise of power" (120).

In-group speakers do not leave their group goals and perceptions behind when they engage in intergroup conversations (where an in-group member speaks with an out-group member). In these settings, "individuals' basic human desire to understand and manage their social standing" (Vorauer and Quesnel 2017, 519), along with "the interplay of social categorization and social identification" (Maitner, Smith, and Mackie 2017, 112), affects what emotions are felt and how discourse will unfold based on those emotions. People are apprehensive, anxious, and uneasy about intergroup settings due to an expectation that "interaction with outgroup members is expected to have negative consequences" (Stephan 2014, 240). In-groupers may worry that any gains made by the out-group will be achieved at their own group's expense (Brewer 2017, 92). More generally, negativity toward and a differential view of out-group members are important parts of in-group bias as a concept, particularly when an individual's group identification is strong (Brewer 2017, 91; Bäck et al. 2018).

As a result, different treatment and hostile communication that favors the in-group, disfavors the out-group, and draws attention to the distinctions between the groups can emerge (Brewer 2017, 92; Keblusek, Giles, and Maass 2017; Lee and Lin 2022). In-group members can use language in an effort to "dehumanize and delegitimize the outgroup" and maintain stereotypes (Keblusek, Giles, and Maass 2017, 637–638). Without the aid of in-group positivity bias, outgroup members are less likely to be trusted than in-group members (Brewer 2017, 98), which can manifest into in-groupers' using language expressing skepticism and uncertainty about outgroup members. Similarly, anger directed at out-group members can lead to a desire to take action in communication through, for example, criticism of the out-group or defense of in-group positions (Maitner, Smith, and Mackie 2017, 116–117).

Even in the absence of actively hostile language, negativity toward the outgroup can be shown by the "absence of positive regard ... for outgroups that is characteristic of most ingroup-outgroup differentiation" (Brewer 2017, 95). This decreased positivity can by itself have powerful discriminatory effects that appear in speech choices: "many forms of racism and sexism are probably attributable to discrimination based on ingroup preference rather than prejudice against outgroups" (Brewer 2017, 95). For power-holding in-groupers, the result is likely to appear in in-group members' word choices when addressing outgroup members, which may be more negative, less positive, and more differential in nature (by focusing on distinctions and clarifications) than they are during a solely intragroup conversation.

Prior research has found evidence of language bias of this nature in educational, legal, and political contexts. In education, where letters of recommendation and admission candidacies provide common occasions for describing students, findings of word choice biases based on gender and race abound.

Research on letters of recommendation, for example, indicates that male and white applicants' letters contain more personalized descriptions of the applicants' intelligence, excellence, exceptionalness, and uniqueness than do letters written for female and Black applicants' (Madera, Hebl, and Martin 2009; Neuendorf 2011; Ross et al. 2017; Schmader et al. 2007; Trix and Psenka 2003).

Political elites and nonelites alike respond to intergroup hostility and perceived threats to their resources and power by "'sounding the alarm' by communicating in an angry, negative tone" (Frimer et al. 2019, 1218). Presidents, Supreme Court justices, and senators vary in their use of positive and negative emotional language depending on the ideological context that they find themselves in (Black et al. 2011; Bryan and Ringsmuth 2016; Collins and Eshbaugh-Soha 2020; Sigelman, Deering, and Loomis 2001).[3] Similarly, media reports about political candidates and Supreme Court nominees are, on average, less positive and more negative toward out-group members—women and people of color—and use high levels of differential words. These media accounts also tend to be less complimentary, contain fewer positive descriptions of the candidate's/nominee's background or experience, and are more negatively toned than coverage of other candidates/nominees (Carlin and Winfrey 2009; Conroy et al. 2015; Gershon 2013; Towner and Clawson 2016). Media reports about legislation also use high levels of differential words when the legislation at issue is perceived as favoring out-group members (Lee and Lin 2022).

## SENATORIAL LANGUAGE DURING SUPREME COURT CONFIRMATION HEARINGS

This theoretical lens, supported by prior research findings from both political and legal arenas, informs our examination of the language choices senators make during the Judiciary Committee's confirmation hearings for Supreme Court nominees. Female nominees and nominees of color, when outside the questioning senators' in-group, are likely to be perceived in more negative, hostile, and skeptical ways than are in-group nominees. As with speakers in other settings, in-group (white and male) senators may manifest this by employing different language when asking questions of in-group nominees than they use when questioning out-group nominees. Indeed, the question-and-answer format of confirmation hearings may be a particularly opportune setting for these types of language differences to emerge since questions in this format allow speakers to "vigilantly attend to their social roles and shape their interactional conduct accordingly" (Hayano 2013, 411). Questions, and in particular negative questions, offer speakers effective tools to implement confrontation and criticism under the neutral guise of doing one's job (Hayano 2013, 411).

If this theoretical expectation is correct, senatorial questioning of female nominees and nominees of color is likely to include the inequitable use of positive and negative tone and more use of differentiation language then when the senator is questioning male or white nominees. Specifically, in-group members are likely to receive questions presented with more positive tone and that give the nominee's explanations and background the benefit of the doubt. By contrast, out-group members will likely face questions with less positive tone, more negative tone, and that are more focused on drawing distinctions or addressing uncertainty about the nominee and her background (i.e., high use of differentiational words).

As Maitner, Smith, and Mackie (2017) argue, the way we perceive and emotionally respond to out-groups is determined by "social identity salience," with the level of negative emotion and tone waxing and waning accordingly (113). In the case of language choices, we expect that an out-group member's status as a woman or person of color will be less salient when the senator and nominee share party affiliation (and the many common ideals and goals that come from that shared group membership). Conversely, just as shown in the Frimer et al. (2019) study, when there is an absence of shared party, the perception of hostility and threat from the out-group nominee will be at its height, resulting in senators "sounding the alarm" (consciously or not) through their word choices.

A few examples from the confirmation hearings illustrate these phenomena. The first example, from Thurgood Marshall's confirmation hearing, shows how Senator Hiram Fong (R-HI), the first person of color to serve on the Senate Judiciary Committee, questioned Marshall. Fong, unlike many other senators, did not question Marshall's competence to serve on the Court. Instead, Fong praised the nominee effusively, with his positive tone apparent in his word choices:

SENATOR FONG: Mr. Chairman and members of the committee, I have no questions to ask. I just want to make a statement.

Judge Marshall, I want to extend to you my warmest congratulations on your nomination to the position of Associate Justice of the U.S. Supreme Court. I believe this to be a great and a historic nomination. It is my conviction,

Judge Marshall, that you were nominated primarily because you have shown that you are a distinguished and an excellent lawyer and jurist. The fact that you are a Negro who has been in the forefront of many of the most significant efforts to secure our ideas of equality and brotherhood to all Americans renders your nomination of a special pride for all Americans.

There is no question in my mind that you are eminently qualified for a seat on the high court....

The name of Marshall is one of the most illustrious in the annals of American constitutional law. From the time of Chief Justice John Marshall to the time of Thurgood Marshall, this Nation has made tremendous strides to make a reality the ringing words of equality in our Declaration of Independence. I am convinced that upon confirmation, another Mr. Justice Marshall will serve with great distinction. I am delighted to strongly support your nomination, to wish you Godspeed, and to extend to you and your family my "Aloha" as you undertake your responsibilities.[4]

In contrast, consider Senator Tom Cotton's (R-AR) questioning of Ketanji Brown Jackson in 2022. Here, the in-group senator's comments to this out-group, different-party nominee not only lack a positive or celebratory discussion of the nomination or nominee's record, they also strike a notably negative, hostile tone:

SENATOR COTTON: Judge, Congress did change the law after sentencing and the First Step Act. That was a terrible mistake. Congress specifically did not make that change retroactively. And you saw that, and you thought it was extraordinary and compelling even though Congress specifically did not make it retroactive. You chose to rewrite the law because you were sympathetic to a fentanyl drug kingpin whom you had expressed frustration at having sentenced him to as to his crim—to his 20 year sentence in the first place.

You twisted the law and you rewrote it so you could cut the sentence of a drug kingpin. That's what you did, Judge.

JUDGE JACKSON: Respectfully, Senator, I disagree. Congress provided judges through the compassionate release motion mechanism with the opportunity to review sentences. Congress, pre—prior to the compassionate release mechanism being enacted, a judge who imposed a sentence would have no opportunity to revisit. In Mr. Young's case, the question was, with this compassionate release motion under a circumstance in which Congress had changed the law, was that an extraordinary and compelling circumstance to revisit his sentence.

And I made a determination that it was.

SENATOR COTTON: So, I—I suppose then if you're confirmed, we can just count on you to always rule in favor of retroactivity, no matter what the facts of the case are, because it was a blatant, blatant rewrite of the law here so you could reduce the sentence of a drug kingpin that you didn't like sentencing to 20 years in the first place.

JUDGE JACKSON: No, Senator it was not.[5]

To explore whether these examples are typical of the experience of Supreme Court nominees, we test the following two hypotheses relating to positive and negative toned questions received by nominees:

HYPOTHESIS 6.1: Female, different-party nominees will receive a lower percentage of positive tone words, relative to negative tone words, than other nominees.

HYPOTHESIS 6.2: Person of color, different-party nominees will receive a lower percentage of positive tone words, relative to negative tone words, than other nominees.

In addition to varying levels of negative and positive tone, we also expect senators to use more differentiation words when questioning out-group nominees. Recall that the higher use of these differentiation words implies "the making of distinctions and clarifying confusions and concerns" (Lee and Lin 2022, 661). This aligns with our theoretical expectation that questions to fellow in-group members will reflect a positive outlook and will give the nominee the benefit of the doubt, while questions to out-group members will lack that same deference and trust and will evidence more intergroup skepticism.

To illustrate the power of differentiation words, we look again to Thurgood Marshall's hearing. In the example below, Senator Sam Ervin's (D-NC) questioning of Marshall included numerous differentiation words, most notably in the use of various forms of "did not." The example shows how the repeated use of these words allows Ervin to both express hostility toward Marshall's lack of responsiveness and also imply that Marshall does not understand the legal issue presented:

SENATOR ERVIN. Do you not consider that in the final analysis, the, Court was laying down rules of conduct for the guidance and control of the officer?

JUDGE MARSHALL. I said, Senator, I respectfully say I am not going to comment or give any interpretation of that opinion. I just cannot do it.

SENATOR ERVIN. I would like to remark in respect to the requirement you did not recall, the words of the Court were that he must expressly state, in substance, that he "is willing to make a statement and does not want an attorney." Will you answer this question: Was not that the first decision of the Supreme Court that ever said any such requirements existed so far as you can recall?

JUDGE MARSHALL. So far as I can recall.

SENATOR ERVIN. Did not the Chief Justice say that an involuntary confession would be inadmissible under these words of the Fifth Amendment that I am quoting, unless "the principles announced today" and "the system of warnings we delineate today" were observed by the officer having the suspect in custody?

JUDGE MARSHALL. I think that was in the opinion.

SENATOR ERVIN. Do you not construe that to be a voluntary confession by the five judges joining in the majority opinion that the Court was on that day adding a new requirement to the provision of the Fifth Amendment that I have read?

JUDGE MARSHALL. I think it speaks for itself.

SENATOR ERVIN. Well, does it not speak to that effect?

JUDGE MARSHALL. It is not—I would rather not comment on the opinion of the Supreme Court in the *Miranda* case in any form or fashion.

SENATOR ERVIN. Can you point out a single syllable in the provision of the Fifth Amendment which says that no person shall be compelled in any criminal case to be a witness against himself that embraces the requirements announced and the system of warnings laid down by the majority opinion in the *Miranda* case for the first time on June 13, 1966?

JUDGE MARSHALL. I have to repeat, sir, I do not want to comment upon that decision.[6]

Applying this example of high rates of differential language in a more general way, we hypothesize the following:

HYPOTHESIS 6.3: Female, different-party nominees will receive a higher percentage of differentiation words than other nominees.

HYPOTHESIS 6.4: Person of color, different-party nominees will receive a higher percentage of differentiation words than other nominees.

## DATA AND METHODOLOGY

To investigate the language of gender and racial bias at Supreme Court confirmation hearings, we use the same data employed in Chapters 4 and 5. As before, the unit of analysis in this chapter is the nominee-senator pair, meaning we have one observation for every senator who questioned each nominee at a confirmation hearing from 1939 to 2022. The major difference between this chapter and the previous two chapters is that here we use the full text of all comments made by senators during the question and answer sessions to generate our dependent variables.[7] This allows us to examine the language used by senators in their interactions with nominees.

To do this, we employ computer-assisted content analysis software. Though there are a growing number of programs that analyze text-as-data (e.g., Lowe 2002; Neuendorf 2017), we utilize Linguistic Inquiry and Word Count (LIWC) (Tausczik and Pennebaker 2010), which has seen substantial adoption in the social scientific study of law (e.g., Bryan and Ringsmuth 2016; Collins, Corley, and Hamner 2015; Corley and Ward 2020; Gleason and Smart 2022; Moyer 2021; Rice and Zorn 2019). For our purposes, the main benefit of LIWC is that we are able to employ its dictionaries, which have been subjected to rigorous validity analyses, to generate our dependent variables.

More specifically, we adopt the LIWC dictionaries related to positive and negative emotion to capture the tone of the senators' remarks. We also use LIWC's dictionary relating to differentiation. Our first dependent variable measures the overall tone of the senator's comments toward nominees. This is calculated by subtracting the percentage of negative emotional words from the percentage of positive emotional words for each senator's remarks toward each nominee they interacted with (e.g., Abe 2011). Positive emotional words include terms such as "good," "great," "best," and "better," while negative emotional words include terms such as "bad," "wrong," "hurt," and "nasty." Our second dependent variable is the percentage of words that capture differentiation, which includes words like "hasn't," "but," "without," and "else."

Because our dependent variables are the relative percentage of senatorial words used in each senator-nominee interaction that falls into each of our categories of interest, we use ordinary least squares regression to estimate our models.[8] Since nominees appear multiple times in the data, we use robust standard errors, clustered on each nominee. As in the previous two chapters, because we are focused on whether in-group members (male senators in the gender models and white senators in the racial models) treat out-group members (female nominees in the gender models and nominees of color in the racial models) differently than white and male nominees, we limit our gender models to male senators and our race models to white senators.

To examine whether female nominees and nominees of color receive less supportive language at the hearings, we follow the approach used in Chapters 4 and 5. In the gender models, we created four regimes. *Female, Same Party* is scored 1 for female nominees who share the party affiliation of the questioning senator. *Male, Different Party* is coded 1 for male nominees of an opposing party from the questioning senator. *Male, Same Party* is scored 1 for male nominees who share the party affiliation of the questioning senator. *Female, Different Party* is coded 1 for female nominees of a different political party than the questioning senator and is used as the baseline for comparison. In the tone model, we expect that the *Female, Same Party*; *Male, Different Party*; and *Male, Same Party* variables will be positively signed, indicating that senators use more positive language toward these nominees relative to female, different-party nominees. In the differentiation model, we expect these variables will be negatively signed, revealing that senators use more words associated with differentiation when interacting with female, different-party nominees.

We set up similar regimes for the racial models. *Nominee of Color, Same Party* is scored 1 for person of color nominees who share the party of the questioning senator. *White, Different Party* is coded 1 for white nominees of a different party than the questioning senator. *White, Same Party* is scored 1 for white nominees who share the political party of the questioning senator. *Nominee of Color, Different Party* is coded 1 for nominees of color of a different political party than the questioning senator and is used as the baseline. We expect the *Nominee of Color, Same Party*; *White, Different Party*; and *White, Same Party* variables will be positively signed in the tone model and negatively signed in the differentiation model.

We also include in the models the control variables from the previous chapters. First, we believe that more qualified nominees and those with previous judicial experience will be viewed more positively by the senators, and receive more positive tone and less differentiation words, than less qualified nominees. Accordingly, we expect the *Nominee Qualifications* and *Nominee Judge* variables will be positively signed in the tone models, and negatively signed in the differentiation model. We also believe that senators up for reelection will seek to use the hearings to generate media attention that might improve their reelection prospects (Collins and Ringhand 2016; Schoenherr, Lane, and Armaly 2020). One mechanism to do this is to be more aggressive toward nominees. Accordingly, we expect the *Senator Reelection Year* variable will be negatively signed in the tone model, and positively signed in the differentiation model.

## EMPIRICAL RESULTS
### *Tone toward Nominees*

Before presenting the results from our statistical models, we begin by examining the underlying gender and racial dynamics of the tone used by senators toward nominees at the hearings, which is presented in Figure 6.1. Recall that tone is scored by subtracting negative tone from positive tone. Thus, higher numbers mean that senators used a higher percentage of positive tone than negative tone for a nominee.

Starting with the top figure, we find strong, though preliminary, support for Hypothesis 6.1. That is, senators use more negative tone toward female, different-party nominees, as compared to each of the other categories of nominees. Substantively, senators use about 1.5 percent more positive than negative words for female, different-party nominees, compared to 2.2 percent for male, different-party nominees; 2.1 percent for female, same-party nominees; and 2 percent for male, same-party nominees. In other words, while senators use more positive words than negative words for all types of nominees, senators use about 30–45 percent less positive language when interacting with female, different-party nominees, compared to other types of nominees (calculated as the percentage increase from 1.5 to 2 and 2.2).

A similar picture emerges for different-party nominees of color. When interrogating person of color nominees from the opposite party, senators use about 1.6 percent more positive than negative words, compared to 2.1 percent for white, different-party nominees; 2.3 percent for same-party nominees of color; and 2 percent for white, same-party nominees. This means that senators use

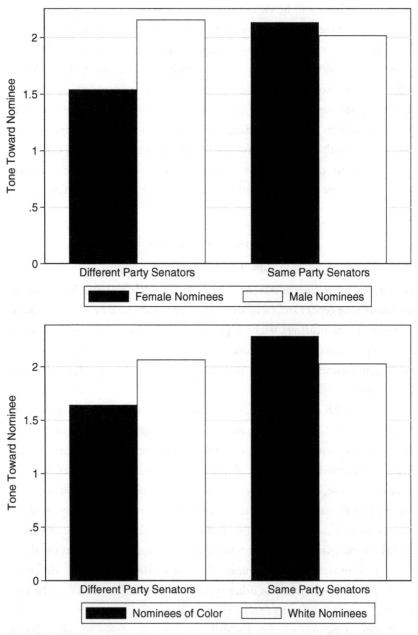

**FIGURE 6.1.** Gender, Race, and Tone toward Nominees at Supreme Court Confirmation Hearings, 1939–2022

about 25–40 percent relatively less positive language when describing different-party nominees of color, as our theory predicted.

Figure 6.2 graphically depicts the results from the regression models. This figure presents the relative increase in the percentage of positive words minus negative words corresponding to a one-unit change in each of the independent variables. The circles represent the coefficient estimates, and the lines coming off the circles are 90 percent confidence intervals. The marginal effects are significant at the 95 percent (one-tailed) level or lower if the confidence intervals do not cross the zero line.

Staring with the top figure, we find strong support for our theoretical expectations. That is, female, different-party nominees receive the most negative tone among all types of nominees. Substantively, female, different-party nominees receive about 0.6 percent fewer positive than negative comments compared to female, same-party nominees and male, different-party nominees, and about 0.4 percent fewer positive comments compared to male, same-party nominees. Because the average of the dependent variable is about 2 percent, these are relatively strong effects, indicating that female, different-party nominees receive about 25–40 percent less positive language than other nominee types. In addition, this figure reveals that for our control variable *Senator Reelection Year*, senators use more positive than negative language during reelection years. This is contrary to what we expected. It suggests that senators see more electoral benefit from using positive tone toward nominees.

The results with respect to race are more modest. The bottom figure indicates that different-party nominees of color receive about 0.7 percent fewer positive than negative words, compared to same-party nominees of color. However, different-party nominees of color do not receive statistically significantly fewer positive comments than white, same-party or different-party nominees. This suggests that copartisanship is a large driving force in the extent to which senators use more negative language toward nominees of color. And, as with the gender figure, we also find that senators use relatively more positive language during reelection years.

### Differentiation

We now turn to our analysis of differentiation, which involves senators challenging nominees by using words associated with casting doubt on their testimony, such as "hasn't" and "but." Figure 6.3 presents the underlying gender and

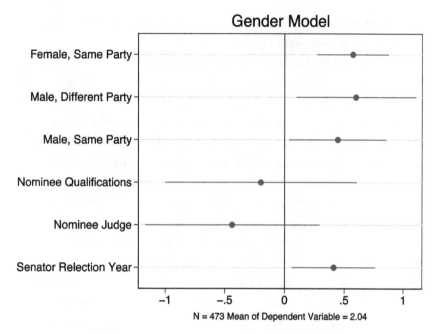

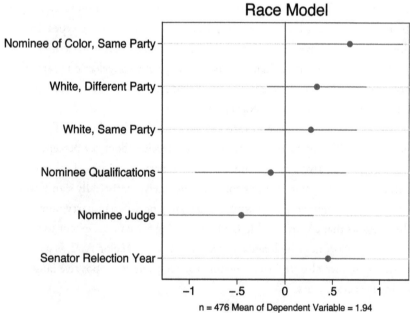

**FIGURE 6.2.** Influences on Senator's Tone toward Supreme Court Nominees, 1939–2022

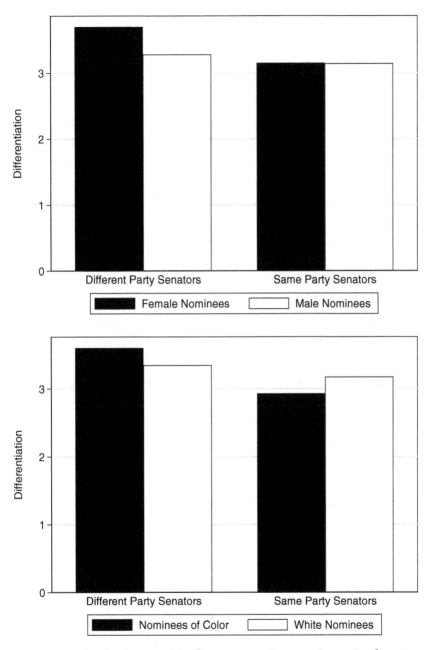

**FIGURE 6.3.** Gender, Race, and Differentiation at Supreme Court Confirmation Hearings, 1939–2022

racial dynamics in the use of differentiation words by senators toward nominees at the hearings. This figure reports the percentage of differentiation words used by senators toward nominees.

Starting with the top figure, we find, as expected, that female, different-party nominees receive the highest amount of differentiation words of all nominee types. About 3.7 percent of senators' comments toward female, different-party nominees involve the use of differentiation terms, compared to 3.3 percent for male, different-party nominees, and 3.2 percent for male and female, same-party nominees. This means that female, different-party nominees get about 12–15 percent more differentiation terms than other types of nominees. Though not as strong an effect as the results of our analysis of senators' tone toward nominees, these findings nonetheless reveal that senators show more skepticism of the testimony of female, different-party nominees.

Similar results can be found in the bottom graph, which plots racial differences related to senators' use of differentiation words. About 3.6 percent of senators' comments include differentiation words when interacting with different-party nominees of color, compared to 3.3 percent for white, different-party nominees; 2.9 percent for person of color, same-party nominees; and 3.2 percent for white, same-party nominees. Thus, while senators use the most differentiation terms when describing different-party nominees, they are especially likely to use these terms that cast doubt when interrogating nominees of color, an increase of about 10–25 percent.

Figure 6.4 reports the results of our regression model of the influences on senator's use of differentiation language. Starting with the gender graph on the top, we find strong support for Hypothesis 6.3. That is, compared to all other categories of nominees, senators use more differentiation words when questioning female, different-party nominees. Substantively, senators employ 0.5 percent more differentiation terms for female, different-party nominees compared to female, same-party nominees and male, same-party nominees; and 0.6 percent more differentiation words compared to male, same-party nominees. Since the average nominee receives 3.25 percent of differentiation words, this means that female, different-party nominees get about 15–20 percent more words that are used to question or undermine their testimony.

A similar picture emerges for nominees of color, as revealed by the bottom graph in Figure 6.4. Here, we find that different-party nominees of color receive more differentiation words than both white and person of color, same-party

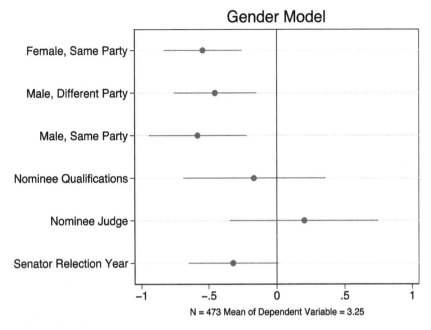

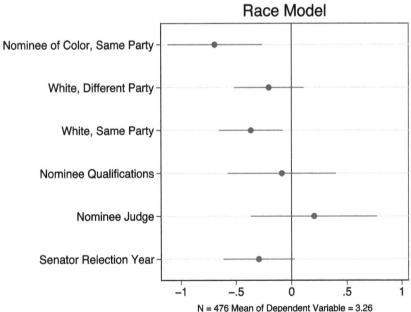

FIGURE 6.4. Influences on the Differentiation of Supreme Court Nominees, 1939–2022

nominees. However, they do not receive more differentiation words than white, different-party nominees, suggesting that the driving force between this disparity may not be a nominee's race, but rather party. Substantively, person of color nominees from the opposite party of the questioning senator are subjected to about 0.7 percent more differentiation words than same-party nominees of color and 0.4 percent more than same-party white nominees. This provides further evidence that senators are skeptical of different-party nominees of color, at least relative to same-party nominees, utilizing words that express this skepticism in their interrogation of these nominees.

### CONCLUSION

As we have argued, word choices matter. Language shapes our society, institutions, and relationships and, at an individual level, language choices allow people to express their identity and their values. This chapter indicates that, within the context of the Senate Judiciary Committee's confirmation hearings for the U.S. Supreme Court, word choices also can be central "to the creation and reproduction of inequality" (Hollander and Abelson 2014, 181). Through the use of less positive, more negative, and more differentiating words, in-group senators can signal their skepticism of female nominees and nominees of color. This is consistent with the empirical findings set out in Chapters 4 and 5: female and person of color nominees face a different confirmation process than do their white and male peers, especially in their interactions with different-party senators when testifying before the Senate Judiciary Committee.

The implications of this chapter's language-based findings are noteworthy, both for the nominees themselves and for the broader public watching the hearings unfold. Words can "inflict harm" since they "have meanings that often carry significant implications for ways persons may think, feel, or act toward others" (Rubini and Kruglanski 1997, 1047). Even subtle linguistic choices, like the selection of a particular verb or term that may occur subconsciously, "can be powerful forces of inequality" (Hollander and Abelson 2014, 188) that communicate stereotypes, denigrate the out-group, and send the message that "the distinction between ingroup and outgroup is based on essential features that make groups profoundly and unchangeably different from each other" (Keblusek, Giles, and Maass 2017, 638). Because Supreme Court confirmation hearings are conducted in such a public and salient forum, this message of inequality is an undeniably loud one.

**APPENDIX TABLE 6.1.** Gender, Race, Party, and Tone toward Nominees at Supreme Court Confirmation Hearings, 1939–2022

| | Gender Model | Race Model |
|---|---|---|
| Female, Same Party | 0.572* | |
| | (0.179) | |
| Male, Different Party | 0.599* | |
| | (0.298) | |
| Male, Same Party | 0.446* | |
| | (0.243) | |
| Nominee of Color, Same Party | | 0.683* |
| | | (0.330) |
| White, Different Party | | 0.335 |
| | | (0.309) |
| White, Same Party | | 0.272 |
| | | (0.287) |
| Nominee Qualifications | -0.199 | -0.149 |
| | (0.475) | (0.468) |
| Nominee Judge | -0.439 | -0.455 |
| | (0.432) | (0.447) |
| Senator Reelection Year | 0.411* | 0.452* |
| | (0.209) | (0.232) |
| Constant | 2.026* | 2.161* |
| | (0.535) | (0.598) |
| AIC | 1986.7 | 1987.0 |
| N | 473 | 476 |

* $p <. 0.05$ (one-tailed). The dependent variable is the percentage of positive words made by senators minus the percentage of negative words made by senators. Entries are ordinary least squares regression coefficients. Numbers in parentheses are robust standard errors, clustered on nominee.

**APPENDIX TABLE 6.2.** Gender, Race, Party, and Differentiation at Supreme Court Confirmation Hearings, 1939–2022

| | Gender Model | Race Model |
|---|---|---|
| Female, Same Party | -0.544* | |
| | (0.171) | |
| Male, Different Party | -0.453* | |
| | (0.181) | |
| Male, Same Party | -0.583* | |
| | (0.214) | |
| Nominee of Color, Same Party | | -0.692* |
| | | (0.254) |
| White, Different Party | | -0.205 |
| | | (0.186) |
| White, Same Party | | -0.365* |
| | | (0.171) |
| Nominee Qualifications | -0.167 | -0.087 |
| | (0.310) | (0.288) |
| Nominee Judge | 0.202 | 0.204 |
| | (0.323) | (0.339) |
| Senator Reelection Year | -0.320 | -0.294 |
| | (0.195) | (0.190) |
| Constant | 3.733* | 3.494* |
| | (0.440) | (0.451) |
| AIC | 1938.9 | 1946.0 |
| N | 473 | 476 |

* p <. 0.05 (one-tailed). The dependent variable is the percentage of comments involving differentiation words made by senators. Entries are ordinary least squares regression coefficients. Numbers in parentheses are robust standard errors, clustered on nominee.

# SEVEN

# GENDER, RACE, AND THE THOMAS-HILL AND KAVANAUGH–BLASEY FORD SPECIAL SESSIONS

*On Oct. 11, 1991, 14 white men grilled African-American law professor Anita Hill in a packed Senate Judiciary Committee hearing room about her allegations of sexual harassment by then-U.S. Supreme Court nominee Clarence Thomas. (Cowan 2018)*

*Judge Brett M. Kavanaugh and his accuser faced off Thursday [September 27, 2018] in an extraordinary, emotional day of testimony that ricocheted from a woman's tremulous account of sexual assault to a man's angry, outraged denial, all of which played out for hours before a riveted nation and a riven Senate. (Stolberg and Fandos 2018)*

As we have seen throughout the pages of this book, gender and race have permeated the Supreme Court confirmation hearings for decades, often in ways that affect how female nominees and nominees of color are questioned and described by members of the Senate Judiciary Committee. But Judiciary Committee members also had to grapple with these issues in a much more explicit way when Anita Hill accused Clarence Thomas of sexual harassment and Christine Blasey Ford accused Brett Kavanaugh of sexual assault. These sexual misconduct allegations plainly put gender issues directly on the table, but race was a potent part of the proceedings as well. This was especially so during the Thomas-Hill hearing, when both accuser and nominee were Black and charges of racialized stereotypes and inequitable treatment of both Thomas and Hill were frequent. Partisanship—as has been the case throughout this book—likewise was a factor in how the special sessions called to address the accusations against these nominees played out (Kaplan 2018).

Any systematic examination of race and gender during Supreme Court confirmation hearings, consequently, would be incomplete without a discussion of these special sessions. The uniqueness of the Thomas-Hill and Kavanaugh–Blasey Ford hearings necessarily renders our analysis narrower and more descriptive. Nonetheless, several questions are important to explore: How did senators handle the explicitly gender and race matters present during these proceedings? In what ways did senators pursue their partisan goals in designing and carrying out these special sessions? And how did the passage of time—and the changes in society's perspectives on sexual misconduct allegations between 1991 and 2018—change the way senators behaved across the two special sessions?

To answer these questions, we use first-of-its-kind data to capture important details about the questions and answers of the senators, nominees, and accusers during these special session hearings. We supplement these data with stories, quotes, and reflections drawn from the hearings and those who participated in them. We begin this chapter by setting the scene, explaining events leading up to the Thomas-Hill and Kavanaugh–Blasey Ford special sessions, including the emergence of allegations against the two nominees and the contentious battles among senators about how the Judiciary Committee would investigate and air the allegations. We then use our original data to empirically analyze the ways gender and race were addressed during the two hearings. Finally, we conclude with a discussion of how significant societal changes between 1991 to 2018 likely account for several of the differences we see between the Thomas-Hill and Kavanaugh–Blasey Ford hearings and explore how our analysis may reveal a path forward for the Committee in the future.

## SETTING THE SCENE: THE TWO SPECIAL SESSIONS

Although the Thomas-Hill and Kavanaugh–Blasey Ford hearings were especially salient events for Supreme Court watchers, allegations of personal misconduct are not new to the Supreme Court confirmation process. Indeed, a study found that twenty-three of the eighty nominations between 1877–1994 involved accusations of personal misconduct (Cameron and Segal 2010). Serious allegations of financial misconduct were raised in 1795 against Washington nominee John Rutledge (for failure to pay personal debts); in 1873 against Grant nominee George Williams (for using public money for private gain); and in 1968 against Johnson nominee Abe Fortas (for taking bribes). More recently, William Rehnquist (Chief Justice) and Douglas Ginsburg were both accused of inappropriate drug use (a prescription pain killer addiction and smoking marijuana with law students, respectively) (Molotsky 1986; Roberts 1987). Allegations of sexual misconduct also have precedent. President Grover Cleveland's 1887 nomination of Lucius Lamar, for example, was stalled by accusations that he gave a woman a government job in exchange for sex, while a whisper campaign in 1967 accused Thurgood Marshall of "womanizing" (Haygood 2015; Lutler 2018; Pretorious 2009).

Plainly, allegations of disqualifying personal misconduct on the part of Supreme Court nominees are not new. Nonetheless, the emergence of accusations of sexual misconduct during the Thomas confirmation hearing presented an unprecedent moment for the Senate Judiciary Committee. Public engagement with the confirmation process had grown over the years, bringing new attention to the Committee's choices. The Thomas nomination in particular was, as we explored in Chapter 1, closely watched and divisive across multiple dimensions, including race and partisanship. How the Committee would handle the accusations against Thomas, including when the details of the accusations would emerge from the Committee and what procedures the Committee would adopt to address them, were hotly debated by partisans both on and outside the Committee. Years later, when similar allegations were made against Brett Kavanaugh, the Committee would have the same debates all over again.

### *Thomas–Hill Special Session (1991)*

Thomas's (standard) confirmation hearings took place before the Judiciary Committee September 10–20, 1991. On September 27, 1991, the Democrat-controlled Committee deadlocked (7–7) on whether to send the Thomas nomination to the Senate floor with a favorable recommendation. Unable to resolve the issue, the Committee later that day voted 13–1 to send the nomination to the floor without a recommendation. Just over a week later—on October 6, 1991—the public would learn for the first time through a leaked report to National

Public Radio (NPR) that Anita Hill, a University of Oklahoma law professor, had accused Thomas of sexual harassment dating back to the early 1980s when he was her boss at two different federal agencies, the Department of Education and the Equal Opportunity Employment Commission.

Unbeknownst to the public, Hill had first spoken to Democratic Senate staffers about her allegations in early September 1991. In light of this information and after urging from colleagues, Committee chairman Joe Biden (D-DE) asked the White House to "authorize a further FBI investigation, this time focused on Hill's charges" (Totenberg 2018). The FBI's investigation of the accusations, which Committee Republicans and Democrats (but not the public or all senators) knew about, included interviews with Hill and Thomas and a detailed statement from Hill outlining her allegations. The FBI report had been provided to Judiciary Committee members before the September 27 Committee vote on the nomination (Mayer and Abramson 1994). Biden voted against forwarding Thomas's nomination with a favorable recommendation but voted for advancing the nomination with no recommendation. Biden, however, made a point at the time to state that his opposition to the nominee was based on "judicial philosophy" and that he had "no question with respect to the nominee's character" (Mayer and Abramson 1994, 251). As Mayer and Abramson would later write:

> If Biden did believe Hill, as he later claimed, he apparently did not see sexual harassment as a disqualifying offense. Even after Hill surfaced, he neither pushed for an investigation to determine if the harassment had in fact taken place nor shared what information was already known with his colleagues before the vote. (1994, 268)

On October 7, the day after the NPR story, Hill gave a press conference indicating that she would be willing to testify about her allegations (Totenberg 2018). The final Senate vote on Thomas's nomination had been scheduled for October 8, but in light of the rapidly developing situation, Republican and Democratic leaders agreed to delay the vote and hold additional hearings investigating the matter. But the Committee had no plan in place about how to proceed with such a hearing. Committee members argued about whether Hill would appear, whether Thomas would be present if she did, whether Thomas would be recalled to reply to her comments, whether the testimony of either or both would be open or closed to the public, and even who should testify first (Hill and Coleman 1995; Kaplan 1991). So Senate leaders began negotiating key details about the hearing's timing and scope. Republicans, the minority party in the Senate at the time, favored a special session that was quick, brief, and limited in scope, and that is (almost) exactly what they got. The reopened hearings would focus tightly on Hill's accusations and would "exclude general questions about Thomas's sexual conduct, such as whether he had a history of interest in pornography" (Mayer and Abramson 1994, 271). As Biden's colleague on the Committee, Senator Metzenbaum (D-OH), would later say, "Joe bent over too far to accommodate the Republicans, who were going to get Thomas on the Court come hell or high water" (quoted in Mayer and Abramson 1994, 271).

The resulting hearing began on Friday, October 11, and adjourned at 2:03 a.m. on October 14. The special session resembled traditional confirmation hearings in many ways. The hearing was held in public, senators on the Committee were present in the hearing room, and they engaged in the traditional type of back-and-forth question and answer session with the individuals testifying. But the hearing also was distinct in important ways. The scope of questions was limited, the nominee and his accuser were the witnesses, and the questioning time of the senators was differently distributed (the Republicans, for example, leaned on former prosecutor Senator Arlen Spector to lead their questioning of Hill). Few people were satisfied with the resulting process, which in the end presented the grim debacle of an exclusively white and male panel of U.S. senators clumsily navigating fault lines of race and gender that they did not understand, or perhaps even see. Ultimately, the allegations of sexual harassment failed to derail Thomas's nomination: on October 15, 1991, he was confirmed by a 52–48 vote, with 11 Democratic senators supporting confirmation, and two Republicans opposing him (Dewar 1991).

### Kavanaugh–Blasey Ford Special Session (2018)

Twenty-seven years later, the same process would play out again, in sometimes excruciatingly similar ways. Brett Kavanaugh's (standard) confirmation hearings took place September 4–7, 2018. The Judiciary Committee had scheduled its vote on his nomination for September 20. Between the close of the hearings and the scheduled vote, however, rumors began to circulate about an unaired accusation against the nominee. A media report in *The Intercept* on September 12 described a letter possessed by then ranking Democratic Committee member, Dianne Feinstein (D-CA). The letter was said to contain information about a sexual assault involving Kavanaugh and a woman while the two were in high school (Bowden 2018). More details about the letter and woman would emerge in the days that followed, although the name of the accuser, Christine Blasey Ford, would not be released until September 16, when she was finally named by the *Washington Post* (Desjardins 2018).

As had been the case during the Thomas hearings, information about the allegation also was not immediately known by all of the senators. Unbeknownst to the public or many of her colleagues, Senator Feinstein had received the letter from Blasey Ford on July 30. Some Democratic Judiciary Committee senators had heard about the letter and its contents in early September, but Republicans on the Committee apparently first learned of it only after Feinstein shared the information with Judiciary Committee Chair Grassley (R-IA) on September 13 (Hemingway and Severino 2019). Feinstein provided the letter to the FBI for inclusion in Kavanaugh's nomination file on that same day in September (Bowden 2018). Grassley would later criticize Feinstein's handling of the accusation:

> SENATOR GRASSLEY: The ranking member took no action. The letter wasn't shared with me or colleagues or my staff. These allegations could have been investigated in a way that maintained the confidentiality that Dr. Ford requested. Before his hearing, Judge Kavanaugh met privately with 65 senators, including the ranking member. But the ranking member didn't ask Judge Kavanaugh about the allegations when she met with him privately in August.[1]

When the accusation became public, Democrats and some Republicans in the Senate (specifically, Jeff Flake [R-AZ], Susan Collins [R-ME], and Bob Corker [R-TN]) pressed their colleagues to delay the vote and hold a special session hearing to take testimony from Blasey Ford and Kavanaugh. Senate Majority Leader Mitch McConnell (R-KY) and Judiciary Committee Chair Chuck Grassley (R-IA) opposed this idea, but their Senate majority was too small to not acquiesce, and they agreed to reopen the hearings (Hemingway and Severino 2019).

Despite having dealt with a virtually identical situation decades before during the Thomas confirmation process, the Judiciary Committee still had no agreed-upon procedures in place to manage this type of allegation. Virtually all of the problems that haunted the Thomas hearing manifested this time as well. The Committee's members argued about the order of appearances, whether any additional witnesses should be called, whether "hearsay" was inappropriately permitted, and who should bear the "burden of proof" in determining what had happened. In the end, the special session lasted just one day. Blasey Ford testified first, followed by Kavanaugh.

As with the Thomas-Hill hearing, the special session was dramatic and highly salient. Blasey Ford's testimony was somber, perhaps because Republicans on the Committee had opted to hire Rachel Mitchell, a special prosecutor with experience prosecuting sex crimes, to question Blasey Ford on their behalf (a topic we return to below). Kavanaugh's testimony, in contrast, was explosive. He accused the Democratic senators of "orchestrating a political hit" with "millions of dollars in money from outside left-wing opposition groups," to get revenge on "behalf of the Clintons." He angrily told senators that "what goes around comes around."[2] When the Committee's ranking member (Senator Feinstein) began the Democratic senators' round of questioning, Kavanaugh repeatedly talked over her.[3] The Democratic senators on the Committee responded with an escalation of their own: on September 28, 2018, the day the Committee was scheduled to vote on the Kavanaugh nomination, four Democratic senators walked out of the proceedings.

Neither the testimony nor the walk-out derailed Kavanaugh's nomination. On September 28, 2018, the Committee voted on strict party lines to advance the nomination to the floor of the Senate with a favorable recommendation. Based on a deal brokered between Senator Flake and Democrats on the Committee, the final Senate vote was delayed an additional week to give the FBI time to supplement its background investigation with details about the sexual misconduct allegations (Bowden 2018). The subsequent FBI report did not generate new information, and Kavanaugh was confirmed by the full Senate on October 6 by a 50–48 vote.

## HOW GENDER AND RACE WERE HANDLED
## DURING THE SPECIAL SESSIONS

The Thomas-Hill and Kavanaugh–Blasey Ford special session hearings involved sexual misconduct allegations by female accusers against male nominees, examined in public by overwhelmingly male members of the Senate Judiciary Committee. During the 1991 Thomas-Hill hearing, the allegations were heard by a Committee made up entirely of white men. During the 2018 Kavanaugh–Blasey Ford hearing, the Republican delegation was made up of 11 men, including one senator of color, while there were four women and three senators of color among the Committee's 10 Democrats. Both sessions obviously raised gender issues. The Thomas-Hill hearing also directly raised the specter of race, through the race of Hill and Thomas, the race of the senators, and the sexual stereotypes in play in regard to both Black men and Black women. How would these complex race and gender dynamics play out in the unchartered territory of these hearings, especially when paired with the partisan dynamics that are almost always present in the Supreme Court confirmation process?

To examine these issues, we collected an original database of all dialogue at the special sessions. We use each statement made at the hearings as the unit of analysis (meaning a new observation occurs each time the identity of the speaker changes). We also include information on the party of the questioning senator and the identity of the speaker. In addition to the senators and the nominees, Christine Blasey Ford, Anita Hill, and Rachel Mitchell (the Republican senators' questioner during part of the Kavanaugh hearing) appear in this data. The unique context of these sessions required us to develop issue area coding protocols somewhat different than those used throughout the book. To maintain the focus of this chapter, we limit our discussion to issue areas that regularly implicated gender and race during the special sessions. A full description of the issue area coding for the special sessions, and a presentation of all the topics discussed, appears in Appendix Tables 7.1 and 7.2.

### Investigation through Factual Questions

According to the Committee members themselves, the Thomas-Hill and Kavanaugh–Blasey Ford special session hearings were designed to "investigate" the accusers' charges (per Chairman Biden[4]) and assess the "credibility" of the victims' sexual misconduct allegations (per Chairman Grassley[5]). As Biden went on to say during the Thomas-Hill hearing, "This is a fact-finding hearing, and our purpose is to help our colleagues in the U.S. Senate determine whether Judge Thomas should be confirmed to the Supreme Court."[6] If the goal of these sessions is indeed this type of investigatory and fact-finding mission, we would expect that many of the senators' questions would involve factual queries about the events and people involved.

As shown in Figure 7.1, factual queries—those questions dealing with specific facts and factual allegations about the alleged incident—constituted 17 percent of questions at the Thomas hearing and 16 percent at the Kavanaugh hearing. Though these queries are generally intended to get at core information in dispute regarding the allegations, there was wide variation in the assertive-ness of the factual questions asked. For instance, compare the following two examples involving senatorial questioning of Anita Hill. The first line of ques-tioning comes from Senator Patrick Leahy (D-VT):

SENATOR LEAHY. Do you remember the type of restaurant?

MS. HILL. No, I don't. It wasn't anything that was memorable to me, the type of food that we had.

SENATOR LEAHY. Do you remember how you got there?

MS. HILL. I believe that the driver for Chairman Thomas or then Chair-man Thomas took us, Mr. Randall, and dropped us off at the restaurant.

SENATOR LEAHY. And you went right from the office?

MS. HILL. Went from the office.

SENATOR LEAHY. After dinner, how did you get home?[7]

The second set of questions to Hill came from Senator Arlen Specter (R-PA):

SENATOR SPECTER. Professor Hill, you testified that you drew an infer-ence that Judge Thomas might want you to look at pornographic films, but you told the FBI specifically that he never asked you to watch the films. Is that correct?

MS. HILL. He never said, "Let's go to my apartment and watch films," or "go to my house and watch films." He did say, "You ought to see this material."

SENATOR SPECTER. But when you testified that, as I wrote it down, "We ought to look at pornographic movies together," that was an expression of what was in your mind when he—

MS. HILL. That was the inference that I drew, yes.

SENATOR SPECTER. The inference, so he—

MS. HILL. With his pressing me for social engagements, yes.

SENATOR SPECTER. That that was something he might have wanted you to do, but the fact is, flatly, he never asked you to look at pornographic movies with him.

MS. HILL. With him? No, he did not.[8]

These two sets of questions show how differently senators asked factual ques-tions of Hill. Senator Leahy's questions were intended to yield basic factual information—a postwork dinner location and transportation logistics—relevant to Hill's accusation. In contrast, Senator Specter's fact-based questions

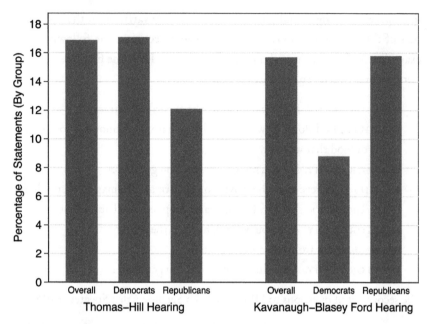

**FIGURE 7.1.** Percentage of Senator Statements in "Factual" Issue Area during Thomas and Kavanaugh Special Session Hearings

were much more assertive in nature, seeming to be focused not only on unearthing the factual allegations in the dispute, but also casting doubt on Hill's version of events.

As Figure 7.1 reveals, both Democratic and Republican senators asked these types of factual questions, but there were some notable differences between the two groups of senators. For Democratic senators, 17 percent of their questions during the Thomas-Hill hearing were in this category, but that number dropped to 9 percent during the Kavanaugh–Blasey Ford hearing. For Republicans (including questioning by their proxy, Rachel Mitchell, during the Kavanaugh hearing), the trend was reversed: 12 percent of their questions were factual during the Thomas-Hill hearing, and 16 percent involved factual allegations during the Kavanaugh–Blasey Ford hearing.

### Accuser Timing and Motives Questions

While there were very few overt attacks directed at the accusers in these two hearings, senators used other techniques to cast doubt on their allegations and stories. Notably, numerous questions were asked related to why the accuser came forward, the timing of the accusations, and behavior following the alleged incident—a category of questions we refer to as *Accuser Timing and Motives*. Some questions that fall within this category, when asked in a particular way and context, can be investigatory in nature. But other questions about allegation timing and motivations are more focused on discrediting or blaming women who report sexual harassment and sexual assault, especially when such accusations are raised some time after the events allegedly occurred (Trope and Liberman 2010, 2003). The key difference between these questions and questions coded as "factual" is that they do not address the alleged incident itself.

At the Thomas-Hill hearing, *Accuser Timing and Motives* questions included exchanges between the senators and Hill about why certain details were not included in her interview with the FBI, why she did not report the alleged harassment at the time it allegedly occurred, why she followed Thomas when he went to work for a different agency, why she continued to engage with him socially when no longer working with him, and why she telephoned him occasionally over the years since the alleged incident. The following example illustrates this type of dialogue and shows how senators expressed their skepticism of the motivation and timing of Hill's accusations. In it, Senator Arlen Specter (R-PA) is asking Hill about her accusation that she witnessed Thomas look at a can of soda and ask "Who put pubic hair on my Coke?" while they were working together:

> SENATOR SPECTER: Let me pick up on Senator Biden's line of questioning. You referred to the "oddest episode I remember" then talked the Coke incident. When you made your statement to the FBI, why was it that that was omitted if it were so strong in your mind and such an odd incident?[9]

In contrast to 1991, many of the *Accuser Timing and Motives* questions asked of Blasey Ford came from same-party senators (Democratic senators) and appear in context to have been asked to give Blasey Ford an opportunity to explain herself, rather than to cast doubt on her account. This is exemplified in one of Senator Feinstein's earliest exchanges with Blasey Ford:

> SENATOR FEINSTEIN: I want to thank you very much for your testimony. I know how very, very hard it is. Why—why have you held it to yourself all these years? As you look back, can you indicate what the reasons are?

DR. BLASEY FORD: Well, I haven't held it all these years. I did disclose it in the—in the confines of therapy, where I felt like it was an appropriate place to cope with the sequelae of the event.[10]

Overall, our data indicate that *Accuser Timing and Motives* questions were asked at both hearings, but this was particularly true during the Thomas-Hill hearing, as displayed in Figure 7.2. In the Thomas hearing, this was the single most common type of senatorial question category, constituting 23 percent of statements. Conversely, at the Kavanaugh hearing, statements about the motivations for, and timing of, Christine Blasey Ford's accusations received far less attention: only 8 percent of statements were devoted to this topic at the later hearing.

The data tell an even more interesting story when we examine the partisan breakdown of the questions asked in this category across the two hearings. As Figure 7.2 indicates, during the Thomas-Hill hearings, this was the most common topic of questioning by Republican senators, who devoted 32 percent of their questioning to grilling Hill about the timing and motives behind her

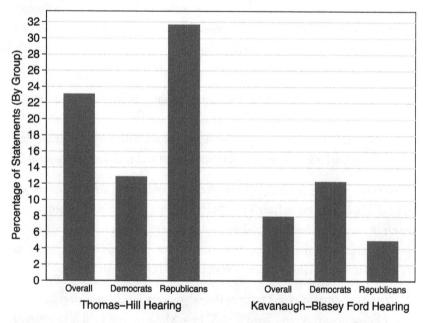

FIGURE 7.2. Percentage of Senator Statements in "Accuser Timing and Motives" Issue Area during Thomas and Kavanaugh Special Session Hearings

accusations. Democratic senators, in contrast, devoted just 13 percent of their comments during the 1991 hearing to this issue. During the Kavanaugh–Blasey Ford hearing, things were quite different. Not only were these questions much less common overall during the 2018 hearing, when they did happen Democrats dominated this conversational space, devoting 12 percent of their questions to this issue area, compared to 5 percent for Republicans. We speculate more below about how cross-time changes plus the Republican senators' use of Rachel Mitchell to ask questions of Blasey Ford together contributed to this stark difference.

### *Coaching Questions*

Closely related to the *Accuser Timing and Motives* category is a set of questions from senators digging into whether the witness was coached or had conversations with senators about the accusations or testimony prior to the hearing (*Coaching Questions*). The underlying intention with these questions, as with the *Accuser Timing* category, often seemed to be to either cast doubt on or to buttress the objectivity of the testimony provided. The following example, from the Republican senator's proxy, Rachel Mitchell, in her questioning of Blasey Ford, shows how questions in this area can explore whether a witness was coached or encouraged to come forward with her accusations:

MS. MITCHELL: OK. Did you talk to any member of Congress—and, again, remember Congress includes the Senate, or the House of Representatives or any congressional staff members—about your allegations between July 10th and the July—and July 30th, which was the date of your letter to Senator Feinstein?

DR. BLASEY FORD: Yes, I met with Congresswoman Eshoo's staff. And I think that's July 18th, the Wednesday, and then on the Friday I met with the congresswoman herself.

MS. MITCHELL: OK. When you met with her, did you meet with her alone or did someone come with you?

DR. BLASEY FORD: I was alone. She had a staff person.

MS. MITCHELL: OK. What did you talk about with Congresswoman Eshoo and her staff on July 18th and the 20th?

DR. BLASEY FORD: I described the night of the incident and we spent time speaking about that. And I asked her how to—what my options were in

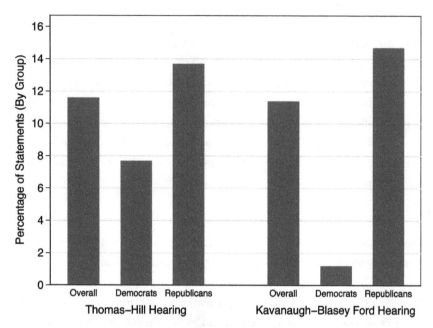

**FIGURE 7.3.** Percentage of Senator Statements in "Coaching" Issue Area during Thomas and Kavanaugh Special Session Hearings

terms of going forward and how to get that information relayed forward. And I also talked to her about fears of whether this was confidential information. And she talked about the constituent confidentiality principle.[11]

Within our data, *Coaching Questions* are common at both hearings, as Figure 7.3 indicates. In the Thomas-Hill hearing, 12 percent of senatorial questions involved this topic, while a similar number, 11 percent, focused on coaching during the Kavanaugh–Blasey Ford hearing. Once again, partisanship differences emerge. For Democrat senators, 8 percent of questions were on coaching in 1991 and just 1 percent of their questions were on this topic in 2018. For Republican senators (and their proxy Rachel Mitchell), their focus in this area was relatively stable across time: 14 percent of questions in 1991 and 15 percent of questions in 2018. That Republican interrogators consistently asked more questions about coaching is not surprising. Both nominees involved in the special sessions were appointed by Republican presidents, and this type of questioning is, in part, intended to cast doubt on the accusations by suggesting that the accusers may have been coached to come forward by outside actors opposed to the nominations.

## Race and Racial Stereotypes

Much of our discussion so far has focused on senatorial questioning strategies relating to how gender dynamics—specifically, how accusations of sexual misconduct brought by female accusers against male nominees—played out in the special session hearings. However, it also is important to consider how the race of the nominee and accuser factor into the senators' questioning behavior. Race was particularly salient in the Thomas-Hill hearing: Thomas was just the second Black person ever nominated to the Supreme Court; Hill, his accuser, was also Black; and both Thomas and Hill faced questions from a panel of all white male senators.

It is unsurprising, then, that race was frequently invoked during the Thomas-Hill hearing, by both the nominee and the senators. Thomas himself was the most explicit about the role he believed race played in Hill's accusations against him and how those accusations were received. On the first evening of the Thomas-Hill special session, Chairman Biden asked Thomas: "Do you have anything you would like to say?" To that open-ended question, Thomas replied:

> JUDGE THOMAS: Senator, I would like to start by saying unequivocally, uncategorically that I deny each and every single allegation against me today that suggested in any way that I had conversations of a sexual nature or about pornographic material with Anita Hill, that I ever attempted to date her, that I ever had any personal sexual interest in her, or that I in any way ever harassed her.[12]

Following that denial of the allegations against him, Thomas quickly turned his testimony to race, explaining how, in his view, his identity as a Black man was likely a driving force behind both the allegations and the way the hearing was proceeding:

> JUDGE THOMAS: Second, and I think a more important point, I think that this today is a travesty. I think that it is disgusting. I think that this hearing should never occur in America. . . . This is a circus. It is a national disgrace. And from my standpoint, as a black American, as far as I am concerned, it is a high-tech lynching for uppity-blacks who in any way deign to think for themselves, to do for themselves, to have different ideas, and it is a message that, unless you kow-tow to an old order, this is what will happen to you, you will be lynched, destroyed, caricatured by a committee of the U.S. Senate, rather than hung from a tree.

Later in the hearing, in an exchange between the nominee and Senator Orrin Hatch (R-UT), Thomas explained the way racial stereotypes, especially as they relate to sex, can disadvantage Black men:

> JUDGE THOMAS: Senator, the language throughout the history of this country, and certainly throughout my life, language about the sexual prowess of black men, language about the sex organs of black men, and the sizes, et cetera, that kind of language has been used about black men as long as I have been on the face of this Earth. These are charges that play into racist, bigoted stereotypes and these are the kind of charges that are impossible to wash off. And these are the kinds of stereotypes that I have, in my tenure in government, and the conduct of my affairs, attempted to move away from and to convince people that we should conduct ourselves in a way that defies these stereotypes. But when you play into a stereotype it is as though you are skiing downhill, there's no way to stop it. And this plays into the most bigoted, racist stereotypes that any black man will face.
>
> SENATOR HATCH: Well, I saw—I didn't understand the television program, there were two black men—I may have it wrong, but as I recall—there were two black men talking about this matter and one of them said, she is trying to demonize us. I didn't understand it at the time. Do you understand that?
>
> JUDGE THOMAS: Well, I understand it and any black man in this country—Senator, in the 1970s I became very interested in the issue of lynching. And if you want to track through this country, in the 19th and 20th centuries, the lynchings of black men, you will see that there is invariably or in many instances a relationship with sex—an accusation that that person cannot shake off. That is the point that I am trying to make. And that is the point that I was making last night that this is high-tech lynching. I cannot shake off these accusations because they play to the worst stereotypes we have about black men in this country.[13]

Hill also experienced the hearings through the prism of race. As a Black woman accusing a Black man of sexual harassment in nationally televised proceedings before an all-white, all-male panel of senators, Anita Hill was in an extremely difficult position, which became even more complex after Thomas's race-laced testimony. Thomas had, in effect, painted Hill as the "black-woman-as-traitor-to-the-race" (Painter 1992, 204; see also Jackson 1992; Smith 1992).

Hill would face many other similar attacks, including from senators inside the hearing room. Senator Alan Simpson (R-WY) would suggest that Hill may suffer from a "delusional disorder,"[14] Senator Spector quoted favorably from an affidavit indicating that Hill might be "somewhat unstable,"[15] and Senator Hatch suggested that Hill may have sourced her allegation details directly from *The Exorcist*.[16] Senators on the Committee portrayed Hill in these and other ways as "an angry and sexually deranged woman" (Crenshaw 2019, 18), evoking racial stereotypes specific to Black women (McGinley 2019).

Racial stereotypes such as these likely played a role in how Hill was perceived, as well as in her credibility as the accuser at the Thomas hearing. Hill noted this herself during a 2002 interview: "How do you think certain people would have reacted if I had come forward and been white, blond-haired and blue-eyed? And I will just give you one name: Strom Thurmond. I do not think [conservative senator] Strom Thurmond would have embraced Clarence Thomas so readily if his accuser had been a white female" (Palmer 2002). Hill's point was perhaps demonstrated years later, when Blasey Ford was perceived by many as credible in part because her "tone, language, and demeanor" made her "the perfect middle-class white mother and wife, accomplished in her own career but not threatening of others" (McGinley 2019, 68). This is, of course, a privilege Anita Hill did not enjoy in 1991.

### Committee Management of Accusations Questions

Another major difference our data reveal between the two special sessions hearings does not directly involve race or gender but instead evidences a deep and unresolved disagreement about how allegations of sexual misconduct should be handled. A number of senators in both hearings focused at least some of their questioning time to this issue, commenting on (and often criticizing) how the Judiciary Committee was conducting its investigation. As Figure 7.4 reveals, in the Thomas-Hill special session, 8 percent of the comments addressed the Committee's process, but in the Kavanaugh–Blasey Ford hearing, that had doubled, constituting 16 percent of the total comments. During the 1991 hearing, there was relatively equal distribution in *Committee Management of Accusations* questions coming from Democratic and Republican senators—11 percent and 13 percent of their questions, respectively. During the 2018 Kavanaugh hearing, 27 percent of Democratic senators' questions and statements involved the Committee's management of the process, while only 14 percent

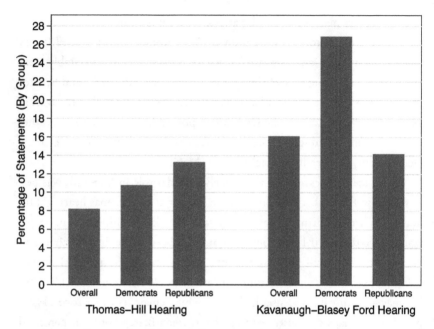

**FIGURE 7.4.** Percentage of Senator Statements in "Committee Management of Accusations" Issue Area during Thomas and Kavanaugh Special Session Hearings

of Republican-attributed statements fell in this category. As highlighted in Figure 7.5, however, when we look at the comments of the Republican senators themselves (excluding Mitchell's questions) this figure jumps to 27 percent, with Republican senator questions largely focused on criticizing the process.

How might we explain this drastic cross-time increase in senators' questions relating to *Committee Management*? Senators were heavily criticized during and after the Thomas-Hill hearing for mishandling the allegations and mistreating Hill—which has been attributed by at least some observers to the racial and gender dynamics of the hearing (e.g., Boyd 1992; Crenshaw 2019; Gilmore 2017; Jordan 1992; Morrison 1992; Palmer 2002). Democratic Senator Dianne Feinstein (CA), recalling her reaction when watching the Thomas-Hill hearing on television, was one of those critics. "What I saw," Feinstein said, "was an attractive woman in a blue suit before an all-male Judiciary Committee, speaking of her experience of sexual harassment. She was treated badly, accused of lying, attacked, and her credibility put to the test throughout the process."[17] Joe Biden, chair of the Committee during the Thomas-Hill hearing, also came to recognize that the Committee mishandled the accusation. Reflecting on his

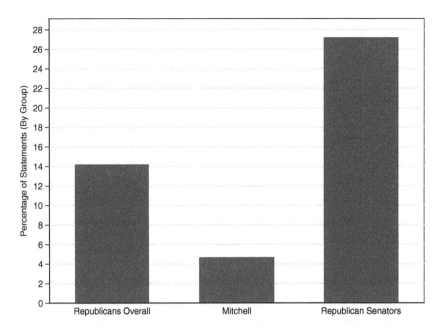

**FIGURE 7.5.** Percentage of Republican Statements in "Committee Management of Accusations" Issue Area during Kavanaugh Special Session Hearings, by Speaker

Committee's treatment of Hill while running for president in 2019, Biden said "To this day, I regret I couldn't give her the kind of hearing she deserved" (Stolberg and Huse 2019).

These concerns about mismanagement of the Thomas-Hill process haunted the Kavanaugh–Blasey Ford hearing. Republican senators repeatedly railed against the Committee's management of the accusations against Kavanaugh. Attacking how Democratic senators, particularly ranking member Senator Feinstein, managed Blasey Ford's allegation allowed Republican senators to criticize their political opponents on a perceived weak point. Importantly, it also allowed them to generate sympathy for the nominee without overtly attacking his accuser, thereby avoiding the type of sharp criticism faced by the senators who had mistreated Hill.

Their criticisms often were quite impassioned:

SENATOR GRAHAM: What you want to do is destroy this guy's life, hold this seat open and hope you win in 2020. You've said that, not me. You've got nothing to apologize for. When you see Sotomayor and Kagan, tell them that Lindsey said hello because I voted for them. I would never do to them what you've done to this guy. This is the most unethical sham since I've been in politics. And if you really wanted to know the truth, you sure as hell wouldn't have done what you've done to this guy.[18]

SENATOR GRASSLEY: Before we take a break, I can't let what Durbin— Senator Durbin said—by the way, he's my friend; we work on a lot of legislation together. But you talked about the obstruction from the other side. I cannot let it go by what you've heard me say so many times, that between July 30th and September 13th, there were 45 days this committee could have been investigating this situation and her privacy would have been produced—protected. So something happened here in between, on your side, that the whole country—well, not the whole country should have known about it—no, not know about it. We should have investigated it.[19]

SENATOR GRAHAM: I cannot imagine what you and your family have gone through. Boy, you all want power. God, I hope you never get it. I hope the American people can see through this sham. That you knew about it and you held it. You had no intention of protecting Dr. Ford; none. She's as much of a victim as you are. God, I hate to say it because these have been my friends. But let me tell you, when it comes to this, you're looking for a fair process? You came to the wrong town at the wrong time, my friend.[20]

Likely in response these strong objections to the process by Republican senators, as well as lingering criticisms stemming from the Democrats' handling of the Thomas-Hill hearing, the Democrats changed their strategy for the Kavanaugh–Blasey Ford special session and met the Republican criticisms head-on by devoting 27 percent of their own statements and questions to defending the way Blasey Ford's allegations were handled.

### NAVIGATING CHANGING TIMES

The above discussion highlights many notable things about the Thomas-Hill and Kavanaugh–Blasey Ford hearings, including the types of questions asked during the hearing, how gender and race may have affected the perceived credibility of the witnesses, and how Democratic and Republican Committee members used different partisan tactics to advance their preferred narratives during the hearings. Our data also show, however, notable variation across time when comparing the 1991 to 2018 hearings. As discussed above, the 1991 Thomas-Hill hearing had a much higher percentage of questions on *Accuser Timing and Motives* relative to the 2018 Kavanaugh–Blasey Ford hearing—23 percent vs. just 8 percent of senator questions. The opposite pattern was true with the *Committee Management of Accusations* category of senatorial statements in our data, with these just accounting for 8 percent in 1991 but 16 percent in the later hearing. We believe changes such as these are largely attributable to two factors: societal changes and Republican senators' use of Rachel Mitchell to question Blasey Ford.

### Societal Changes

The cross-time shift we observe in the data lines up with larger societal changes, some of which were driven by the Thomas-Hill hearings themselves. In 1991, when Anita Hill testified before the Senate Judiciary Committee, our national understanding of sexual harassment and the harm it causes was in its infancy. As Hill herself put it, looking back to that era it in a 2019 interview with the *New York Times*:

> Most of the people viewing the hearings [in 1991] didn't even realize that sexual harassment was something that was actionable, that they could file a complaint about. They had no idea what the concept was about. So we were at a very different point. (Bennett 2019)

After the Thomas-Hill hearing, however, activism and awareness around sexual harassment increased significantly. The hearings provoked public and private conversations about the harassment women too often faced in the workplace (Allen 1995). The number of sexual harassment claims filed with the federal Equal Employment Opportunities Commission exploded. Congress enacted the Civil Rights Act of 1991 to provide more legal remedies for people who suffered sexual harassment at work. And 1992 was deemed the "Year of the Woman," with an unprecedented number of women elected to public office in part because of the galvanizing effect of Hill's testimony (Totenberg 2011).[21]

So when Blasey Ford came forward with her accusations in 2018, the context was different than it had been when Hill gave her testimony before the Senate Judiciary Committee. Sexual harassment and sexual assault, and the harm caused by such behaviors, was much better understood in 2018 than it had been in 1991. The #MeToo movement had gone viral just a few years earlier, empowering millions of women to share their stories of harassment on social media.

Prominent men, such as movie producer Harvey Weinstein and federal judge Alex Kozinski, had been held to account for various types of sexual misconduct, assault, or abuse. With this deepened dialogue came a better understanding of why victims of sexual harassment and abuse do not always immediately report their experiences.

With such fundamental changes occurring in society at large, it is no surprise that senators also changed their questioning style on sexual misconduct matters and their overall treatment of the accusers in the almost thirty years between the Thomas-Hill and Kavanaugh–Blasey Ford special sessions. Senators from both parties during the Kavanaugh–Blasey Ford hearing appeared more aware of the harm imposed by sexual harassment and sexual assault. At least as evidenced by their questioning, senators of both parties also appeared to show more sensitivity to the difficulties and challenges faced by the women who brought these accusations forward. Senator Richard Blumenthal (D-CT) captured this change in his comment at the Kavanaugh–Blasey Ford special session, recalling an earlier conversation with a prosecutor:

> SENATOR BLUMENTHAL: He said, quote, of his prosecutions of rape cases, "I learned how much unexpected courage from a deep and hidden place it takes for a rape victim or sexually abused child to testify against their assailant." If we agree on nothing else today, I hope on a bipartisan basis, we can agree on how much courage it has taken for you to come forward, and I think you have earned America's gratitude.[22]

### A Shift in Republican Senators' Strategy: Rachel Mitchell

These societal changes also likely contributed to the choice made by Republican senators to alter their tactics when the Blasey Ford allegations emerged. As in 1991, the Republican members of the Senate Judiciary Committee were all men. In an attempt to avoid some of the bad optics and backlash this had caused in the Thomas-Hill hearings, Republican senators hired Rachel Mitchell, a prosecutor with extensive experience on sex crimes, to ask questions on their behalf during the Kavanaugh–Blasey Ford special session. A *Washington Post* story described the Republican's decision to use Mitchell:

> They are turning to her to ask what are expected to be personal and potentially painful questions about the woman's youth on live television, sparing

the all-male panel of 11 Republican senators on the committee some uncomfortable exchanges that could sway the public's opinion about the session. (Sullivan et al. 2018)

As planned, Mitchell questioned Blasey Ford on behalf of the Republican senators. But Mitchell immediately was criticized by those on the right for her respectful handling of Kavanaugh's accuser. Commentator Andrew Napolitano put it like this on *Fox News*:

> Mitchell not only is not laying a glove on her, but, in my view, is actually helping her credibility by the gentility with which these questions are being asked and the open-ended answers that the witness is being permitted to give. The president cannot be happy with this. (Breshnahan, Bade, and Gerstein 2018)

Perhaps in response to these concerns, Republican senators changed tactics during Kavanaugh's testimony, quickly taking over the questioning of him themselves. The difference in substance between Mitchell's questions (to Blasey Ford) and those of the Republican senators (to Kavanaugh) is interesting. As shown on Figure 7.6, most of Mitchell's questioning involved factual questions about the alleged incident itself, coaching, or the timing of the accuser coming forward. To wit, Mitchell devoted 23 percent of her questions to facts about what happened. In contrast, only 7 percent of questions from Republican Committee members addressed these topics.

Mitchell also asked the bulk of the Republican's questions on *Accuser Timing and Motives* (8 percent of her questions compared to less than 1 percent for the senators). These differences are predictable, given that Mitchell was the only Republican representative to question Blasey Ford, while the Republican senators conducted most of their side's questioning of Kavanaugh themselves. Recall also that there were fewer of these questions overall in the Kavanaugh–Blasey Ford session than during the Thomas-Hill session (23 percent of total questions vs. just 8 percent). Mitchell's *Accuser Timing and Motives* questions also tended to strike a different, less accusatory tone than did the skeptical senators' questions in the Thomas-Hill hearing, evidencing again the different societal contexts in which the special sessions occurred. The contrast is at times sharp, as shown in the following two exchanges. The first comes from the 1991

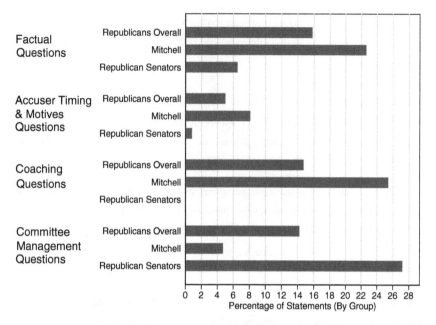

**FIGURE 7.6.** Percentage of Statements Made by Rachel Mitchell and Republican Senators, by Issue Area, during Kavanaugh Special Session Hearings

Thomas-Hill special session and the second from the Kavanaugh–Blasey Ford session:

> SENATOR SPECTER: Thank you, Mr. Chairman. Professor Hill, now that you have read the FBI report, you can see that it contains no reference to any mention of Judge Thomas's private parts or sexual prowess or size, et cetera. My question to you would be, on something that is as important as it is in your written testimony and in your responses to Senator Biden, why didn't you tell the FBI about that?

> MS. HILL: Well, it was a very trying and difficult decision for me not to say anything further. I can only say that when I made the decision to just withdraw from the situation and not press a claim or charge against him, that I may have shirked a duty, a responsibility that I had, and to that extent I confess that I am very sorry that I did not do something or say something, but at the time that was my best judgment. Maybe it was a poor judgment, but it wasn't dishonest and it wasn't a completely unreasonable choice that I made, given the circumstances.[23]

Our second example comes from Rachel Mitchell's questioning of Blasey Ford in 2018:

> MS. MITCHELL: OK. Now, you've talked about attending therapy. In your text to *The Washington Post* dated 7/6—so that's the very first statement we have from you—you put in there, quote, "have therapy records talking about it." . . . Would it be fair to say that Brett Kavanaugh's name is not listed in these notes?[24]

In contrast to Mitchell, the Republican senators directed most of their substantive questioning to airing disputes or complaints about the way the Senate Judiciary Committee handled the accusation and the hearing. Over 27 percent of the Republican senators' statements fell into the *Committee Management of Accusations* category, but less than 5 percent did for Mitchell. As noted above, Democratic senators shared at least some of these frustrations, having devoted a plurality of their comments at the Kavanaugh hearing to those disputes (27 percent). It appears, therefore, that *both* parties are frustrated by the current system of handling accusations of personal misconduct.

## CONCLUSIONS

When the Thomas-Hill and Kavanaugh–Blasey Ford special session hearings are viewed in combination with the other empirical evidence this book has provided on the treatment of gender and race during Supreme Court confirmation hearings, a more complete picture of the hearings emerges. As our discussion in this chapter shows, the special sessions forced the Senate Judiciary Committee to directly grapple with controversial gender and racial issues well beyond what is typically required of it during the confirmation process. Perhaps because of this, the Committee leadership, in the lead up to both hearings, failed to take allegations of sexual misconduct sufficiently seriously and had no plan in place for how to deal with them. Instead, the Committee engaged in on-the-fly negotiations about how the special session hearings should be conducted. It is unsurprising, then, that the hearings left all parties unsatisfied. Nominees and witnesses alike were awkwardly asked by senators to elaborate on explicit details of the allegations, the female accusers were required to defend their motivations for coming forward with their allegations, and both parties were accused of engaging in gender and race stereotyping.

When comparing 1991's hearing to 2018's, though, we did see some small but important improvements in the sensitivity in questioning and Committee strategies. This included, in the latter hearing, a marked decrease in questions toward the accuser relating to the timing and motivation for coming forward with her allegations, as well as the unusual decision by the all-male Republican side of the Committee to bring in an outsider, Rachel Mitchell, to question Blasey Ford on their behalf. Multiple factors likely contributed to these cross-time differences, including the different races of the accusers in the two hearings, societal changes in awareness about sexual misconduct allegations, and reactions by Republican senators to the backlash Committee members had received for their questioning behavior during the Thomas-Hill hearing.

Despite the dramatic Thomas-Hill and Kavanaugh–Blasey Ford special session hearings, and the very real potential that something similar could happen again, the Senate Judiciary Committee continues to lack stable, depoliticized procedures for handling future allegations of nominee misconduct. This should change. Plainly, both parties are frustrated by the way the Judiciary Committee handles accusations of potentially disqualifying personal conduct. By developing stable procedures that will govern this type of situation in the future, regardless of which party controls the Senate or the presidency, senators will no longer be expected to develop ad hoc procedures in the midst of a high-stakes nomination. While developing these procedures will not be easy, the Committee need not start from scratch. Recently developed changes to the Code of Conduct for federal judges (U.S. Courts 2019) may be informative. Senate Rule XXVI, which permits hearings to be closed to the public when they invade personal privacy, damage reputation, or involve charges of a crime or misconduct (U.S. Senate 2013), offers another foundation on which better procedures can be built.[25] Striking the right balance between personal privacy and public accountability is difficult in this context, but it is essential to maintain public confidence in the confirmation process.

**APPENDIX TABLE 7.1.** Issue Area Coding of the Special Sessions of Clarence Thomas and Brett Kavanaugh

| Issue | Description |
|---|---|
| Hearing Administration | Introductions, scheduling, hearing process |
| Accuser Timing and Motives | Why the accuser came forward, timing of accusations, postincident behavior |
| Factual | Specific factual allegations regarding the incident |
| Nominee Background | Aspects of nominee's background and relationship to accuser |
| Accuser Background | Aspects of accuser's background and relationship to nominee |
| Nominee Suffering | Suffering and harm caused to nominee and family |
| Accuser Suffering | Suffering and harm caused to accuser and family |
| Nominee Attacks | Attacks on nominee's character or motivations |
| Accuser Attacks | Attacks on accuser's character or motivations |
| Coaching | Coaching or conversations regarding testimony |
| Committee Management | The Judiciary Committee's handling of the accusations |
| Media Coverage | Media coverage of the allegation |
| Other | Statute of limitations, praise of nominee or accuser, investigative agencies |

**APPENDIX TABLE 7.2.** The Issues Addressed at the Special Sessions of Clarence Thomas and Brett Kavanaugh

| Issue | Overall | Thomas | Kavanaugh |
|---|---|---|---|
| Hearing Administration | 18.5% (762) | 16.1% (395) | 21.9% (367) |
| Accuser Timing and Motives | 17% (700) | 23.1% (566) | 8.0% (134) |
| Factual | 16.4% (678) | 16.9% (415) | 15.7% (263) |
| Nominee Background | 13.5% (555) | 12.9% (317) | 14.2% (238) |
| Coaching | 11.5% (475) | 11.6% (284) | 11.4% (191) |
| Committee Management | 11.4% (471) | 8.2% (202) | 16.1% (269) |
| Accuser Background | 9.1% (374) | 9.8% (241) | 7.9% (133) |
| Nominee Suffering | 2.3% (94) | 2.7% (66) | 1.7% (28) |
| Accuser Suffering | 2.2% (92) | 1.7% (42) | 3.0% (50) |
| Nominee Attacks | 1.2% (48) | 0% (0) | 2.9% (48) |
| Media Coverage | 1.2% (48) | 1.4% (33) | 0.9% (15) |
| Accuser Attacks | 0.6% (25) | 1.0% (25) | 0% (0) |
| Other | 1.6% (65) | 2.2% (53) | 0.7% (12) |
| Total | 106.5% (4,127) | 107.6% (2,452) | 104.4% (1,675) |

Entries are the percentage of statements in each category. Numbers in parentheses are the total number of statements in each category. Total percentage does not sum to 100 due to rounding and because a single statement can be coded in more than one category.

# EIGHT

## REFLECTING AND LOOKING FORWARD

During her opening statement at her Supreme Court confirmation hearing in 2022, Ketanji Brown Jackson reflected on the historic nature of her nomination and explained the dedication she would bring to her role as a Supreme Court justice:

> JUDGE JACKSON: During this hearing, I hope that you will see how much I love our country and the Constitution, and the rights that make us free. I stand on the shoulders of so many who have come before me, including Judge Constance Baker Motley, who was the first African-American woman to be appointed to the Federal bench and with whom I share a birthday.
>
> And like Judge Motley, I have dedicated my career to ensuring that the words engraved on the front of the Supreme Court building, "Equal Justice Under Law," are a reality and not just an ideal. Thank you for this historic chance to join the highest court, to work with brilliant colleagues, to inspire future generations and to ensure liberty and justice for all.[1]

As Jackson's hearing continued into Day 2, the optimism of the nominee's opening statement would give way to a contentious question-and-answer session between the Senate Judiciary Committee senators and Jackson. To many watching the hearings, Jackson's confirmation experience reflected larger societal patterns of bias toward women and people of color. For example, as one commentator noted:

> [The Supreme Court] confirmation hearings for Judge Ketanji Brown Jackson cast a spotlight on the challenges women of color face in the workplace,

from having their qualifications scrutinized, to enduring microaggressions, to feeling the pressure of representing an entire race in their responses and behavior. (Purushothaman 2022)

The empirical analyses presented in this book bears out these concerns, for Jackson and the other women and people of color Supreme Court nominees in our data. In Chapter 4, we found evidence of higher levels of competency-related (judicial philosophy) questions for women nominees. We also observed that both women and nominees of color face more extensive questioning than other nominees in areas falling within their stereotyped strengths. In Chapter 5, we showed that senators more frequently interrupt women and person of color nominees than male and white nominees. And in Chapter 6, we found that female nominees and nominees of color receive less positive, more negative, and more differentiating words from senators than do other nominees.

As we conclude, we broaden our discussion by looking at how race and gender bias might manifest during Supreme Court confirmation hearings in the future, and what might be done to combat it. To explore those issues, we begin by examining the work of the Senate Judiciary Committee in a way that we have not yet done: by tracking the addition of women and people of color to the Committee's membership over time and analyzing these senators' behaviors toward nominees during the hearings. As we discuss, the diversification of the Judiciary Committee is a relatively recent development. Our analysis of the questioning practices of these newer senators therefore may be able to shed light on how female nominees and nominees of color will be treated by more diverse Committees in future hearings. We then explore other changes, both at the individual and institutional levels, that might further reduce or eliminate biased behaviors. Finally, we end by discussing the importance of combating bias, in future Supreme Court confirmation hearings and beyond.

## BEYOND THE IN-GROUP: THE OTHER PARTICIPANTS ON THE SENATE JUDICIARY COMMITTEE

In the empirical analyses presented in this book so far, we have focused on the questioning behavior of "in-group" senators: for gender analysis, the male senators; and for race and ethnicity analysis, the white senators. This focus has allowed us to test the group-based theory we outline in Chapter 3. It also makes sense, given the dominance of white men on the Senate Judiciary Committee across time. But, the confirmation hearings *have* changed over the past few decades, even if those changes have been subtle and sometimes difficult to see. One important such change is the addition of more women and people of color participating in the hearings as members of the Committee.

We begin our look to the future by exploring the effect, if any, the addition of these senators has had on the confirmation experience of female nominees and nominees of color. We begin by briefly discussing the women and men who have diversified the Senate and the Senate Judiciary Committee. We then analyze these senators' behaviors toward nominees. In doing so, we revisit the main issues featured in Chapters 4, 5 and 6: presumptions of competence, intrusive interruptions, and tone. Because of the relatively few numbers of Judiciary Committee members who have been women or people of color, the analysis presented in this chapter is necessarily limited in its scope. Nonetheless, it provides intriguing insights into how future nominees may experience their confirmation hearings.

### Diversifying the Senate and the Judiciary Committee

The first woman to ever serve in the U.S. Senate was Rebecca Latimer Felton (D-GA). Felton was appointed (not elected) to her seat in 1922. The incumbent Georgia senator had died and his successor would be sworn in in a matter of weeks. The governor of Georgia, Thomas Hardwick, who had opposed enactment of the Nineteenth Amendment (which prohibited sex-based discrimination in voting), was looking for a way to appeal to the newly enfranchised female voters he had just spurned. Appointing Felton, who was eighty-seven years old at the time, seemed a promising, albeit largely symbolic, strategy (Solowiej and Brunell 2003). She was a suffragist, which allowed the governor to give a nod to the success of the campaign to extend voting rights to women.[2] She served for fifty days; the Senate was in session for just one of them. Sixteen more women were elected or appointed to the Senate in the sixty years following Felton's brief service, beginning with Hattie Caraway (D-AR) who was elected in 1932.[3]

As shown on Figure 8.1, it took until 1993—177 years after it was established— for two women, Diane Feinstein (D-CA) and Carol Moseley Braun (D-IL) to be seated on the Senate Judiciary Committee (United States Senate 2021a).[4] Like Felton, their appointment to the Committee came only after external events forced their male colleagues to grapple with the limitations of excluding women

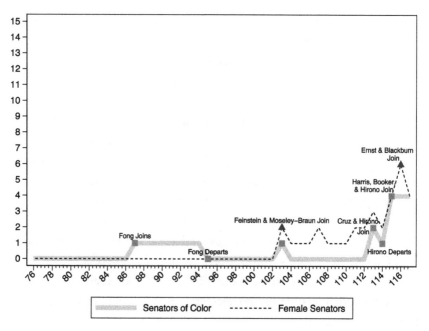

FIGURE 8.1. Number of U.S. Senators of Color and Women Senators Serving on the Senate Judiciary Committee from the 76th to 117th Congresses, 1939–2022

and people of color—in this case the widely panned performance of the all-male and all-white Committee members during the Thomas-Hill special session hearing. Female Republican senators had to wait a bit longer for their opportunity to serve on the Committee, with Joni Ernst (R-IA) and Marsha Blackburn (R-TN) finally becoming the first female Republican members on the Committee in 2019. Once again, their addition was triggered by external events: this time, the awkwardness of having no female Republican senators on the Committee to help their male partisans question Christine Blasey Ford about her sexual assault allegations against Brett Kavanaugh (Everett 2018).

People of color served earlier in the Senate than did women, but they continue to be underrepresented both in the Senate and on the Judiciary Committee. Two Black men, Hiram Revels and Blanche Bruce, were appointed by their state legislatures to serve in the Senate during Reconstruction (in the 1870s), but this inclusion was short lived. After the end of Reconstruction, no African American served in the Senate until 1966 when Edward Brook (R-MA) became the first African American elected to the Senate by popular vote (United States Senate 2021b). In 1993, the same year she was appointed to the

Judiciary Committee, Moseley-Braun became the first Black woman to serve in the Senate, and in 2013 Tim Scott (R-SC) became the first African American to be elected to the Senate from a former Confederate state. The first Hispanic American was elected in 1928, but Asian Americans were not represented in the upper house until 1959, when Republican Hiram Fong was elected from the newly minted state of Hawaii. Finally, three Native Americans have served in the Senate, starting with Charles Curtis (R-KA) in 1907.[5]

Overall, of the almost 2,000 individuals who have served in the U.S. Senate from 1789 to 2022, only 33 have been people of color, and only 11 have been African Americans (Brudnick and Manning 2020; United States Senate 2021b). As dismal as these numbers are, the representation of women and people of color on the Judiciary Committee has been even worse. As shown in Figure 8.1, Fong was appointed to the Committee in 1961, but it took more than fifty years for Mazie Hirono (D-HI) to, in 2012, become both the first Asian American woman to serve on the Judiciary Committee and the first to be elected to the U.S. Senate. No African American, male or female, served on the Committee until Mosley-Braun took her seat in 1993, and the first African American man to serve on the Committee, Cory Booker (D-NJ), was not appointed until 2018.

## THE BEHAVIOR OF WOMEN SENATORS AND SENATORS OF COLOR ON THE SENATE JUDICIARY COMMITTEE

Now that female senators and senators of color have finally appeared as questioners in the Senate Judiciary Committee hearing room, we can begin examining whether their behavior will be different than that of their white and male counterparts. Unlike the large and interdisciplinary body of literature about the behavior of in-group members we have discussed so far, there is little existing work examining how traditional out-group members are likely to behave in a variety of circumstances. While we expect a senator's political party to continue to play a major role in driving behavior on the Committee, we have few other settled expectations about how these senators will behave. Will female senators and senators of color favor their fellow group members? Will they behave in ways that are equally assertive toward all or some nominees, without regard to shared gender, race, or ethnicity? Or might they follow the same behaviors seen from white male senators and be more assertive and forceful toward nontraditional nominees?

Any of these alternatives are theoretically supportable. As with traditional in-group members, we might expect shared group favoritism to affect the behavior of women and person of color senators. Some of the same literature we discuss for this in Chapter 3 applies here as well, since people crave group inclusion and the effect of grouping tends to accentuate similarities between those in one's group and differences from outsiders (Hogg and Abrams 1988). Discrimination toward those not in one's group can then develop, not because of animosity, but rather because positive associations like sympathy, trust, and admiration are reserved for fellow group members (Brewer 2001). This may be particularly likely in the case of shared racial identity, which can foster racial consciousness in behavior and interactions (McClain et al. 2009).

On the other hand, especially in settings like the Senate Judiciary Committee, we may see women and person of color senators behaving in ways that don't align with standard in-group theory. After all, unlike with white and male senators, as explained in Chapter 3, women and people of color, acting alone or in groups, generally do not hold the same societal status, power, and resources that undergirds much of the theoretical basis of the existing in-group literature. This may result in less reliance on stereotypes when assessing and interacting with others. We may even see signs of a concerted partisan strategy on the Judiciary Committee to use the party's female senators and senators of color to engage in the party's more assertive questioning behavior, including toward their fellow group members. Particularly in the years following the Thomas nomination, such a strategy would align with increased consciousness about and desire to avoid being perceived as biased against women and people of color.

The next section begins to explore these possibilities by examining the Supreme Court confirmation hearing behavior of the women and people of color who have served on the Senate Judiciary Committee during the years covered by our data. To do this, we focus on the main analyses appearing in Chapters 4, 5, and 6, examining questions relating to nominee competence, the intrusive interruptions of nominees, and the tone used by senators when they question nominees.

### Questions of Competence

In Chapter 4, we examined how presumptions of incompetence and subject matter stereotypes can negatively affect women and people of color. We expected that in-group senators would be more skeptical of out-group nominees' professional qualifications, while white and male nominees' competency to serve would be presumed. This, in turn, would lead white and male senators to spend more of their hearing time asking questions of a woman or person of color nominee relating to this area of competence. Our empirical results supported this expectation with respect to nominee gender but not race.

Do these same patterns hold when the questioning senators themselves are not members of the dominant in-group? Senator Marsha Blackburn's (R-TN) interrogation of Ketanji Brown Jackson regarding her judicial philosophy indicate they might:

> SENATOR BLACKBURN: Okay. Well, I—I've got some serious concerns about that. I do want to go to your judicial philosophy and back to the Ninth Amendment. President Biden said he was looking for a judicial nominee with a judicial philosophy that is more of one that suggests that there are unenumerated rights in the Constitution.
>
> And all the amendments mean something, including the Ninth Amendment. You told Senator Lee that you didn't discuss this statement with President Biden. But I want to know whether you agree with it. Do you share the judicial philosophy that President Biden is looking for? And Senator Kennedy tried to walk through some of this with you.
>
> Do you believe that the Ninth Amendment is a source of unenumerated rights?
>
> JUDGE JACKSON: Senator, the Supreme Court has not found any unenumerated rights that derive from the Ninth Amendment. And so that's not the precedent of the court and there aren't any rights that have been established under that provision of the Constitution.
>
> SENATOR BLACKBURN: Okay. White House Chief of Staff, Ron Klain, has written that the Supreme Court should intervene whenever the nation's conscience and laws need a jolt in a progressive direction. Presumably, that is what he and his boss, President Biden, expect a justice to do. So do you believe that the role of the court is to intervene whenever we need a jolt in a progressive direction?
>
> And would you do that through the unenumerated rights? Would you do it on issues like abortion or any other issue?[6]

Blackburn's questioning of Jackson about whether she would use the Ninth Amendment to enact a progressive political agenda exemplifies how senators might express stereotyped skepticism of the competence of a Black woman to correctly interpret the Constitution; their shared status as women did not change the dynamic described in Chapter 4. But there are counter examples in the data as well. As discussed in Chapter 6, Senator Fong, the first person of color to serve on the Committee, did not—unlike many other senators—question Thurgood Marshall's competence to serve on the court. Instead, he praised the nominee unequivocally, noting the historical nature of the nomination and describing Marshall as "an excellent lawyer and jurist."[7]

Which example is more typical of the behavior of female senators and senators of color, Blackburn's questioning of Jackson or Fong's of Marshall? To address that question systemically, we turn to our data. Figure 8.2 presents the proportion of judicial philosophy questions asked by female senators (top graph) and senators of color (bottom graph) based on the nominees' gender, race, and partisanship.

Starting with the top graph, this figure shows that female senators generally follow the same questioning patterns we would expect of male senators. They ask female nominees more judicial philosophy questions than male nominees. Overall, female senators used 8.3 percent of their questions to interrogate female nominees on their judicial philosophies, compared to 6.5 percent for male nominees. This difference also holds when we account for partisanship. Judicial philosophy questions constitute 8.8 percent of the questions female senators asked female, different-party nominees, compared to 6.8 percent for male, different-party nominees; 8 percent for female, same-party nominees; and 5 percent for male, same-party nominees. Thus, while shared partisanship slightly mitigates the volume of judicial philosophy questioning, female senators, like their male counterparts, appear skeptical of female nominees' competence for the Court, asking them more questions about how they approach constitutional interpretation, the core task of a Supreme Court justice.

The bottom graph in Figure 8.2 reveals the extent to which senators of color query nominees about their judicial philosophies. Here, we do not see the same pattern. Instead, the results are flipped: senators of color ask white nominees more judicial philosophy questions than they ask nominees of color. More specifically, senators of color asked virtually no judicial philosophy questions of different-party nominees of color and devoted only 4.6 percent of their questioning of same-party nominees of color to matters of judicial philosophy, compared to 6.5 percent for white, different-party nominees and 5 percent for white,

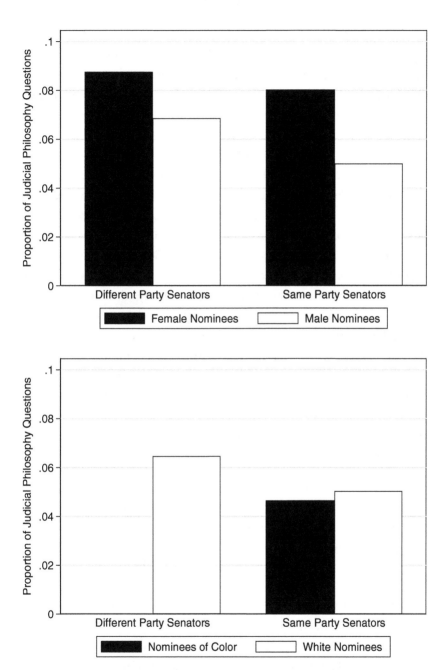

**FIGURE 8.2.** Gender, Race, and Judicial Philosophy Questions from Female and Person of Color Senators at Supreme Court Confirmation Hearings, 1939–2022

same-party nominees. However, it is important to note that the data underlying these findings are very limited. There have been only two senators of color who have questioned a different-party nominee of color: Fong (who questioned Thurgood Marshall) and Ted Cruz (R-TX) (who questioned Ketanji Brown Jackson). These findings, consequently, may have limited predictive value.

### Interruptions

Chapter 5 focused on whether female nominees and nominees of color are interrupted more during their hearings than are other nominees. As we discussed, interruptions can have a powerful effect on the conversational dynamic, both by silencing the original speaker and by placing the interrupter in a dominant position over the direction the conversation takes. We found strong evidence of gender and race effects in the senators' interruption patterns, especially for intrusive interruptions. As predicted by in-group theory, white and male nominees were granted more conversational deference (and were interrupted less often) than other nominees. Will female senators and senators of color show the same race and gender biased patterns in their questioning of nominees?

The hearings provide numerous examples indicating they might. Ketanji Brown Jackson was repeatedly interrupted at her hearing, including by fellow person of color, Senator Cruz. Cruz's questioning of Jackson about her trial court record sentencing child pornography offenders stood out for many reasons, including the senator's repeated interruptions of Jackson (marked in the transcript excerpt with "—").

> JUDGE JACKSON: Thank you, senator. You've picked out, I don't know, seven, eight cases. I've sentenced more than 100 people, but not to child pornography.
>
> SENATOR CRUZ: But, not to child pornography. These are your child porn cases.
>
> JUDGE JACKSON: And in every case—in every case, Senator I look at the evidence, I look at the recommendations of not just the government because my duty as a judge—a judge is to consider all of the arguments that are made in a case. I look at the evidence, I talk to the defendants about the harms that they have engaged in. Many of these defendants are people who—
>
> SENATOR CRUZ: Ok, judge, with respect, you're not answering my question. . . .

Shortly after, the tense exchange continued:

> JUDGE JACKSON: Senator, I didn't say I'm not going to answer. I said my
> answer—
> SENATOR CRUZ: Ok, well then, please tell us in these facts, in this case
> *Chazin*, why did you sentence him to just 28 months.
> JUDGE JACKSON: Senator, you're looking at the record; I don't have the record
> here. What I will say, is that in every case I looked at the recommendations
> of not only the government but also the probation office, the defendant, the
> record, the evidence I took into account the seriousness of the offense—[8]

Through his repeated interruptions of Jackson's answers, Senator Cruz was able to cut off Jackson's attempts to offer a nuanced defense of her sentencing practices.[9] While interruptions cannot be fully avoided during dynamic question-and-answer sessions like confirmation hearings, as we saw in Chapter 5, when they happen repeatedly, they aid a speaker to gain control over a conversation—just as Senator Cruz did in this example.

A confirmation hearing exchange between Senator Amy Klobuchar (D-MN) and Amy Coney Barrett shows a similar dynamic. Klobuchar is asking the nominee about her Seventh Circuit Court of Appeals dissenting opinion in *Kanter v. Barr* (2019). In that opinion, Barrett differentiated between the types of rights that former felons hold. In pushing Barrett to defend the lines she drew in that case, Klobuchar interrupted Barrett multiple times:

> SENATOR KLOBUCHAR: And it says felons could be disqualified from ex-
> ercising certain rights like the rights to vote and serve on juries. But apart
> from that clause, you said these rights belong only to virtuous citizens.
> That's what I'm trying to understand, what that means.
> JUDGE BARRETT: So, the argument in the case, those who were challeng-
> ing *Heller* and those who were arguing on the side of the government in
> the *Kanter* case, is that the seventh—the Second Amendment is a civic
> right. And that is how the Supreme Court itself frames the debate, as a
> distinction between civic rights and individual rights with voting being
> a civic right. And in literature, you know, in the historical literature, that
> was—which was at play in the case. That was drawn—
> SENATOR KLOBUCHAR: Okay. But how would you define the word virtu-
> ous? Because it doesn't appear in the Constitution.

JUDGE BARRETT: Well, senator, this—

SENATOR KLOBUCHAR: —I'm just trying to know what that means because we're—we have—we're living in a time where a lot of people are
having their voting rights taken away from them. So, what's virtuous?

JUDGE BARRETT: Okay. Well, senator, I want to be clear that that is not
an opinion designed to denigrate the right to vote, which is fundamental.
The distinction between civic and individual rights is one that's present in
the court's decisions and it has to do with kind of a jurisprudential view
of what rights are.

And the virtuous citizenry idea is a historical and jurisprudential one. It
certainly does not mean that I think that anybody gets a measure of virtue
on whether they're good or not and whether they're allowed to vote. That's
not what I—

SENATOR KLOBUCHAR: Okay. . . .[10]

These examples from Klobuchar and Cruz also raise an additional possibility:
are the Judiciary Committee Democrats and Republicans intentionally leaving
the most rigorous questioning of women and person of color nominees to female
senators and senators of color? While we do not know if the Democrats on the
Committee explicitly strategized to place female senators like Amy Klobuchar,
instead of male senators such as Sheldon Whitehouse (D-RI) and Patrick Leahy
(D-VT), in the aggressor position during the Barrett hearing, these examples
support the possibility, as does the following example, again from Senator Blackburn's questioning of Jackson, regarding the definition of the word "woman":

SENATOR BLACKBURN: . . . Do you agree with Justice Ginsburg that there
are physical differences between men and women that are enduring?

JUDGE JACKSON: Senator, respectfully, I—I'm not familiar with that particular quote or case, so it's hard for me to comment as to whether—

SENATOR BLACKBURN: All right, I'd love to get your—your opinion
on—on that. And you can submit that. Do you interpret Justice Ginsburg's meaning of men and women as male and female?

JUDGE JACKSON: Again, because I don't know the case, I don't know how
I interpret it. I need to read the whole thing.

SENATOR BLACKBURN: Okay. Can you provide a definition for the word
woman?

JUDGE JACKSON: Can I provide a definition?

SENATOR BLACKBURN: Yeah.

JUDGE JACKSON: I can't.

SENATOR BLACKBURN: You can't?

JUDGE JACKSON: Not in this context, I'm not a biologist.

SENATOR BLACKBURN: So you believe meaning the word woman is so unclear and controversial that you can't give me a definition?

JUDGE JACKSON: Senator, in my work as a judge, what I do is I address disputes. If there's a dispute about a definition, people make arguments, and I look at the law, and I decide—so I'm not—

SENATOR BLACKBURN: The fact that you can't give me a straight answer about something as fundamental as what a woman is, underscores the dangers of the kind of progressive education that we are hearing about. Just last week, an entire generation of young girls watched as our taxpayer funded institutions permitted a biological man to compete and beat a biological woman in the NCAA swimming championships.

What message do you think this sends to girls who aspire to compete and win in sports at the highest levels?

JUDGE JACKSON: Senator, I'm not sure what message that sends. If you're asking me about the legal issues related to it, those are topics that are being hotly discussed, as you say, and could come to the court. So I'm—

SENATOR BLACKBURN: And I think it tells our girls that their voices don't matter.[11]

It is difficult to imagine a male, different-party senator questioning Jackson as effectively on this issue as Blackburn did, indicating the utility of using senators from the nominee's in-group to engage in the most aggressive questioning of nontraditional nominees.

A final example, involving then Senator Kamala Harris (D-CA) and Brett Kavanaugh, illustrates a different dynamic: the disruptive effect of interruptions by a female senator of color in her interrogation of a white, male nominee. During this exchange, Harris is questioning the nominee on his views on state voting restrictions and race, including the phrase "racial spoils system":

SENATOR HARRIS: Can you define the term as you used it? What does it mean to you?

JUDGE KAVANAUGH: But I need to—you raised the case. And it—the state voting restriction in that case denied Hawaiians—residents of Hawaii the ability to vote on the basis of their race. So if you were Latino or African-American, you could not vote in the election—

SENATOR HARRIS: And I heard your response to that earlier, and I appreciate the point that you made then. My question is, you used this term twice. And I'm asking, what does the term mean to you?

JUDGE KAVANAUGH: I'm not sure what I was referring to then, to be—to be entirely frank. So I would have to see the context of it. But what I do know is that the Supreme Court by a 7–2 margin agreed with the position articulated in the amicus brief, in that the voting restriction there was for a state office and denied people the ability to vote on account of their race. So it was—

SENATOR HARRIS: Sir, I appreciate that. You have been very forthcoming about the amount of work and preparation that you put into everything you do. You have certainly led me to believe that you're very thoughtful about the use of your words and your knowledge that words matter, especially words coming from someone like you or any one of us.

And so I would like to know what you meant when you used that term. But we can move on. But I will say this. Are you aware that the term is commonly used by white supremacists?[12]

As these examples show, Senators Cruz, Klobuchar, Harris, and Blackburn each engaged in the same type of aggressive interruption strategy we saw white and male senators engage in in Chapter 5. They also support the possibility, noted above, that copartisans on the Committee strategize their questioning to ensure that at least some of the most contentious questioning of nominees who are not white men comes from female senators or senators of color.

Despite some salient examples, however, the data do not support this conclusion. As Figure 8.3 reveals, female senators more frequently interrupt male, different-party nominees than they do female, different-party nominees; senators of color do the same with respect to different-party, white nominees compared to different-party nominees of color. The top graph reveals that female senators intrusively interrupt male, different-party nominees in 20 percent of their opportunities to do so, as compared to 16 percent for female,

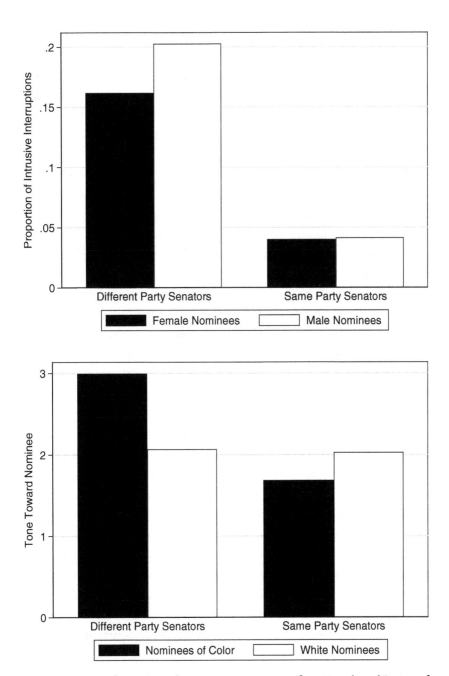

**FIGURE 8.3.** Gender, Race, and Intrusive Interruptions from Female and Person of Color Senators at Supreme Court Confirmation Hearings, 1939–2022

different-party nominees. As found in Chapter 5, this is mitigated heavily by shared partisanship. Female senators only interrupt same-party nominees (male and female) about 4 percent of the time. Thus, it is clear that partisanship plays a major role in the extent to which women senators intrusively interrupt nominees. Gender does as well—with female senators interrupting male nominees from the opposite party more often than they do similarly situated female nominees.

A slightly more complicated picture emerges for senators of color. While they interrupt white, different-party nominees much more frequently than other types of nominees—in 18 percent of their statements—they also interrupt same-party nominees of color more frequently than white, same-party nominees (9 percent compared to 2 percent). Also, senators of color intrusively interrupt different-party nominees of color relatively infrequently, at 4 percent. Considered collectively, the evidence in Figure 8.3 reveals that female and person of color senators most frequently interrupt different-party members of their out-group, which is similar to the behavior of white male senators (but with a different out-group). This suggests that in-group theory is applicable in this context and that it is amplified when the senator and the nominee are not copartisans.

### The Language Used by Senators

Our final examination of the questioning practices of female senators and senators of color looks at the language used when Judiciary Committee members describe and speak to nominees. As explained in Chapter 6, biases based on race and gender can lead to significant differences in the language used to talk to and about people. We expected that in-group senators would use more positive tone (and less differentiation words) when interacting with nominees who share their in-group status. Our results bore this out and showed that male senators use the least positive tone toward female, different-party nominees and that white senators used less positive tone toward different-party nominees of color, as compared to same-party nominees of color. Will female senators and senators of color be similarly generous in their use of positive language when talking to or about nominees who are in their in-groups?

Senator Feinstein certainly was, in her opening statement at Ruth Bader Ginsburg's hearing:

SENATOR FEINSTEIN. . . . For me, this is a very special opportunity, because while several of my colleagues spoke of the fact that they have been
present during many of these hearings, for myself and Senator Moseley-
Braun, this is our first. And it is no coincidence that, as our first, it is someone such as yourself.

We are contemporaries, Judge, and many women of our generation
struggled against significant odds to educate themselves and to balance
career and family. To be honest, though, until I began to prepare for these
hearings, I really didn't realize the depth and the extent to which you have
played a very critical role in breaking down the barriers that have barred
women from public and private sectors for centuries. So now I know just
how really fitting and proper and how significant this vote is going to be
for me. And I want to thank President Clinton for nominating you.

I noted, for example, that as one of only 9 women in a class of 400 at
Harvard, you were asked by the dean to justify taking a place in the class
that otherwise would have gone to a man. That despite graduating at the
top of your law school class, only two law firms in the entire city of New
York offered you second interviews, and neither offered you a job. And
that even after you became a litigator, you were given sex discrimination
cases to handle, because they were viewed at the time as women's work.

You met each of these challenges and indignities and, no doubt, many
more, Judge Ginsburg, with intellect, with determination, and grace. And
not only did you justify your admission to law school, but you blazed a
trail that thousands of women have followed.[13]

While describing a nominee as a "role model" is not uncommon for senators, Feinstein's use of effusive language went far beyond that. To see if the
Feinstein-Ginsburg language pattern holds more broadly among women and
person of color senators, both of the same and different party as the nominee,
we look one final time to our data.

Figure 8.4 reports the tone used by female senators and senators of color
when interacting with and describing nominees. Beginning with the top graph,
we find support for the Feinstein-Ginsburg model. Female senators do indeed
use more positive language toward female nominees, particularly if they are
copartisans. Different-party female senators use about 12 percent more positive language toward female nominees compared to male nominees, while

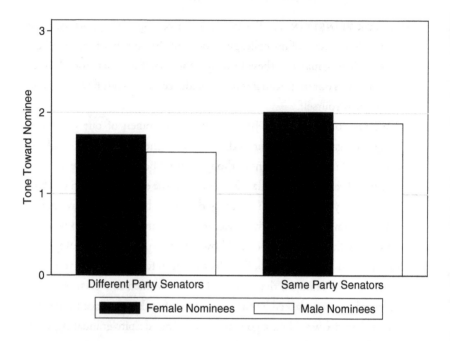

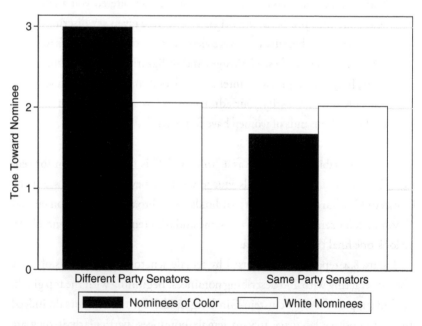

**FIGURE 8.4.** Gender, Race, and Tone toward Nominees from Female and Person of Color Senators at Supreme Court Confirmation Hearings, 1939–2022

same-party female senators use about 7 percent more positive language in questioning female nominees than male nominees. Thus, female senators are more complimentary toward members of their in-group, as evidenced by the use of more positive language toward female nominees.

Turning now to the bottom graph, we see that the results are more mixed for senators of color. In our limited data, senators of color use the most positive language for nominees of color appointed by a different-party president. This is notable because it suggests that being a member of a racial in-group outweighs partisanship. But as noted above, this finding is based on the questioning of only two senators, Fong and Cruz. Senator Fong was especially positive in his questioning of Thurgood Marshall, which is likely driving the results we see here. Also interesting is that same-party senators of color use about 20 percent more positive language when interacting with white nominees compared to their interactions with nominees of color. They are not, therefore, more effusive toward members of their racial in-group, even when they share a party affiliation.

What should we make of these results examining the behavior of the small number of female senators and senators of color who have sat on the Senate Judiciary Committee so far? It appears female senators, like their male counterparts, tend to question the competence of female nominees more often than male nominees. But, unlike their male colleagues, they interrupt male nominees more frequently than female nominees, and use more positive language toward female nominees. These latter two findings suggest that female senators behave more favorably to members of their in-group, especially but not only when they share those nominees' party affiliations. Senators of color, who have not been as fully represented on the Judiciary Committee, show some of the same patterns. They question the competence of white nominees more often than nominees of color, and interrupt white, different-party nominees much more than other nominee types. Their use of tone, in contrast, is more mixed.

Based on this limited evidence, it appears that increasing the diversity of the membership of the Judiciary Committee could help reduce the risk that gender and racial biases will manifest during the Supreme Court confirmation hearing process. Female senators and senators of color do not, it appears, consistently defer to white, male nominees by assuming their competence, giving them more space to speak, and praising them in their language, all of which are patterns we observed from the white, male senators who have historically dominated the hearings. Thus, the subtle forms of gender and racial bias we have documented throughout this book are less likely to be present in the future with a more diversified Judiciary Committee.

## PATHWAYS TO MITIGATE BIAS IN THE FUTURE

Additional steps to reduce bias at the confirmation hearings also are worth considering, including both individual and institutionally focused changes. Perhaps the most obvious individual-focused way to mitigate bias is through implicit bias training and education. Sometimes termed *unconscious bias training*, these programs vary in length and intensity and are designed to "make individuals aware of their unintentional involvement in the perpetuation of discrimination and inequity" (Pritlove et al. 2019). When effective and well designed, implicit bias training helps participants recognize their own biases and group privileges and can also provide participants with effective "strategies aimed at reducing discriminatory thoughts and practices" (Pritlove et al. 2019).

Implicit bias training requirements for many organizations in the United States have grown exponentially in recent years. Many major corporations, like Starbucks, Facebook, Delta Airlines, and Google, now put their employees through such training (Delta Airlines 2020; Umoh 2018). A similar trend toward more bias training requirements can be seen in governmental organizations and regulations. A majority of major police departments around the United States provide some form of implicit bias training for their officers (CBS News 2019). There is also a move toward requiring more state-licensed professionals in fields like public health, real estate, and sales to receive similar training (State of California 2021; State of Michigan 2021). Additionally, several judiciaries throughout the nation host implicit bias training for their judges and other court personnel (Bennett 2017; Hoover 2021; Miller 2020), something that is encouraged by the American Bar Association (Stanzione 2020).

Despite the growth of implicit bias training in private and public sectors, it remains controversial. Critics argue that it is ineffective, in part because some organizations attempt to avoid employee backlash by making the training voluntary rather than mandatory. The result is that the training is "embraced only by people who are already familiar with bias and interested in reducing it" (Gino and Coffman 2021). The training programs also can fail to help participants identify bias (Kim and Roberson 2022) and may lack concrete tips for how to reduce future bias (Gino and Coffman 2021).

Views toward implicit bias training efforts also are often deeply politicized. This has been particularly clear in the federal government's adoption and reversal of policies with regard to training in this area. While the Obama administration moved the federal government's executive branch toward more diversity and implicit bias training, President Trump's administration reversed course: near the end of the Trump presidency, in September 2020, the Office of Management and Budget director issued a memo to federal executive branch agencies informing them that President Trump had directed federal agencies to "cease and desist from using taxpayer dollars to fund" antiracism training. The memo referred to such training as "divisive, anti-American propaganda" (Vought 2020). The Biden administration shifted direction once again, rescinding these restrictions in a January 20, 2021 executive order (the very first executive order of the administration) and then expanding bias trainings in June 2021 (Biden 2021a, 2021b).

Given all of this, requiring implicit bias training for members of the Senate Judiciary Committee and their staff is unlikely to be a feasible solution for mitigating bias in the near future. It is notable, however, that state legislatures have slowly been adopting diversity initiatives, and not just in "blue" states. Diversity, nondiscrimination, and implicit bias training for legislators and legislative staff has been adopted in states as diverse as Alabama, California, Connecticut, Maine, Massachusetts, Minnesota, New Jersey, New York, Oregon, Vermont, Washington, and Wyoming (Saucedo and Hentze 2020). These state efforts may provide fruitful examples for reformers pushing for the adoption of similar programs in the Senate.

Another individual-level way to combat bias is for individuals on the Senate Judiciary Committee to call it out when it occurs. An example from 2022 shows how effective individual interventions can be. At that time, the Committee was considering Andre Mathis, a Black lawyer, for an appointment to the Sixth Circuit Court of Appeals. During Mathis's short round of questioning before the Committee, Senator Blackburn cited the nominee's "rap sheet" of legal citations (for, it was later revealed, failure to pay traffic tickets) (Sneed 2022). Later, fellow Judiciary Committee member Alex Padilla (D-CA) called out this type of questioning "demeaning" and "offensive," specifically noting how frequently it is directed at nominees of color:

It's not lost on me that [it's] nominees of color that have been treated differently in our hearings, whether it's insinuations of rap sheets, or hostility

about their qualifications or views, or undue scrutiny of their personal religious faith. (Sneed 2022)

Padilla would go on to ask his Judiciary Committee colleagues to be "cognizant
of this disparity" in how they treat nominees of color versus other nominees
(Sneed 2022).

Senator Patrick Leahy (D-VT) did something similar in 2021, during the
joint confirmation hearing for Jennifer Sung (for the Ninth Circuit Court of
Appeals) and Beth Robinson (for the Second Circuit Court of Appeals). Senator
John Kennedy (R-LA) had ended a tense question-and-answer exchange with
Sung by interrupting the nominee to declare that she is not impartial. Earlier,
Senator Cruz had interrupted Robinson multiple times to make a similar point.
When Kennedy had finished his questioning, then Committee Chairman Leahy
drew attention to his colleagues' frequent interruptions of female nominees:

> This idea that especially if we have a woman nominee you can interrupt her
> anytime you want and state your own things . . . I would hope we can get
> back and show some respect to those who are answering questions under
> oath. (Benninghoff 2021)

Interest groups may be able to play a similar role by calling out biased behavior toward nominees in nearly real time. This type of strategy has been used since
2020 by numerous organizations, working in tandem, as a tool to encourage fair
media coverage toward women and people of color in salient federal political
positions (UltraViolet 2022b). In February 2022, the coalition of groups working toward this goal released a forty-two-page guide for the media designed to
ensure that the coverage of Biden's Black woman nominee (later announced to
be Ketanji Brown Jackson) would be fair and free from sexist and racist biases
and stereotypes (UltraViolet 2022a). One could imagine these or similar groups
using the same strategy—a combination of a prehearing guide provided to senators' offices plus widespread real-time efforts to publicize biased behaviors—to
attempt to steer senators toward more equitable behavior in the future.

Institutional-level reforms also should be considered. To see what institutional reforms in response to documented systematic bias looks like in a political
institution, one need just look across the street from the U.S. Capitol building
to the U.S. Supreme Court building. In response to empirical research findings
that female justices on the Court are interrupted more frequently than male

justices during oral arguments (Feldman and Gill 2019; Jacobi and Schweers 2017), Chief Justice Roberts, according to Justice Sotomayor, started "playing referee when interruptions happened and ensuring that people got back to the judges who were interrupted" (Liptak 2021). When the Court resumed in-person proceedings in the October 2021 term toward the end of the COVID-19 pandemic, Roberts also made modest alterations to the Court's traditional oral argument procedures (United States Supreme Court 2021). SCOTUSblog's Amy Howe described those changes like this:

> Instead of reverting entirely to the traditional "free for all" format for asking questions, the justices will adopt a hybrid approach that sets aside time for the justices to take turns asking questions. (Howe 2021)

While it may be too soon to fully assess the effects of Roberts's institutional reform on interruption rates during oral arguments, Court watchers have noted that the changes already have resulted in a much more active questioning style of Justice Thomas (who had earlier expressed his disdain for interruptions during oral arguments) (Howe 2021; Johnson et al. 2021). Justice Sotomayor believes there also have been other changes, saying, "My colleagues are much more sensitive than they were before. You will see us, even now when we're speaking, a judge will say, 'Sorry, did I interrupt you?'" (Liptak 2021).

For those concerned with bias in our political institutions, these institutional reforms to the Supreme Court's processes are positive developments. Would something similar work in the Senate's Judiciary Committee? A direct import of the Supreme Court's model seems unlikely, given the stark differences between the two institutions and their actors. While justices are ideologically diverse and sometimes issue starkly divided opinions and scathing dissents, they also have relative independence from daily politics. By contrast, senators have institutional incentives to regularly score political points, gain media attention, and find ways to satisfy the partisan inclinations of their voters. Supreme Court justices are consequently likely more willing to engage in collegial intrainstitutional behavior than are senators. Institutional-level reforms to encourage more equitable behaviors at confirmation hearings might therefore better focus on reducing the political tension built into the Committee's work.

The Judiciary Committee has made institutional-level changes to the Supreme Court confirmation process many times. Some of these changes—such as deciding to no longer wait for "blue slips" to be returned from a federal circuit court's home state senators before proceeding with a Committee vote on the nominee (Ruger 2019) and abandoning the Committee quorum requirement for moving nominations out of Committee (Hannon 2020)—have reflected and likely exacerbated political tension rather than reducing it. But other changes have been generally bipartisan efforts to make the process more democratic and inclusive, the most notable of which is the opening of the hearings to the public.

As we reviewed in Chapter 2, public hearings and nominee testimony did not become common until after 1937, when the Senate faced severe backlash for failing to publicly disclose or discuss Hugo Black's ties to the Ku Klux Klan before confirming him in a closed-door session (Maltese 1998). This deeply secretive process was roundly criticized, and the Judiciary Committee quickly agreed to adopt more inclusive procedures in the future. Nonetheless, some groups have suggested that returning to a less public confirmation process today could improve the process by reducing the senators' incentives to engage in sharply partisan behaviors. In 1988, for example, the Twentieth Century Fund task force, composed of lawyers, academics, and retired politicians, argued that that the Judiciary Committee's confirmation process was "dangerously close to looking like the electoral process" (Maltese 1998, 9) and recommended that nominee testimony be eliminated (with senators relying instead on written materials and non-nominee testimony) or, if nominees were to testify, that their testimony should focus exclusively on "the ability and capacity of the nominee to carry out the high tasks of serving on the Supreme Court" (Maltese 1998, 9).

If closing the hearings or eliminating nominee testimony would lower performative partisanship on the part of the senators, it could perhaps modestly reduce activation of biases at the hearings. But it also could simply render these biases invisible to the larger public, making them more difficult to call out and contest. Returning the Supreme Court confirmation process to the backroom dealings of less democratic eras, when women and people of color had little or no voice in the process, also would likely reduce the influence of advocates for those groups, who continue to be underrepresented in the Senate and on the Senate Judiciary Committee. Finally, closing the hearings would eliminate one of the main mechanisms the public uses to evaluate nominees and hold senators accountable for their confirmation choices (Collins and Ringhand 2013a; Greenberg 2005). It is unlikely, in our opinion, that any potential benefits of closed hearings would outweigh these significant costs.

A different institutional change, however, could potentially reduce the intense partisanship of the current process without these accompanying costs: imposing limited terms on Supreme Court justices. With life tenure and thirty or more years of potential service on the Supreme Court on the line, every confirmation hearing that takes place today is a high-stakes affair. Presidents, senators, interest groups, and voters understand that who sits on the Court matters and that it may be years before another vacancy emerges. Recall, for example, that it was eleven years between Stephen Breyer's appointment in 1994 and the next appointment, of Chief Justice John Roberts, in 2005. Given these high stakes, it is hardly surprising that every confirmation becomes a trial by ordeal. In times of high partisan strife, there is little incentive for anyone involved to treat it as anything else. Tweaking the confirmation process will not change that, but limiting the terms of Supreme Court justices could.

The imposition of fixed eighteen-year terms for justices would give each elected president two seats to fill per term, with a midterm election in between.[14] This predictability would bring down the temperature of the confirmation process by reducing the consequences of filling any single seat. Because confirming a Supreme Court nominee would become a routine process, it would also decrease the incentives for senatorial grandstanding, which, as noted above, could reduce the activation of biases and result in a more equitable process. It also would lessen the likelihood of more controversial changes, like expanding the number of justices, while keeping the Court well within our system of checks and balances by ensuring that the composition of the Court reflects the democratic choices of the American people. Unlike "court packing" proposals, term limiting Supreme Court justices enjoys broad bipartisan support, with 2020 and 2022 polling showing that a vast majority of the public—around 70 percent—support term limiting Supreme Court justices (Jackson 2022), with little variation by party (Fix the Court 2020).

Despite this overwhelming public support, there are constitutional and political challenges to the imposition of term limits, and it seems unlikely Congress will take up this reform anytime soon. But there is another way it could be implemented: by the justices themselves. Absolutely nothing prevents the sitting justices from publicly announcing that they have agreed to begin stepping down, every two years, in order of seniority. If regularly followed, this practice could quickly become a professional norm that new members of the Court are expected to follow. And if a later justice deviated from the practice, that settled

expectation would ease the path to formalizing the arrangement through a stat-
ute or constitutional amendment, much like consensus formed around the imposition of presidential terms after President Franklin D. Roosevelt ran for and
won an unprecedented fourth term in office.


## WHY BIAS MATTERS

Throughout this book, we have provided consistent evidence that not all nominees to the U.S. Supreme Court experience equivalent confirmation hearings.
We have seen notable variation in the questioning received by women nominees
and nominees of color relative to white and male nominees, which, at times,
is further heightened by the Senate's strong partisan dynamics. Some of these
differences are positive, with the senators serving on the Judiciary Committee
often praising female nominees and nominees of color for being role models and
representing increased inclusiveness for countless Americans. But our examination of the empirical evidence also reveals other, less positive differences in how
nominees are treated. Female nominees and nominees of color are interrupted
more, are described in less positive terms, are asked more questions in areas they
are stereotyped to have different opinions in, and are subjected to more negatively toned senatorial questioning. In addition, female nominees have their
competence to fulfill the core tasks of a Supreme Court justice questioned more
often than do their male colleagues.

This disparate behavior toward women and people of color during their
confirmation hearings matters because the Supreme Court matters. Supreme
Court justices serve at the pinnacle of the judicial branch. Their decisions establish national law and policy—from "defining privacy rights, interpreting the
First Amendment, setting guidelines for the treatment of criminal defendants,
and exercising [the] power of judicial review" in other areas (Maltese 1998, 2)—
that affect the lives of millions of Americans. The senators who sit on the Judiciary Committee understand this and take their vetting of Supreme Court
nominees seriously. The questions asked and answers given at the hearings can
affect the fate of the nominee in the full Senate (Collins and Ringhand 2013a;
Farganis and Wedeking 2014), shape the ideological orientation of the Supreme
Court (Epstein and Segal 2007), and contribute to our understanding of what
is and is not "settled" as a matter of contemporary constitutional law (Collins
and Ringhand 2013a).

The Supreme Court confirmation hearings also have profound symbolic value. The U.S. Supreme Court is one of the least public political institutions in the United States, and much of its work occurs far outside of the public's eye. The confirmation hearings provide a unique view into this otherwise elusive entity. Indeed, these hearings are a national event, attracting substantial media attention, reporting, and gavel-to-gavel television coverage (Bybee 2011; Collins and Ringhand 2013a; Farganis and Wedeking 2014; Vining 2011). As such, they provide an important opportunity for Americans to directly observe nominees and, in many cases, develop opinions about the nominees and about the Court (Gimpel and Wolpert 1996).

Because of this, the hearings allow average citizens to see and learn from how the nominees are treated and assessed by other high-profile elites—in this case, the senators serving on the Senate's Judiciary Committee. Justices Thurgood Marshall, Sandra Day O'Connor, Clarence Thomas, Ruth Bader Ginsburg, Sonia Sotomayor, Elena Kagan, Amy Coney Barrett, and Ketanji Brown Jackson may have been repeatedly extolled as role models at their hearings,[15] but acknowledgments of the importance of appointing these women and people of color to the U.S. Supreme Court have been repeatedly counterbalanced by the bias they are exposed to at the hearings.

Because confirmation hearings are such highly salient public events, race and gender bias at the hearings can cause real harm. Women and people of color who are future lawyers, lawyers, or lower court judges may see such bias and shy away from opportunities to join the federal judiciary, including the U.S. Supreme Court. "Perceptual barriers" affect women's likelihoods of pursuing judicial seats (Williams 2008, 75), and until those barriers are removed, women are less likely to pursue their ambition in the field. A similar effect has been observed with Black women pursuing law degrees, with high rates of perceived unfair treatment contributing to heightened considerations of leaving law school (Johnson 2022; NALP 2020). Beyond affecting personal ambition to serve on the Court or work in the legal field, biased confirmation hearings, visible for the nation to observe, may also aggravate a sense among women and people of color that our country's governing institutions do not represent them or understand their concerns (Campbell and Wolbrecht 2006; Lazurus and Steigerwalt 2018; Moyer et al. 2021).

A biased Supreme Court confirmation process may also perpetuate negative stereotypes about women and people of color in general, casting doubt on their ability to serve in elite institutions like the Supreme Court, now and in the future. Specifically, by shaping negative perceptions of a future justice's fitness to serve on the Court, senatorial bias toward certain nominees could contribute to increased questions among the general public regarding that specific nominee's qualifications to be a Supreme Court justice. Even if a nominee is successfully confirmed, this public skepticism could persist for years into her service on the Court. These perpetuated stereotypes even hold the potential to affect those who interact with a justice on the Court—such as advocates and other justices—in effect fostering a culture of incivility that welcomes disrespect for and questions of credibility about their female and person of color colleagues (Feldman and Gill 2019; Jacobi and Schweers 2017).

As we have discussed, most Senate Judiciary Committee members (like most people) may not be aware of their biases and may not be "consciously disrespectful" during the confirmation hearings of women and people of color. But conscious or not, biased behavior toward women and people of color in the nomination process sends a powerful message. This type of behavior can have "the 'real world' consequence of delegitimizing knowledge, experience, and ultimately, leadership" (Han and Heldman 2007, 22). This book joins a large literature documenting race and gender bias in various settings and raising the alarm on the harm such bias can cause.

Race and gender bias matter wherever they occur, including at the highest institutions of power. The potential implications of an inequitable Supreme Court confirmation process are far reaching. Displays of bias in such a high-profile setting risk sending women and people of color what Justice Sonia Sotomayor once described as the "crippling" message that "I do not belong here."[16] That possibility should trouble Americans of all colors and creeds who care about the powerful promise, inscribed on the face of the Supreme Court building itself, that in this country, we strive for Equal Justice Under Law.

# NOTES

## Introduction

1. Barrett Transcript, questioning by Senator Kennedy (R-LA) at 102.

2. Marshall Transcript, questioning by Senator Eastland (D-MS) at 161.

3. Thomas Transcript, questioning by Senator Biden (D-DE) at Part 4, 157.

4. Notably, employers who claimed to be "pro-diversity" showed this type of bias as much as did employers who did not mention diversity goals in their postings (Kang et al. 2016).

5. Whenever possible, we used the text of the official government transcripts as the source for the statement text. This was possible for all hearings through Neil Gorsuch using transcripts made available from Mersky and Jacobstein (1977) for hearings from 1939 to 1970 and R Street Institute (2019) for hearings from 1971 to 2017. As of this writing, the government has yet to release the official transcripts of the three most recent nominees, Brett Kavanaugh, Amy Coney Barrett, and Ketanji Brown Jackson. Accordingly, we use the text of the unofficial transcripts available from CQ Transcripts (2022) as the source of text from these hearings. The data from 1939 to 2010 are based on data collected by Collins and Ringhand (2013b), which we extended to include the text of all statements and information on interruptions at the hearings. The data from 2017 to 2022 were collected specifically for this book, using the coding rules developed by Collins and Ringhand (2013b) for variables included in their data.

6. Barrett transcript, questioning by Senator Cruz (R-TX) at Day 2, 54.

## Chapter 1

1. Article III judges are appointed by the president, confirmed by the Senate, have lifetime appointments, and serve on courts authorized under Article III of the Constitution. These courts are the federal district courts, federal courts of appeals, U.S. Court

of International Trade, and U.S. Supreme Court. In contrast, Article I judges serve on courts created by Congress under Article I of the Constitution. The selection of these judges varies, and they do not enjoy life tenure. Article I courts include administrative courts, legislative courts, territorial courts, and military tribunals (Pfander 2004).

2. Nominees Thurgood Marshall and Clarence Thomas faced similar accusations that they would somehow function as mere lackeys of then sitting, and presumptively more intelligent, white male justices. Critics dismissed Marshall as a mere junior partner of liberal justice William Brennan (Eastland 1991), and Thomas as just "tagging along" behind conservative justice Antonin Scalia (Primus 2016).

3. Elena Kagan, who clerked for Justice Marshall, followed this same path.

4. Johnson's greater commitment to appoint a Black man and "do this job that Abraham Lincoln started" is further illustrated by Johnson's "backup" appointment if Marshall's nomination failed: William Coleman, another prominent African American lawyer at the time (Haygood 2015b).

5. The type of media coverage we have described of Sotomayor and Jackson was predictable. Empirical research confirms that female and person of color nominees tend to receive more media coverage than other nominees, and that coverage often focuses on race and ethnicity (Brenner and Knake 2012; Towner and Clawson 2016). Studies on media attention on leaders of color find similar patterns (e.g., Jeffries 2002; Schaffner and Gadson 2004).

6. Eisenhower's disinterest in Allen and other potential female nominees (to the Supreme Court or other federal courts, as we shall see below) may have had just as much to do with his Republican Party (and the role of women within that party) than it did with Allen's record. As Goldman (1997) put it, "Women seemed to have less clout within the Republican president's party than they had had with Democrats under Roosevelt and Truman" (143).

7. ABA ratings have been criticized for putting "nontraditional" nominees at a disadvantage, often because of the organization's emphasis on lengthy legal experience (Clark 2003). There is evidence that the ABA rates female nominees and nominees of color lower than white male nominees (Haire 2001; Sen 2017). In the case of Lillie's potential nomination to the Court, the ABA said the rating was due to her "relations on the court, her inability to get along with other judges, . . . her rate of reversal and so forth" (Dean 2001, 191). "Relations on the court" and an "inability to get along" are hardly neutral criteria. Even the final item on the list—her reversal rate by higher courts—is not as "objective" of a measure as it may at first appear. In initial discussions with the Nixon administration, Lillie claimed that her appeal and reversal rates were similar to other judges on her court and were largely present in cases where she had upheld the trial court decision (Dean 2001, 177). In other words, her reversal rate was unlikely to be a reliable proxy for the quality of her judicial thinking.

8. O'Connor transcript, prepared statement by Judge Joan Dempsey Klein at 303.

9. O'Connor transcript, prepared statement by Judge Joan Dempsey Klein at 303.

10. The "woman's seat" argument had emerged even before O'Connor's selection to the Court. Back in 1971 when Nixon considered appointing Mildred Lillie to the

Supreme Court, he remarked that if he did so, her seat would "always be a woman's seat from then on" (Dean 2001, 111).

11. Barrett transcript, questioning by Senator Blackburn (R-TN) at 132.

12. The data in Figures 1.3 and 1.4 were compiled from Federal Judicial Center (2021). These figures exclude the partial appointment data available for the Biden administration as we write. However, the text below provides details on the Biden administration's notable nomination patterns in its first year.

13. Highlights of note in early efforts to diversify the lower federal courts include Truman's 1949 selection of Burnita Shelton Matthews to serve on the U.S. District Court for the District of Columbia, Kennedy's 1966 appointment of Constance Baker Motley to the Southern District of New York (Motley was the first Black female Article III judge), and Kennedy's 1961 selection of three judges of color (James Parsons, Reynaldo Garza, and Wade McCree Jr.) to the federal district courts (Brazelton and Chaffin-DeHaan 2018; Federal Judicial Center 2021; Fix and Johnson 2017; Means 2018; Means, Eslich, and Prado 2019). Asmussen (2011) highlights the frequent tug-of-war between the president and Senate in the appointment of female and person of color nominees to the federal circuit and district courts.

14. With only one full year of Biden administration nomination data available to us at the time of this writing and Biden's nomination trends still under development, we opt to exclude them from Figures 1.3 and 1.4 to avoid misinterpretations relative to prior administrations.

15. Bush was praised for his selection of Hispanic district and circuit court judges (Scherer 2011).

16. Empirical evidence is mixed when it comes to judicial gender diversity and perceptions of courts (e.g., Chen and Bryan 2018, 2021; Ono and Zilis 2022; Redman 2017; Nelson 2015).

17. During her confirmation hearing, Ketanji Brown Jackson echoed Kang's sentiment about the creation of role models: "One of the things that having diverse members of the court does is it provides for the opportunity for role models. Since I was nominated to this position, I have received so many notes and letters and photos from little girls around the country who tell me that they are so excited for this opportunity, and that they have thought about the law in new ways" (Jackson transcript, at Day 2, 41–42).

18. For an excellent, thorough summary of research in this area, we recommend Harris and Sen's (2019) annual review on "Bias and Judging."

19. Although there has been less social science research examining the effects of judges' Latino ethnicity relative to race, what we know so far points to a promising avenue for future study. Compare Hofer and Casellas (2020) and Morin (2014) (finding differences) to Haire and Moyer 2015 (finding no differences).

20. Further, Collins, Manning, and Carp (2010) find that, in the context of trial courts in which cases are presided by a single judge, working with a critical mass of female judges in a single courthouse can influence the decision of male judges. Harris (2018, 37) finds that, specifically in trial courts' sentencing of criminal defendants, "the presence of Black judges alters individual judges' behavior, making both Black and

White judges less punitive in cases with Black defendants and increasing equality in sentencing outcomes for Black and White defendants" but only "when judges work in close proximity with their Black colleagues."

### Chapter 2

1. This seems an apt and understandable desire for Ginsburg, who had dedicated much of her career to advancing equal rights for women.

2. Most ABA evaluation work has come after a Supreme Court nomination is made. However, Eisenhower (1957), Nixon (1971), and Ford (1975) allowed the ABA to pre-vet potential nominees (Rutkus 2010).

3. Presidents are likely to also consider the ideological positions of senators (Epstein et al. 2006).

4. President Trump was quite clear he expected his nominees to overturn the Affordable Care Act (Bedford 2016), while President Franklin Roosevelt was equally clear that he was looking for nominees who would uphold his New Deal agenda (Roosevelt 1937).

5. One of the primary ways this happens is in discussion of the Supreme Court's precedents, which are routinely debated at the hearings, with senators regularly asking nominees about their perspectives on some of the Court's most iconic decisions, such as *Brown, Roe v. Wade* (1973), *Griswold v. Connecticut* (1965), *District of Columbia v. Heller* (2008), and many others (Collins and Ringhand 2013a). Indeed, since the 1960s, one out of every five questions at the hearings has involved senators asking about the Court's precedents (Batta et al. 2012).

6. Marshall transcript, questioning by Senator Eastland (D-MS) at 161.

7. Stewart transcript, questioning by Senator McClellan (D-AR) at 40.

8. Stewart transcript, questioning by Senator Eastland (D-MS) at 124.

9. See, for example, Sotomayor transcript, questioning by Senator Cornyn (R-TX) at 4.22.

10. White transcript, questioning by Senator Hart (D-PA) at 22.

11. Carswell transcript, questioning by Senator Bayh (D-IN) at 489.

12. Carswell transcript, questioning by Senator Cook (R-KY) at 490.

13. Johnson (2011) has drawn out this contrast, characterizing O'Connor's hearing as a "coronation."

14. Barrett transcript, questioning by Senator Ernst (R-IA), at 79.

15. Barrett transcript, questioning by Senator Blackburn (R-TN), at 131.

16. Jackson transcript, questioning by Senator Cruz (R-TX), at 77.

17. Justice Thomas was confirmed by a vote of 52–48. Justice Alito was confirmed by a vote of 58–42.

### Chapter 3

1. Sotomayor transcript, questioning by Senator Graham (R-SC) at 137.

2. Kar (2009) provides a more in-depth and balanced set of quotes about Sotomayor from the 2000 edition of the *Almanac*.

3. Frankfurter Transcript, statement of Charles Carroll at 95.

*Chapter 4*

1. Marshall transcript, questioning by Senator Eastland (D-MS) at 160–61.

2. Gorsuch transcript, questioning by Senator Franken (D-MN) at 129.

3. The impact of candidate sex on voters is "complex" and "nuanced" (Dolan 2014). Female political candidates face numerous other electoral challenges relative to their male counterparts including higher quality and larger challenger pools (Lawless and Pearson 2008; Palmer and Simon 2006).

4. Interestingly, these gendered stereotypes about judges may be less likely to hold in civil law countries, where judges are viewed to hold less power. Remiche (2015) notes that over 60 percent of the judges in the ordinary court system in France are women (compared to approximately 32 percent of federal judges in the United States). Underlying these frequency differences, Remiche argues, are legal cultures that assign different levels of "power" to judges. The French judge is viewed as "a knowledgeable automaton mechanically applying the law entirely created by the Parliament," (96) while the American judge has more discretion and decision-making power.

5. Sotomayor transcript, statement by Senator Hatch (R-UT) at 11.

6. Marshall transcript, questioning by Senator Thurmond (R-SC) at 523.

7. Jackson transcript (Day 1), questioning by Senator Cornyn (R-TX) at 17.

8. Alito transcript, statement by Senator Schumer (D-NY) at 37.

9. Sotomayor transcript, statement by Senator Sessions (R-AL) at 8.

10. Alito transcript, statement by nominee Alito at 465.

11. Sotomayor transcript, questioning by Senator Kyl (R-AZ) at 123.

12. The data used in this chapter exclude the special sessions devoted to allegations of sexual harassment at the Clarence Thomas hearing and sexual assault at the Brett Kavanaugh hearing because the special sessions focused solely on those allegations. We analyze the Thomas and Kavanaugh special sessions in Chapter 7.

13. Although female and person of color nominees appear before the Judiciary Committee far less frequently than white, male nominees, there is ample variation to make statistical investigation appropriate. For example, female nominees make up 24 percent of observations in the data and person of color nominees constitute 13 percent of observations in the data.

14. In the models that test for gender differences, the dataset excludes the 27 observations pertaining to female senators. In the models that test for racial differences, the dataset excludes the 24 observations relating to senators of color.

15. When we include all senators in the models, we obtain substantively and statistically similar results. However, doing so likely masks any unique behavior of female and person of color senators due to the very small number of these senators on the Judiciary Committee.

16. We also ran the models in Chapters 4, 5, and 6 classifying Southern Democrats as Republicans in the race models, which did not substantially change the results.

17. Because Epstein et al. (2022) do not report a qualification score for Homer Thornberry or Ketanji Brown Jackson (at the time of this writing), we calculated the qualification score for Thornberry (0.6875) and Jackson (1) based on Segal's coding protocols. We are grateful to Jeff Segal for sharing his coding rules with us.

18. To be clear, this variable is distinct from a nominee's qualifications. The two variables are correlated at -0.13. Simply put, judicial experience does not in and of itself make one qualified for the Supreme Court.

19. We also considered including a temporal control variable in the models in Chapters 4, 5, and 6, but excluded it because such a variable would only vary among (not within) nominees. It would therefore function akin to an indicator variable for each nominee, and would indirectly capture a nominee's party affiliation, race, and gender, which are the key independent variables of interest. For this same reason, we excluded a measure of congressional polarization (calculated as the distance between Senate party means based on first dimension DW-NOMINATE scores), which is correlated with the year of hearing of 0.94 and consequently also essentially functions as an indicator variable for nominees.

20. The fractional logit model is a quasi-likelihood method that is estimated as a generalized linear model and allows us to account for the bounded nature of the dependent variable (Papke and Wooldridge 1996). We obtain substantively and statistically similar results when we employ ordinary least squares regression, Tobit, and random effects models, and when we do not cluster on the nominee.

21. In prior analyses of a more limited set of confirmation hearing data (1981–2010) we found that *Female, Same Party* nominees received fewer judicial philosophy questions than *Female, Different Party* nominees (Boyd, Ringhand, and Collins 2018). Here, examining the full set of confirmation hearings available to us (1939–2022), we find no evidence of a difference between the number of judicial philosophy questions for *Female, Same Party* and *Female, Different Party* nominees. This difference is likely due to cross-time changes in the Judiciary Committee and/or the nominees.

### Chapter 5

1. Kagan transcript, questioning by Senator Coburn (R-OK) at 175.

2. Not all research finds that women receive more interruptions than men. Some studies find no statistical differences (see James and Clarke's [1993] review), while others find that men receive more interruptions (see, e.g., Kathleen's [1994] study of committee members in the Colorado legislature). Despite these findings, the bulk of the literature and theory tends to expect interruption behavior differences in many circumstances, particularly outside of casual conversations (Feldman and Gill 2019).

3. Thomas transcript, questioning by Senator DeConcini (D-AZ) at 207–8.

4. Sotomayor transcript, questioning by Senator Hatch (R-UT) at 86.

5. Jackson transcript (Day 2), questioning by Senator Graham (R-SC) at 30.

6. Thomas transcript, questioning by Senator Thurmond (R-SC) at 218.

7. Ginsburg transcript, questioning by Senator DeConcini (D-AZ) at 169.

8. Kagan transcript, questioning by Senator Kyl (R-AZ) at 106.

9. When we provided coders the option of a "neutral" category of interruptions during pilot data collection, coders tended to overrely on that category in somewhat unpredictable ways, which resulted in low intercoder reliability scores (see also Mendelberg, Karpowitz, and Oliphant 2014). As a result, we dropped the neutral category in the final data collection.

10. Kagan transcript, questioning by Senator Feinstein (D-CA) at 96.

11. When we use all interruptions, instead of just intrusive interruptions, we obtain substantively similar results, which is not surprising given that 92 percent of interruptions are intrusive interruptions.

12. Research on interruptions at Supreme Court oral arguments demonstrates that female attorneys are afforded less speaking time than male attorneys owing to being interrupted more (Patton and Smith 2017). Computing an analogous measure for confirmation hearings is very challenging due to several factors, including (1) variation in the length of confirmation hearings and insufficient records of the exact length of hearings prior to 1981, when they were first televised; (2) variation in the speed at which senators and nominees speak (which has substantial implications for testimony that lasts over the course of days relative to thirty-minute oral arguments); (3) differences in senators' questioning styles (some of whom give lengthy speeches instead of questioning nominees, such as Senator Whitehouse [D-RI] during the first day of the questioning of Amy Coney Barrett); and (4) variation in senators' use of their questioning time (particularly in early hearings when some senators occasionally ceded their time or made very short statements without questioning nominees).

## Chapter 6

1. Kagan transcript, questioning by Senator Sessions (R-AL) at 76.

2. Roberts transcript, questioning by Senator Schumer (D-NY) at 406.

3. Among justices and senators, there is also preliminary evidence to indicate that women serving in those roles are less likely to utilize negative emotional language than their male counterparts (Black et al. 2011; Sigelman, Deering, and Loomis 2001). The evidence is limited at this stage due to small numbers of women serving in these salient political and legal roles.

4. Marshall transcript, questioning by Senator Fong (R-HI) at 16–17.

5. Jackson transcript (Day 2), questioning by Senator Cotton (R-AR) at 144–45.

6. Marshall transcript, questioning by Senator Ervin (D-NC) at 56–57.

7. We considered including the senators' opening statements in the coding of the dependent variable, but ultimately declined to do so since opening statements started in 1981 and would thus create an imbalance in the data under analysis before and after this date.

8. The tone dependent variable ranges from -9.09 to 33.3. The differentiation dependent variable ranges from 0 to 33.3. When we calculate the differentiation dependent variable as a proportion and use a fractional logit model in place of the regression model, we obtain substantively and statistically similar results.

## Chapter 7

1. Kavanaugh special session transcript, questioning by Senator Grassley (R-IA) at 2.

2. Kavanaugh special session transcript, questioning by Senator Grassley (R-IA) at 3.

3. A week after his special session testimony, Kavanaugh penned an op-ed for the *Wall Street Journal* explaining his conduct and partially apologizing for it. His testimony, he wrote, was "forceful and passionate" because the allegations against him

were "completely contrary" to his record and character. His passion "reflected his deep distress at the unfairness" of how the allegation was handled. He was, he conceded, "very emotional," perhaps "too emotional at times." He asked for our understanding, explaining that he was there as a "son, husband and dad" (Kavanaugh 2018).

4. Thomas special session transcript, questioning by Senator Biden (D-DE) at 1.

5. Kavanaugh special session transcript, questioning by Senator Grassley (R-IA) at 3.

6. Thomas special session transcript, questioning by Senator Biden (D-DE) at 2.

7. Thomas special session transcript, questioning by Senator Leahy (D-VT) at 71–72.

8. Thomas special session transcript, questioning by Senator Specter (R-PA) at 62.

9. Thomas special session transcript, questioning by Senator Specter (R-PA) at 60.

10. Kavanaugh special session transcript, questioning by Senator Feinstein (D-CA) at 15.

11. Kavanaugh special session transcript, questioning by Rachel Mitchell for Republican senators at 39.

12. Thomas special session transcript, questioning by Senator Biden (D-DE) at 157.

13. Thomas special session transcript, questioning by Senator Hatch (R-UT), at 202.

14. Thomas special session transcript, questioning by Senator Simpson (R-WY) at 373.

15. Thomas special session transcript, questioning by Senator Specter (R-PA) at 97.

16. Thomas special session transcript, questioning by Senator Hatch (R-UT), at 206.

17. Kavanaugh special session transcript, statement by Senator Feinstein (D-CA) at 5.

18. Kavanaugh special session transcript, questioning by Senator Graham (R-SC) at 22.

19. Kavanaugh special session transcript, questioning by Senator Grassley (R-IA) at 27.

20. Kavanaugh special session transcript, questioning by Senator Graham (R-SC) at 26.

21. Dianne Feinstein was one of four female Senators to be elected in the "year of the woman" following Anita Hill's testimony before the all-male Senate Judiciary Committee. The others were Carol Moseley-Braun (D-IL), Patty Murray (D-WA), and Barbara Boxer (D-CA).

22. Kavanaugh special session transcript, questioning by Senator Blumenthal (D-CT) at 45.

23. Kavanaugh special session transcript, questioning by Senator Specter (R-PA) at 68.

24. Kavanaugh special session transcript at 29.

25. A more complete discussion of this proposal can be found in Ringhand and Collins (2021).

## Chapter 8

1. Jackson transcript at Day 1, 64.

2. She also was a white supremacist and an avowed segregationist, which demonstrated the practical limitations of that victory (Talmadge 1960).

3. Caraway was a popular candidate, but her gender was an issue in her campaigns. Her opponent in the 1938 Democratic primary campaigned with the motto that "Arkansas Needs Another Man in the Senate." Caraway won that race but lost her seat after serving just one more term (Hendricks 2013).

4. While total Committee membership is as high as 22 senators during this time span, we restrict Figure 8.1's y-axis to 15 to improve readability.

5. Curtis, whose maternal great-great-grandfather was a Kansa-Kaw chief, spoke Kansa and identified with the Kaw tribe. He went on to serve as Herbert Hoover's vice president (United States Senate 2021b).

6. Jackson transcript (Day 2), questioning by Senator Blackburn (R-TN) at 180.

7. Marshall transcript, questioning by Senator Fong (R-HI) at 16–17.

8. Jackson transcript (Day 3), questioning by Senator Cruz (R-TX) at 80–81.

9. In the case of Cruz's numerous interruptions of Jackson, Senate Judiciary Committee Chair Dick Durbin (D-IL) took the unusual step of speaking up during Cruz's questioning to say "Senator, would you please let her respond?," "Please, allow her to answer the question," and "Just say to the judge, there's no point in responding. He's going to interrupt you." Jackson transcript (Day 3), questioning by Senator Cruz (R-TX) at 81–82.

10. Barrett transcript (Day 2), questioning by Senator Klobuchar (D-MN) at 59.

11. Jackson transcript (Day 2), questioning by Senator Blackburn (R-TN) at 178–79.

12. Kavanaugh transcript (Day 2, Part 2), questioning by Senator Harris (D-CA) at 131.

13. Ginsburg transcript, questioning by Senator Feinstein (D-CA) at 40.

14. Various proposals for implementing eighteen-year fixed terms have been around for some time (e.g., Calabresi and Lindgren 2005; DiTullio and Schochet 2004) and are discussed in the 2022 report of President Biden's Presidential Commission on the Supreme Court of the United States.

15. See, for example, Barrett transcript (Day 2), questioning by Senator Cruz (R-TX) at 54; Kagan transcript, questioning by Senator Feinstein (D-CA) at 243; and Sotomayor transcript, questioning by Senator Leahy (D-VT) at 389.

16. *Schuette v. Coalition to Defend Affirmative Action*, 572 U.S. 291 (2014), Sotomayor dissenting at 381.

# REFERENCES

ABC News. 2006. "Who Is Emilio Garza?" January 6, 2006. https://abcnews.go.com/ Politics/SupremeCourt/story?id=952158/.

Abe, Jo Ann A. 2011. "Changes in Alan Greenspan's Language Use across the Economic Cycle: A Text Analysis of His Testimonies and Speeches." *Journal of Language and Social Psychology* 30: 212–23.

Abraham, Henry J. 2008. *Justices, Presidents, and Senators: A History of the U.S. Supreme Court Appointments from Washington to Clinton.* Lanham, MD: Rowman & Littlefield.

Abramson, Alana. 2017. "Neil Gorsuch Confirmation Sets Record for the Longest Vacancy on 9-Member Supreme Court," Time, April 7, 2017. https://time .com/4731066/neil-gorsuch-confirmation-record-vacancy/.

Allen, Robert. 1995. "Stopping Sexual Harassment: A Challenge for the Community Education." In *Race, Gender and Power in America*, edited by Anita Faye Hill and Emma Jordan Coleman. New York: Oxford University Press.

American Bar Association. 2020. *Standing Committee on the Federal Judiciary: What It Is and How It Works.* https://www.americanbar.org/content/dam/aba/adminis trative/government_affairs_office/backgrounder-9-21-2020.pdf.

Anderson, Kristin J., and Campbell Leaper. 1998. "Meta-analyses of Gender Effects on Conversational Interruption: Who, What, When, Where, and How." *Sex Roles* 39: 225–52.

Anonymous. 2004. "'Just One More Vote for Frankfurter': Rethinking the Jurisprudence of Judge William Hastie." *Harvard Law Review* 117: 1639–60.

Aridi, Sara. 2020. "How Ruth Bader Ginsburg Lives On in Pop Culture," New York Times, September 26, 2020. https://www.nytimes.com/2020/09/26/at-home/ruth -bader-ginsburg-pop-culture-rbg.html.

Aries, Elizabeth. 1996. *Men and Women in Interaction: Reconsidering the Differences.* New York: Oxford University Press.

Arvey, Richard D. 1979. "Unfair Discrimination in the Employment Interview: Legal and Psychological Aspects." *Psychological Bulletin* 86: 736–65.

Asmussen, Nicole. 2011. "Female and Minority Judicial Nominees: President's Delight and Senators' Dismay?" *Legislative Studies Quarterly* 36: 591–619.

Bäck, Emma A., Hanna Bäck, Marie Gustafsson Sendénc, and Sverker Sikström. 2018. "From I to We: Group Formation and Linguistic Adaptation in an Online Xenophobic Forum." *Journal of Social and Political Psychology* 6: 76–91.

Badas, Alex, and Katelyn E. Stauffer. 2018. "Someone Like Me: Descriptive Representation and Support for Supreme Court Nominees." *Political Research Quarterly* 71: 127–42.

Barr, Andy. 2009. "Rush: Sotomayor a 'Reverse Racist.'" Politico, May 26, 2009. https://www.politico.com/story/2009/05/rush-sotomayor-a-reverse-racist-022983.

Barrow, Deborah J., Gary Zuk, and Gerard S. Gryski. 1996. *The Federal Judiciary and Institutional Change.* Ann Arbor: University of Michigan Press.

Basinger, Scott, and Maxwell Mak. 2012. "The Changing Politics of Supreme Court Confirmations." *American Politics Research* 40: 737–63.

Basow, Susan, Stephanie Codos, and Julie Martin. 2013. "The Effects of Professors' Race and Gender on Student Evaluations and Performance." *College Student Journal* 47: 352–63.

Batson, C. Daniel, Marina P. Polycarpou, Eddie Harmon-Jones, Heidi J. Imhoff, Erin C. Mitchener, Lori L. Bednar, Tricia R. Klein, and Lori Highberger. 1997. "Empathy and Attitudes: Can Feeling for a Member of a Stigmatized Group Improve Feelings toward the Group?" *Journal of Personality and Social Psychology* 72: 105–18.

Batta, Anna, Paul M. Collins, Jr., Tom Miles, and Lori A. Ringhand. 2012. "Let's Talk: Judicial Decisions at Supreme Court Confirmation Hearings." *Judicature* 96: 7–15.

Baumgartner, Frank R., Derek A. Epp, and Kelsey Shoub. 2018. *Suspect Citizens: What 20 Million Traffic Stops Tell Us about Policing and Race.* New York: Cambridge University Press.

Bavishi, Anish, Juan M. Madera, and Michelle R. Hebl. 2010. "The Effect of Professor Ethnicity and Gender on Student Evaluations: Judged Before Met." *Journal of Diversity in Higher Education* 3: 245–56.

Bazelon, Emily. 2009. "The Place of Women on the Court." New York Times, July 12, 2009. https://www.nytimes.com/2009/07/12/magazine/12ginsburg-t.html.

Bazelon, Emily. 2020. "Why Ruth Bader Ginsburg Refused to Step Down." New York Times, September 21, 2020. https://www.nytimes.com/2020/09/21/magazine/ginsburg-successor-obama.html.

BBC. 2005. "'Woman Needed' for Top US Court." July 12, 2005. http://news.bbc.co.uk/2/hi/americas/4675757.stm.

BBC. 2020. "Ruth Bader Ginsburg Death: Trump to Nominate Woman to Fill Supreme Court Seat." September 20, 2020. https://www.bbc.com/news/world-us-canada-54216710.

Beattie, Geoffrey W. 1982. "Turn-Taking and Interruption in Political Interviews: Margaret Thatcher and Jim Callaghan Compared and Contrasted." *Semiotica* 39: 93–114.

Bedford, Tori. 2016. "Donald Trump: Litmus Tests for Supreme Court Justices, Less Taxes for Big Business." *WGBH*, February 8, 2016. https://www.wgbh.org/news/2016/02/08/news/donald-trump-litmus-tests-supreme-court-justices-less-taxes-big-business-0.

Bennett, Jessica. 2019. "How History Changed Anita Hill." New York Times, June 17, 2019, https://www.nytimes.com/2019/06/17/us/anita-hill-women-power.html).

Bennett, Mark W. 2017. "The Implicit Racial Bias in Sentencing: The Next Frontier." *The Yale Law Journal Forum* 126: 391–405.

Benninghoff, Grace. 2021. "Senate Judiciary Committee Takes Up Beth Robinson's Nomination to Federal Appellate Court." VT Digger, September 14, 2021. https://vtdigger.org/2021/09/14/senate-judiciary-committee-takes-up-beth-robinsons-nomination-to-federal-appellate-court/.

Besnier, Niko. 1990. "Language and Affect." *Annual Review of Anthropology* 19:419–451.

Biden, Joseph R. 2021a. "Executive Order On Advancing Racial Equity and Support for Underserved Communities Through the Federal Government." Executive Order 13985, January 20, 2021.

Biden, Joseph R. 2021b. "Executive Order on Diversity, Equity, Inclusion, and Accessibility in the Federal Workforce." Executive Order 14035, June 25, 2021.

Biden, Joseph R. 2022. "Remarks by President Biden on His Nomination of Judge Ketanji Brown Jackson to Serve as Associate Justice of the U.S. Supreme Court" February 25, 2022. https://www.whitehouse.gov/briefing-room/speeches-remarks/2022/02/25/remarks-by-president-biden-on-his-nomination-of-judge-ketanji-brown-jackson-to-serve-as-associate-justice-of-the-u-s-supreme-court/.

Biernat, Monica, and Kathleen Fuegen 2001. "Shifting Standards and the Evaluation of Competence: Complexity in Gender-based Judgment and Decision Making." *Journal of Social Issues* 57: 707–24.

Biernat, Monica, and Diane Kobrynowicz. 1997. "Gender-and Race-based Standards of Competence: Lower Minimum Standards but Higher Ability Standards for Devalued Groups." *Journal of Personality and Social Psychology* 72: 544–57.

Biskupic, Joan. 2005. *Sandra Day O'Connor: How the First Woman on the Supreme Court Became Its Most Influential Justice*. New York: Harper Collins.

Black, Ryan C., Timothy R. Johnson, and Justin Wedeking. 2012. *Oral Arguments and Coalition Formation on the U.S. Supreme Court: A Deliberate Dialogue*. Ann Arbor: University of Michigan Press.

Black, Ryan C., and Ryan J. Owens. 2016. "Courting the President: How Circuit Court Judges Alter Their Behavior for Promotion to the Supreme Court." *American Journal of Political Science* 60: 30–43.

Black, Ryan C., Sarah A. Treul, Timothy R. Johnson, and Jerry Goldman. 2011. "Emotions, Oral Arguments, and Supreme Court Decision Making." *Journal of Politics* 73: 572–81.

Bland, Randall W. 1973. *Private Pressure on Public Law: The Legal Career of Justice Thurgood Marshall*. Port Washington, NY: Kennikat.

Boddery, Scott S., Laura P. Moyer, and Jeff Yates 2019. "Naming Names: The Impact of Supreme Court Opinion Attribution on Citizen Assessment of Policy Outcomes." *Law & Society Review* 53: 353–85.

Bogoch, Bryna. 1999. "Judging in a 'Different Voice': Gender and the Sentencing of Violent Offences in Israel." *International Journal of Sociology of Law* 27: 51–78.

Boldt, Ethan D., Christina L. Boyd, Roberto F. Carlos, and Matthew E. Baker. 2021. "The Effects of Judge Race and Sex on Pretrial Detention Decisions." *Justice System Journal* 42: 341–58.

Borrelli, Maryanne 1997. "Gender, Credibility, and Politics: The Senate Nomination Hearings of Cabinet Secretaries-Designate, 1975–1993." *Political Research Quarterly* 50: 171–97.

Bowden, John. 2018. "Timeline: Brett Kavanaugh's Nomination to the Supreme Court." The Hill, October 6, 2018. https://thehill.com/homenews/senate/410217/time line-brett-kavanaughs-nomination-to-the-supreme-court/.

Bowie, Jennifer Barnes, Donald R. Songer, and John Szmer. 2014. *The View from the Bench and Chambers: Examining Judicial Process and Decision Making on the US Courts of Appeals*. Charlottesville: University of Virginia Press.

Bowman, Cynthia Grant. 2014. "Mary Donlon Alger: A Strong Pair of Shoulders." *Cornell Law Forum* 40: 16–25.

Boyd, Christina L. 2013. "She'll Settle It?" *Journal of Law and Courts* 1: 193–219.

Boyd, Christina L. 2016. "Representation on the Courts? The Effects of Trial Judges' Sex and Race." *Political Research Quarterly* 69: 788–99.

Boyd, Christina L., Paul M. Collins, Jr., and Lori A. Ringhand. 2018. "The Role of Nominee Gender and Race at U.S. Supreme Court Confirmation Hearings." *Law & Society Review* 52: 871–901.

Boyd, Christina L., Lee Epstein, and Andrew D. Martin. 2010. "Untangling the Causal Effects of Sex on Judging." *American Journal of Political Science* 54: 389–411.

Boyd, Christina L., and Adam G. Rutkowski. 2020. "Judicial Behavior in Disability Cases: Do Judge Sex and Race Matter?" *Politics, Groups, and Identities* 8: 834–44.

Boyd, Melba Joyce. 1992. "Collard Greens, Clarence Thomas, and the High-tech Rape of Anita Hill." *The Black Scholar* 22: 25–27.

Branton, Regina, Ashley English, Samantha Pettey, and Tiffany D. Barnes 2018. "The Impact of Gender and Quality Opposition on the Relative Assessment of Candidate Competency." *Electoral Studies* 54: 35–43.

Brazelton, Shenita, and LaTasha Chaffin-DeHaan 2018. "Diversity Abound: Will Federal Judicial Appointees Mirror a Changing Citizenry?" In *Race, Gender, Sexuality, and the Politics of the American Judiciary*, edited by Sharon Navarro and Samantha Hernandez. New York: Cambridge University Press.

Brenner, Hannah, and Renee Newman Knake. 2012. "Rethinking Gender Equality in the Legal Profession's Pipeline to Power: A Study on Media Coverage of Supreme Court Nominees (Phase I, the Introduction Week)." *Temple Law Review* 84: 325–84.

Bresnahan, Josh, Rachael Bade, and Josh Gerstein. 2018. "Rachel Mitchell's Disappearing Act Confirms GOP Blunder." Politico, September 27, 2018. https://www.politico.com/story/2018/09/27/gop-senators-outside-ford-questioner-mistake-849246.

Bresnahan, Mary I., and Deborah H. Cai. 1996. "Gender and Aggression in the Recognition of Interruption." *Discourse Processes* 21: 171–89.

Brewer, Marilynn B. 2001. "Ingroup Identification and Intergroup Conflict: When Does Ingroup Love Become Outgroup Hate?" In *Social Identity, Intergroup Conflict, and Conflict Reduction*, edited by Richard D. Ashmore, Lee Jussim, and David Wilder. Oxford: Oxford University Press.

Brewer, Marilynn B. 2017. "Intergroup Discrimination: Ingroup Love or Outgroup Hate?" In *The Cambridge Handbook of the Psychology of Prejudice.*, edited by Chris G. Sibley and Fiona Kate Barlow. Cambridge: Cambridge University Press.

Brown, DeNeen L. 2017. "LBJ's Shrewd Moves to Make Thurgood Marshall the Nation's First Black Supreme Court Justice." Washington Post, October 2, 2017. https://www.washingtonpost.com/news/retropolis/wp/2017/10/02/lbjs-shrewd-moves-to-make-thurgood-marshall-the-nations-first-black-supreme-court-justice/.

Brown, Rupert, and Dora Capozza. 2006. "Motivational, Emotional, and Cultural Influences in Social Identity Processes." In *Social Identities: Motivational, Emotional, and Cultural Influences*, edited by Rupert Brown and Dora Capozza. New York: Psychology Press.

Brown v. Board of Education of Topeka, 347 U.S. 483 (1954).

Browning, Sandra Lee, Francis T. Cullen, Liqun Cao, and Renee Kopache. 1994. "Race and Getting Hassled by the Police: A Research Note." *Police Studies* 17: 1–12.

Brudnick, Ida A., and Jennifer E. Manning. 2020. *African American Members of the U.S. Congress: 1870–2020*. CRS Report for Congress RL30378. https://crsreports.congress.gov/product/pdf/RL/RL30378.

Bryan, Amanda C., and Eve M. Ringsmuth. 2016. "Jeremiad or Weapon of Words?: The Power of Emotive Language in Supreme Court Dissents." *Journal of Law and Courts* 4: 159–85.

Buchanan, Patrick J. 2009. "Obama's Idea of Justice." May 29, 2009. https://buchanan.org/blog/pjb-obamas-idea-of-justice-1553.

Bullock, Charles S., III. 1985. "U.S. Senate Committee Assignments: Preferences, Motivations, and Success." *American Journal of Political Science* 29: 789–808.

Bush, George W. 2005. "Remarks Announcing the Nomination of Harriet E. Miers To Be an Associate Justice of the United States Supreme Court." The American Presidency Project, October 3, 2005. https://www.presidency.ucsb.edu/node/214493.

Bybee, Keith. 2011. "Will the Real Elena Kagan Please Stand Up? Conflicting Public Images in the Supreme Court Confirmation Process." *Wake Forest Journal of Law & Policy* 1: 137–56.

Calabresi, Steven G., and James Lindgren. 2005. "Term Limits for the Supreme Court: Life Tenure Reconsidered." *Harvard Journal of Law and Public Policy* 29: 769–877.

Caldwell, Charles M. 1978. "Dedication: These Do We Honor." *Black Law Journal* 6: 165–71.

Cameron, Charles M., Albert D. Cover, and Jeffrey A. Segal 1990. "Senate Voting on Supreme Court Nominees: A Neoinstitutional Model." *American Political Science Review* 84: 525–34.

Cameron, Charles M., and Jeffrey A. Segal. 2010. "The Politics of Scandals: The Case of Supreme Court Nominations, 1877–1994." Presented at the Annual Meeting of the Midwest Political Science Association, Chicago, IL.

Campbell, David E., and Christina Wolbrecht 2006. "See Jane Run: Women Politicians as Role Models for Adolescents." *Journal of Politics* 68: 233–47.

Cannon, Lou. 1980. "Reagan Pledges He Would Name a Woman to the Supreme Court." Washington Post, October 15, 1980. https://www.washingtonpost.com/archive/politics/1980/10/15/reagan-pledges-he-would-name-a-woman-to-the-supreme-court/844817dc-27aa-4f5d-8e4f-0ab3a5e76865/.

Carlin, Diana B., and Kelly L. Winfrey. 2009. "Have You Come a Long Way, Baby? Hillary Clinton, Sarah Palin, and Sexism in 2008 Campaign Coverage." *Communication Studies* 60: 326–43.

Carroll, Royce, Jeff Lewis, James Lo, Nolan McCarty, Keith Poole, and Howard Rosenthal. 2015. "DW-NOMINATE Scores with Bootstrapped Standard Errors." https://voteview.com/data.

Carter, Jimmy. 1978b. "Statement on Signing H.R. 7843 Into Law: Appointments of Additional District and Circuit Judges." The American Presidency Project, October 20, 1978. https://www.presidency.ucsb.edu/documents/statement-signing-hr-7843-into-law-appointments-additional-district-and-circuit-judges.

Carter, Jimmy. 1979. "The State of the Union Annual Message to the Congress." The American Presidency Project, January 25, 1979. https://www.presidency.ucsb.edu/node/250253.

Carter, Jimmy. 1995. *Keeping Faith: Memoirs of a President.* Fayetteville: University of Arkansas Press.

Carter, Stephen L. 1995. *The Confirmation Mess: Cleaning up the Federal Appointments Process.* 1995. New York: Basic Books.

Carter, Stephen L. 2021. "What Thurgood Marshall Taught Me." New York Times, July 14, 2021. https://www.nytimes.com/2021/07/14/magazine/thurgood-marshall-stories.html.

Cassese, Erin C. 2019. "Intersectional Stereotyping in Political Decision Making." In *Oxford Research Encyclopedia of Politics*, edited by David P. Redlawsk. New York: Oxford University Press.

Castilla, Emilio. 2008. "Gender, Race, and Meritocracy in Organizational Careers." *American Journal of Sociology* 113: 1479–526.

CBS News. 2019. "We Asked 155 Police Departments about Their Racial Bias Training. Here's What They Told Us." August 7, 2019. https://www.cbsnews.com/news/racial-bias-training-de-escalation-training-policing-in-america/.

CBS News. 2020. "Read the Full Transcript of the South Carolina Democratic Debate." February 25, 2020. https://www.cbsnews.com/news/south-carolina-democratic-debate-full-transcript-text/.

Chafetz, Josh. 2017. "Unprecedented? Judicial Confirmation Battles and the Search for a Usable Past," *Harvard Law Review* 131: 96–132.

Chen, Philip G., and Amanda C. Bryan. 2018. "Judging the 'Vapid and Hollow Charade': Citizen Evaluations and the Candor of U.S. Supreme Court Nominees." *Political Behavior* 40: 495–520.

Chen, Philip, and Amanda Bryan. 2021. "The Legal Double Standard: Gender, Personality Information, and the Evaluation of Supreme Court Nominees." *Justice System Journal* 42: 325–40.

Chew, Pat K., and Robert E. Kelley. 2009. "Myth of the Color-Blind Judge: An Empirical Analysis of Racial Harassment Cases." *Washington University Law Review* 86: 1117–66.

Chowdhury, Shammur Absar, Morena Danieli, and Giuseppe Riccardi. 2015. "The Role of Speakers and Context in Classifying Competition in Overlapping Speech." Proceedings of Interspeech: 1844–1848.

Christensen, Robert K., John Szmer, and Justin M. Stritch. 2012. "Race and Gender Bias in Three Administrative Contexts: Impact on Work Assignments in State Supreme Courts." *Journal of Public Administration Research and Theory* 22: 625–48.

Clark, Mary L. 2003. "Carter's Groundbreaking Appointment of Women to the Federal Bench: His Other 'Human Rights' Record." *American University Journal of Gender, Social Policy and the Law* 11: 1131–63.

Clark, Mary L. 2004. "One Man's Token in Another Woman's Breakthrough? The Appointment of the First Women Federal Judges." *Villanova Law Review* 49: 487–550.

Clarke, Jessica A. 2018. "Explicit Bias." *Northwestern University Law Review* 113: 505–86.

Clayton, Amanda, Diana Z. O'Brien, and Jennifer M. Piscopo. 2018. "All Male Panels? Representation and Democratic Legitimacy." *American Journal of Political Science* 63: 113–29.

Clement, Scott, Emily Guskin, Dan Keating, Kevin Uhrmacher, and Chris Alcantara. 2020. "Exit Polls from the 2020 South Carolina Democratic Primary." Washington Post, February 29, 2020. https://www.washingtonpost.com/graphics/politics/exit-polls-2020-south-carolina-primary/.

CNN Staff. 2018. "Starbucks CEO Calls Arrest of Two Black Men at Philadelphia Store 'Reprehensible.'" *CNN*, April 15, 2018. https://www.cnn.com/2018/04/15/us/starbucks-statement-philadelphia-arrest/index.html.

Cole, Devan, Ariane de Vogue, and Katelyn Polantz. 2020. "Barbara Lagoa, One of Trump's Top Contenders for the Supreme Court." *CNN*, September 21, 2020. https://www.cnn.com/2020/09/21/politics/barbara-lagoa-trump-supreme-court/index.html.

Collins, Patricia Hill. 1990. *Black Feminist Thought: Knowledge, Consciousness, and the Politics of Empowerment*. Boston: Unwin Hyman.

Collins, Paul M., Jr. 2020. "Amy Coney Barrett Was Next-level Evasive." New York Daily News, October 16, 2020. https://www.nydailynews.com/opinion/ny-oped-barretts-evasiveness-was-next-level-20201016-ucd7ujnyl5b6lmxqojyu6fwtoe-story.html.

Collins, Paul M., Jr., Pamela C. Corley, and Jesse Hamner. 2015. "The Influence of Amicus Curiae Briefs on U.S. Supreme Court Opinion Content." *Law & Society Review* 49: 917–44.

Collins, Paul M., Jr., and Matthew Eshbaugh-Soha. 2020. *The President and the Supreme Court: Going Public on Judicial Decisions from Washington to Trump.* New York: Cambridge University Press.

Collins, Paul M., Jr., Kenneth L. Manning, and Robert A. Carp. 2010. "Gender, Critical Mass, and Judicial Decision Making." *Law & Policy* 32: 260–81.

Collins, Paul M., Jr., and Lori A. Ringhand. 2013a. *Supreme Court Confirmation Hearings and Constitutional Change.* New York: Cambridge University Press.

Collins, Paul M., Jr., and Lori A. Ringhand 2013b. U.S. Supreme Court Confirmation Hearing Database. http://blogs.umass.edu/pmcollins/data/.

Collins, Paul M., Jr., and Lori A. Ringhand. 2016. "The Institutionalization of Supreme Court Confirmation Hearings." *Law & Social Inquiry* 41: 126–51.

Collins, Paul M., Jr., and Lori A. Ringhand. 2019. "Creating Databases in Sociolegal Research: *The U.S. Supreme Court Confirmation Hearings Database.*" In *Research Handbook on Law and Courts,* edited by Susan M. Sterett and Lee D. Walker. Cheltenham, UK: Edward Elgar.

Collins, Todd A., Tao L. Dumas, and Laura P. Moyer. 2017. "Being Part of the 'Home Team': Perceptions of Professional Interactions with Outsider Attorneys." *Journal of Law and Courts* 5: 141–71.

Collins, Todd, and Laura Moyer. 2008. "Gender, Race, and Intersectionality on the Federal Appellate Bench." *Political Research Quarterly* 61: 219–27.

Comparative Agendas Project. 2022. https://www.comparativeagendas.net/.

Conroy, Meredith, Sarah Oliver, Ian Breckenridge-Jackson, and Caroline Heldman. 2015. "From Ferraro to Palin: Sexism in Coverage of Vice Presidential Candidates in Old and New Media." *Politics, Groups, and Identities* 3: 573–91.

Corley, Pamela, and Artemus Ward. 2020. "Intracourt Dialogue: The Impact of US Supreme Court Dissents." *Journal of Law and Courts* 8: 27–50.

Cortina, Lilia M., Kimberly A. Lonsway, Vicki J. Magley, Leslie V. Freeman, Linda L. Collinsworth, Mary Hunter, and Louise F. Fitzgerald. 2002. "What's Gender Got to Do with It? Incivility in the Federal Courts." *Law & Social Inquiry* 27: 235–70.

Cottrill, James B., and Terri J. Peretti. 2013. "The Partisan Dynamics of Supreme Court Confirmation Voting." *Justice System Journal* 34: 15–37.

Cowan, Richard. 2018. "Senate's Judiciary Committee, Then and Now." Reuters, September 26, 2018. https://www.reuters.com/article/us-usa-court-kavanaugh-committee/senates-judiciary-committee-then-and-now-idUSKCN1M635A.

Cox, Adam B., and Thomas J. Miles. 2008. "Judging the Voting Rights Act." *Columbia Law Review* 108: 1–54.

CQ Transcripts. 2022. https://info.cq.com/legislative-news/cq-transcripts-testimony/.

Cray, Ed. 1997. *Chief Justice: A Biography of Earl Warren.* New York: Simon & Schuster.

Crenshaw, Kimberlé. 1989. "Demarginalizing the Intersection of Race and Sex." *University of Chicago Legal Forum* 1989: 139–67.

Crenshaw, Kimberlé W. 2019. "We Still Have Not Learned from Anita Hill's Testimony." *UCLA Women's Law Journal* 26: 17–20.

Cuddy, Amy J. C., Susan T. Fiske, and Peter Glick. 2008. "Warmth and Competence as Universal Dimensions of Social Perception: The Stereotype Content Model and the BIAS Map." *Advances in Experimental Social Psychology* 40: 61–149.

Dancey, Logan, Kjersten R. Nelson, and Eve M. Ringsmuth. 2020. *It's Not Personal: Politics and Policy in Lower Court Confirmation Hearings.* Ann Arbor: University of Michigan Press.

Davis Sue, Susan Haire, and Donald R. Songer. 1993. "Voting Behavior and Gender on the U.S. Courts of Appeals." *Judicature* 77: 129–33.

Davison, Heather K., and Michael J. Burke 2000. "Sex Discrimination in Simulated Employment Contexts: A Meta-analytic Investigation." *Journal of Vocational Behavior* 56: 225–48.

Dawson, April G. 2017. "Laying the Foundation: How President Obama's Judicial Nominations Have Paved the Way for a More Diverse Supreme Court." *Howard Law Journal* 60: 685–706.

De Vogue, Ariane, and Theresa Cook. 2009. "Sotomayor Under Fire for Discrimination Case." *ABC News,* July 15, 2009. https://abcnews.go.com/Politics/SoniaSotomayor/story?id=8093893&page=1.

Dean, John W. 2001. *The Rehnquist Choice: The Untold Story of the Nixon Appointment that Redefined the Supreme Court* New York: Simon & Schuster.

Delta Airlines. 2020. "Promoting Inclusion: New Training to Reach 75,000 Delta Employees." *Delta Airlines News Hub,* November 18, 2020. https://news.delta.com/promoting-inclusion-new-training-reach-75000-delta-employees.

Desjardins, Lisa. 2018. "How the Sexual Assault Accusation against Kavanaugh Unfolded, in One Timeline." *PBS News Hour,* June 6, 2022. https://www.pbs.org/newshour/nation/how-the-sexual-assault-accusation-against-kavanaugh-unfolded-in-one-timeline.

Desmon, Stephanie. 2005. "O'Connor: He's Good . . . but He's Not a Woman." South Florida Sun Sentinel, July 21, 2005. https://www.sun-sentinel.com/news/fl-xpm-2005-07-21-0507201453-story.html.

Dewar, Helen. 1991. "Senate Confirms Thomas By 52 to 48 to Succeed Marshall on Supreme Court." Washington Post, June 6, 2022. https://www.washingtonpost.com/archive/politics/1991/10/16/senate-confirms-thomas-by-52-to-48-to-succeed-marshall-on-supreme-court/ddbeeaba-bd5b-464a-b0bd-600ab2d0dfd7/.

Diaz, Daniella, and Veronica Stracqualursi. 2022. "Cory Booker Reflects on Ketanji Brown Jackson Hearings: 'This Is Not about Racism. It's about Decency.'" *CNN,* March 27, 2022. https://www.cnn.com/2022/03/27/politics/cory-booker-jackson-supreme-court-confirmation-hearings-cnntv/index.html.

District of Columbia v. Heller, 554 U.S. 570 (2008).

DiTullio, James E., and John B. Schochet. 2004. "Saving This Honorable Court: A Proposal to Replace Life Tenure on the Supreme Court with Staggered, Nonrenewable Eighteen-Year Terms." *Virginia Law Review* 90: 1093–49.

Dolan, Kathleen. 2014. "Gender Stereotypes, Candidate Evaluations, and Voting for Women Candidates: What Really Matters?" *Political Research Quarterly* 67: 96–107.

Dovidio, John F., and Samuel L. Gaertner. 2000. "Aversive Racism and Selection Decisions: 1989 and 1999." *Psychological Science* 11: 315–19.

Dovidio, John F., Samuel L. Gaertner, Phyllis A. Anastasio, and Rasyid Sanitioso. 1992. "Cognitive and Motivational Bases of Bias: Implications of Aversive Racism for

Attitudes Toward Hispanics." In *Hispanics in the Workplace*, edited by Stephen B. Knouse, Paul Rosenfeld, and Amy L. Culbertson. Newbury Park, CA: Sage.

Dowd, Maureen. 1991. "The Supreme Court; Conservative Black Judge, Clarence Thomas, Is Named to Marshall's Court Seat." New York Times, July 2, 1991. https://www.nytimes.com/1991/07/02/us/supreme-court-conservative-black-judge-clarence-thomas-named-marshall-s-court.html.

Eagly, Alice H., and Steven J. Karau. 2002. "Role Congruity Theory of Prejudice Toward Female Leaders." *Psychological Review* 109: 573–98.

Eagly, Alice H., Mona G. Makhijani, and Bruce G. Klonsky. 1992. "Gender and the Evaluation of Leaders: A Meta-Analysis." *Psychological Bulletin* 111: 3–22.

Eastland, Terry. 1991. "Only a Footnote—but a Monumental One: A Middling Justice Is Best Honored for His Heroic Work at the Bar, Leading to the Brown Ruling." Los Angeles Times, June 28, 1991. https://www.latimes.com/archives/la-xpm-1991-06-28-me-1205-story.html.

Ekström, Mats. 2009. "Power and Affiliation in Presidential Press Conferences." *Journal of Language and Politics* 8: 386–415.

Ellison, Loria and Carol M. Smith 2013. "Dancing Backwards in High Heels: Balancing Traditionally Male Academic within Feminine Life." In *Women's Retreat: Voices of Female Faculty in Higher Education*, edited by Mary Alice Bruce. Lanham, MD: University Press of America.

Elving, Ron. 2018. "What Happened with Merrick Garland in 2016 and Why It Matters Now." *National Public Radio*, June 29, 2018. https://www.npr.org/2018/06/29/624467256/what-happened-with-merrick-garland-in-2016-and-why-it-matters-now.

Epner, Janet E. 2006. *Visible Invisibility: Women of Color in Law Firms*. Chicago, IL: ABA Commission on Women in the Profession.

Epstein, Cynthia, Robert Saute, Bonnie Oglensky, and Martha Gever. 1995. "Glass Ceilings and Open Doors: Women's Advancement in the Legal Profession: A Report to the 'Committee on Women in the Profession,' the Association of the Bar of the City of New York." *Fordham Law Review* 64: 192–378.

Epstein, Lee, René Lindstädt, Jeffrey A. Segal, and Chad Westerland. 2006. "The Changing Dynamics of Senate Voting on Supreme Court Nominees." *Journal of Politics* 68: 296–307.

Epstein, Lee, Jack Knight, and Andrew D. Martin. 2003. "The Norm of Prior Judicial Experience and Its Consequences for Career Diversity on the U.S. Supreme Court." *California Law Review* 91: 903–66.

Epstein, Lee, Andrew D. Martin, Kevin M. Quinn, and Jeffrey A. Segal. 2005. "Ideological Drift Among Supreme Court Justices: Who, When, and How Important." *Northwestern University Law Review* 101: 1483–541.

Epstein, Lee, and Jeffrey A. Segal. 2007. *Advice and Consent: The Politics of Judicial Appointments*. New York: Oxford University Press.

Epstein, Lee, Thomas G. Walker, Nancy Staudt, Scott Hendrickson, and Jason Roberts. 2022. *The U.S. Supreme Court Justices Database*. https://epstein.usc.edu/justicesdata/.

Essed, Philomena. 1991. *Understanding Everyday Racism: An Interdisciplinary Theory.* Newbury Park, CA: Sage.

Everett, Burgess. 2018. "GOP Eyes Marsha Blackburn in Bid to Add Woman to Senate Judiciary." Politico, November 15, 2018. https://www.politico.com/story/2018/11/15/gop-blackburn-senate-judiciary-991334.

Fandos, Nicholas. 2020a. "Hearings Behind Them, Republicans Close In on Barrett Confirmation," New York Times, October 15, 2020. https://www.nytimes.com/2020/10/15/us/politics/senate-amy-coney-barrett-confirmation.html.

Fandos, Nicholas. 2020b. "Senate Confirms Barrett, Delivering for Trump and Reshaping the Court," New York Times, October 26, 2020. https://www.nytimes.com/2020/10/26/us/politics/senate-confirms-barrett.html.

Farganis, Dion, and Justin Wedeking. 2014. *Supreme Court Confirmation Hearings in the U.S. Senate: Reconsidering the Charade.* Ann Arbor: University of Michigan Press.

Farhang, Sean, and Gregory Wawro. 2004. "Institutional Dynamics on the U.S. Court of Appeals: Minority Representation under Panel Decision Making." *Journal of Law, Economics, & Organization* 20: 299–330.

Federal Judicial Center. 2021. History of the Federal Judiciary. http://www.fjc.gov.

Feldman, Adam, and Rebecca D. Gill. 2019. "Power Dynamics in Supreme Court Oral Arguments: The Relationship between Gender and Justice-to-Justice Interruptions." *Justice System Journal* 40: 173–95.

Firth, Michael 1982. "Sex Discrimination in Job Opportunities for Women." *Sex Roles* 8: 891–901.

Fiske, Susan T. 1993. "Controlling Other People: The Impact of Power on Stereotyping." *American Psychologist* 48: 621–28.

Fiske, Susan T., Amy J. C. Cuddy, Peter Glick, and Jun Xu. 2002. "A Model of (Often Mixed) Stereotype Content: Competence and Warmth Respectively Follow from Perceived Status and Competition." *Journal of Personality and Social Psychology* 82: 878–902.

Fiske, Susan T., and Shelley E. Taylor. 2013. *Social Cognition: From Brains to Culture.* 2nd ed. Newbury Park, CA: Sage.

Fix, Michael P., and Gbemende E. Johnson. 2017. "Public Perceptions of Gender Bias in the Decisions of Female State Court Judges." *Vanderbilt Law Review* 70: 1845–86.

Fix the Court. 2020. "New Poll Shows SCOTUS Term Limits Still Popular Across Party Lines." June 10, 2020. https://fixthecourt.com/2020/06/latest-scotus-term-limits-poll/.

Foschi, Martha. 2000. "Double Standards for Competence: Theory and Research." *Annual Review of Sociology* 26: 21–42.

Foy, Steven L., and Rashawn Ray. 2019. "Skin in the Game: Colorism and the Subtle Operation of Stereotypes in Men's College Basketball." *American Journal of Sociology* 125: 730–85.

Fried, Charles. 1991. *Order and Law: Arguing the Reagan Revolution—A Firsthand Account.* New York: Simon & Schuster.

Friedrich, Paul. 1972. "Social Context and Semantic Feature: The Russian Pronominal Usage." In *Directions in Sociolinguistics: The Ethnography of Communication.*, edited by John J. Gumperz and Dell Hymes. New York: Holt, Rinehart, Winston.

Frimer, Jeremy A., Mark J. Brandt, Zachary Melton, and Matt Motyl. 2019. "Extremists on the Left and Right Use Angry, Negative Language." *Personality and Social Psychology Bulletin* 45: 1216–31.

Gaddis, S. Michael. 2015. "Discrimination in the Credential Society: An Audit Study of Race and College Selectivity in the Labor Market." *Social Forces* 93: 1451–79.

Galinsky, Adam D., Joe C. Magee, M. Ena Inesi, and Deborah H. Gruenfeld. 2006. "Power and Perspectives Not Taken." *Psychological Science* 17: 1068–74.

Galinsky, Adam D., and Gordon B. Moskowitz. 2000. "Perspective-Taking: Decreasing Stereotype Expression, Stereotype Accessibility, and In-Group Favoritism." *Journal of Personality and Social Psychology* 78: 708–24.

Gershon, Sarah Allen. 2013. "Media Coverage of Minority Congresswomen and Voter Evaluations: Evidence from an Online Experiential Study." *Political Research Quarterly* 66: 702–24.

Gibson, James L., and Caldeira, Gregory A. 2009. *Citizens, Courts, and Confirmations: Positivity Theory and the Judgments of the American People.* Princeton, NJ: Princeton University Press.

Gibson, James L., Gregory A. Caldeira, and Lester Kenyatta Spence. 2003. "The Supreme Court and the US Presidential Election of 2000: Wounds, Self-Inflicted or Otherwise?" *British Journal of Political Science* 33: 535–56.

Gill, Rebecca D., Michael Kagan, and Fatma Marouf. 2019. "The Impact of Maleness on Judicial Decision Making: Masculinity, Chivalry, and Immigration Appeals," *Politics, Groups, and Identities* 7: 509–28.

Gill, Rebecca D., Sylvia R. Lazos, and Mallory M. Waters 2011. "Are Judicial Performance Evaluations Fair to Women and Minorities? A Cautionary Tale from Clark County, Nevada." *Law & Society Review* 45: 731–59.

Gilmore, Leigh. 2017. *Tainted Witness: Why We Doubt What Women Say about Their Lives.* New York: Columbia University Press.

Gimpel, James G., and Robin M. Wolpert. 1996. "Opinion-Holding and Public Attitudes toward Controversial Supreme Court Nominees." *Political Research Quarterly* 49: 163–76.

Gino, Francesca, and Katherine Coffman. 2021. "Unconscious Bias Training that Works." *Harvard Business Review* 99: 114–23.

Ginsburg, Ruth Bader. 2001. "The Supreme Court: A Place for Women." Address to Washington University, St. Louis, Missouri (Apr. 4, 2001), in *Vital Speeches of the Day* 67: 420–24.

Ginsburg, Ruth Bader. 2007. "Remarks on Women's Progress at the Bar and the Bench for Presentation at the American Sociological Association Annual Meeting, Montreal, August 11, 2006." *Harvard Journal of Law & Gender* 30: 1–9.

Glass, Andrew. 2018a. "LBJ Nominates Thurgood Marshall to Supreme Court, June 13, 1967." Politico, June 13, 2018. https://www.politico.com/story/2018/06/13/lbj-nominates-thurgood-marshall-to-supreme-court-june-13-1967-636880.

Glass, Andrew. 2018b. "Reagan Nominates First Woman to High Court, July 7, 1981." Politico, July 7, 2018. https://www.politico.com/story/2018/07/07/reagan-nominates-first-woman-to-high-court-july-7-1981-694902.

Gleason, Shane A., Jennifer J. Jones, and Jessica Rae McBean. 2019. "The Role of Gender Norms in Judicial Decision-Making at the U.S. Supreme Court: The Case of Male and Female Justices." *American Politics Research* 47: 494–529.

Gleason, Shane A., and EmiLee Smart. 2022. "You Think; Therefore I Am: Gender Schemas and Context in Oral Arguments at the Supreme Court, 1979–2016." *Political Research Quarterly*, https://doi.org/10.1177%2F10659129211069176

Goldberg, Julia A. 1990. "Interrupting the Discourse on Interruptions: An Analysis in Terms of Relationally Neutral, Power and Rapport Oriented Acts." *Journal of Pragmatics* 14: 883–903.

Goldman, Seth K. 2017. "Explaining White Opposition to Black Political Leadership: The Role of Fear of Racial Favoritism." *Political Psychology* 38: 721–39.

Goldman, Sheldon. 1978. "A Profile of Carter's Judicial Nominees." *Judicature* 62: 246–54.

Goldman, Sheldon. 1997. *Picking Federal Judges: Lower Court Selection from Roosevelt through Reagan*. New Haven, CT: Yale University Press.

Graber, Mark. 2007. "No Better than They Deserve: Dred Scott and Constitutional Democracy." *Northern Kentucky Law Review* 34: 589–617.

Graham, Lindsey. 2022a. "If media reports are accurate, and Judge Jackson has been chosen as the Supreme Court nominee to replace Justice Breyer, it means the radical Left has won President Biden over yet again. The attacks by the Left on Judge Childs from South Carolina apparently worked." Twitter, February 23, 2022. https://twitter.com/LindseyGrahamSC/status/1497218172071645195.

Graham, Lindsey. 2022b. "I expect a respectful but interesting hearing in the Senate Judiciary Committee. The Harvard-Yale train to the Supreme Court continues to run unabated." Twitter, February 23, 2022. https://twitter.com/LindseyGrahamSC/status/1497218325394374709.

Greenberg, David. 2005. "The New Politics of Supreme Court Appointments." *Daedalus* 134: 5–12.

Greenhouse, Linda, and Reva Siegel. 2019. "The Unfinished Story of *Roe v. Wade*." In *Reproductive Rights and Justice Stories*, edited by Melissa Murray, Kate Shaw, and Reva Siegel. St. Paul, MN: Foundation.

Griswold v. Connecticut, 381 U.S. 479 (1965).

Haire, Susan B. 2001. "Rating the Ratings of the American Bar Association Standing Committee on Federal Judiciary." *Justice System Journal* 22: 1–17.

Haire, Susan B., and Laura P. Moyer. 2015. *Does Diversity Matter? Judicial Policy Making in the U.S. Courts of Appeals*. Charlottesville: University of Virginia Press.

Hajnal, Z. H. 2007. *Changing White Attitudes Toward Black Political Leadership*. New York: Cambridge University Press.

Han, Lori Cox, and Caroline Heldman, eds. 2007. *Rethinking Madam President*. Boulder, CO: Lynne Rienner.

Hancock, Adrienne B., and Benjamin A. Rubin. 2014. "Influence of Communication Partner's Gender on Language." *Journal of Language and Social Psychology* 34: 46–64.

Hannon, Elliot. 2020. "Republicans Bulldoze Senate Rules to Advance Amy Coney Barrett Supreme Court Nomination," Slate, October 22, 2020. https://slate.com/news-and-politics/2020/10/republicans-senate-quorum-rules-vote-amy-coney-barrett-supreme-court-nomination.html.

Harris, Allison P. 2018. "Can Racial Diversity among Judges Affect Sentencing Outcomes?" Working Paper, Penn State University. https://www.allisonpharris.com/uploads/1/0/7/3/107342067/harris_diversitysentencing.pdf.

Harris, Allison P., and Maya Sen. 2019. "Bias and Judging." *Annual Review of Political Science* 22: 241–59.

Hart, Roderick P. 2001. "Redeveloping Diction: Theoretical Considerations." In *Theory, Method, and Practice in Computer Content Analysis*, edited by Mark D. West. Westport, CT: Ablex.

Harwood, Jake. 2018. "Communication and Intergroup Relations." In *Oxford Research Encyclopedia of Psychology*, edited by Oliver Braddick. https://oxfordre.com/psychology/view/10.1093/acrefore/9780190236557.001.0001/acrefore-9780190236557-e-290.

Hayano, Kaoru. 2013. "Question Design in Conversation." In *The Handbook of Conversation Analysis*, edited by Jack Sidnell and Tanya Stivers. West Sussex, UK: John Wiley & Sons.

Haygood, Wil. 2015a. "For High Court's First Black Justice, Road to Confirmation Wasn't Simple." Interview by Arun Rath, *All Things Considered*, National Public Radio, August 30, 2015. https://www.npr.org/2015/08/30/436107514/for-high-courts-first-black-justice-road-to-confirmation-wasnt-simple.

Haygood, Wil. 2015b. *Showdown: Thurgood Marshall and the Supreme Court Nomination that Changed America*. New York: Vintage.

Haynie, Kerry L. 2002. "The Color of Their Skin or the Content of Their Behavior? Race and Perceptions of African American Legislators." *Legislative Studies Quarterly* 27: 295–314.

Heilman, Madeline E. 2001. "Description and Prescription: How Gender Stereotypes Prevent Women's Ascent Up the Organizational Ladder." *Journal of Social Issues* 57: 657–674.

Heilman, Madeline E., and Michelle C. Haynes. 2005. "No Credit Where Credit Is Due: Attributional Rationalization of Women's Success in Male-Female Teams." *Journal of Applied Psychology* 90: 905–16.

Heith, Diane J. 2001. "Footwear, Lipstick, and an Orthodox Sabbath: Media Coverage of Non-traditional Candidates." *White House Studies* 1: 35–49.

Hemingway, Mollie, and Carrie Severino. 2019. *Justice on Trial: The Kavanaugh Confirmation and the Future of the Supreme Court*. Washington, DC: Regnery.

Hendricks, Nancy. 2013. *Senator Hattie Caraway: An Arkansas Legacy*. Charleston, SC: History Press.

Hill, Anita, and Emma Coleman Jordan, eds. 1995. *Race, Gender, and Power in America: The Legacy of the Hill-Thomas Hearings*. New York: Oxford University Press.

Hilton, Katherine. 2016. "The Perception of Overlapping Speech: Effects of Speaker Prosody and Listener Attitudes." *Interspeech* 2016: 1260–64.

Hofer, Scott, and Jason Casellas. 2020. "Latino Judges on the Federal District Court: ¿Cómo Deciden?" *American Politics Research* 48: 343–54.

Hogg, Michael A., and Dominic Abrams. 1988. *Social Identifications: A Social Psychology of Intergroup Relations and Group Processes*. London: Routledge.

Hollander, Jocelyn A., and Miriam J. Abelson. 2014. "Language and Talk." In *Handbook of the Social Psychology of Inequality*, edited by Jane D. McLeod, Edward J. Lawler, and Michael Schwalbe. Dordrecht, Netherlands: Springer.

Hollis-Brusky, Amanda. 2015. *Ideas with Consequences: The Federalist Society and the Conservative Counterrevolution*. New York: Oxford University Press.

Hollis-Brusky, Amanda, and Joshua C. Wilson. 2020. *Separate But Faithful: The Christian Right's Radical Struggle to Transform Law and Legal Culture*. New York: Oxford University Press.

Holman, Mirya R., Jennifer L. Merolla, and Elizabeth J. Zechmeister 2011. "Sex, Stereotypes, and Security: A Study of the Effects of Terrorist Threat on Assessments of Female Leadership." *Journal of Women, Politics & Policy* 32: 173–92.

Hoover, Amanda. 2021. "N.J.'s Top Court Acknowledges Racism, Bias in Criminal Justice System. Here's Its Plan to Change It," NJ.com, August 25, 2022. https://www.nj.com/news/2021/08/njs-top-court-acknowledges-racism-bias-in-criminal-justice-system-heres-its-plan-to-change-it.html.

Howe, Amy. 2021. "Justices Tweak Format of In-Person Oral Arguments to Allow Time for Taking Turns." *SCOTUSblog*, September 21, 2021. https://www.scotusblog.com/2021/09/justices-tweak-format-of-in-person-oral-arguments-to-allow-time-for-taking-turns/.

Huddy, Leonie, and Nayda Terkildsen 1993a. "Gender Stereotypes and the Perception of Male and Female Candidates." *American Journal of Political Science* 37: 119–47.

Huddy, Leonie, and Nayda Terkildsen 1993b. "The Consequences of Gender Stereotypes for Women Candidates at Different Levels." *Political Research Quarterly* 46: 503–25.

Huey-Burns, Caitlin. 2022. "Republicans Try Out Midterm Messages During Ketanji Brown Jackson Hearings." *CBS News*, March 28, 2022. https://www.cbsnews.com/news/republicans-supreme-court-ketanji-brown-jackson-hearings/.

Hutchings, Vincent L. 2001. "Political Context, Issue Salience, and Selective Attentiveness: Constituent Knowledge of the Clarence Thomas Confirmation Vote." *Journal of Politics* 63: 846–68.

Hutchinson, Dennis J. 1997. "The Ideal New Frontier Judge." *Supreme Court Review* 9: 373–402.

Inesi, M. Ena, and Daniel M. Cable. 2015. "When Accomplishments Come Back to Haunt You: The Negative Effect of Competence Signals on Women's Performance Evaluations." *Personnel Psychology* 68: 615–57.

Jackson, Jacquelyne Johnson. 1992. "'Them Against Us': Anita Hill v. Clarence Thomas." *The Black Scholar* 22: 48–52.

Jackson, Joe. 2022. "Support for Supreme Court Term Limits Grows, Survey Shows." *Newsweek*, March 15, 2022. https://www.newsweek.com/support-supreme-court-term-limits-grows-survey-shows-1688308.

Jacobi, Tonja, Timothy R. Johnson, Eve Ringsmuth, and Matthew Sag. 2021. "Oral Argument in the Time of COVID: The Chief Plays Calvinball." *Southern California Interdisciplinary Law Journal* 30: 399–459.

Jacobi, Tonja, and Dylan Schweers. 2017. "Justice, Interrupted: The Effect of Gender, Ideology and Seniority at Supreme Court Oral Arguments." *Virginia Law Review* 103: 1379–496.

James, Deborah, and Sandra Clarke. 1993. "Women, Men, and Interruptions: A Critical Review." In *Gender and Conversational Interaction*, edited by Deborah Tannen. New York: Oxford University Press.

Jefferson, Renee Knake, and Hannah Brenner Johnson. 2020. *Shortlisted: Women in the Shadows of the Supreme Court*. New York: New York University Press.

Jeffries, Judson L. 2002. "Press Coverage of Black Statewide Candidates: The Case of L. Douglas Wilder of Virginia." *Journal of Black Studies* 32: 673–97.

Johnson, Cathryn. 1994. "Gender, Legitimate Authority, and Leader-Subordinate Conversations." *American Sociological Review* 59: 122–35.

Johnson, Gbemende. 2022. "Why Aren't There More Black Female Judges on the Federal Bench?" Washington Post: The Monkey Cage, February 22, 2022. https://www.washingtonpost.com/politics/2022/02/22/biden-black-woman-supreme-court/.

Johnson, Kevin R. 2011. "An Essay on the Nomination and Confirmation of the First Latina Justice on the U.S. Supreme Court: The Assimilation Demand at Work." *Chicana/o Latina/o Law Review* 30: 97–162.

Johnson, Theodore. 2022 "What Biden's SCOTUS Nominee Will Face." The Bulwark, February 18, 2022. https://www.thebulwark.com/what-bidens-scotus-nominee-will-face/.

Johnson, Timothy R., Ryan C. Black, and Justin Wedeking. 2009. "Pardon the Interruption: An Empirical Analysis of Supreme Court Justices' Behavior during Oral Arguments." *Loyola Law Review* 55: 331–51.

Johnson, Timothy R., Maron Sorenson, Maggie Cleary, and Katie Szarkowicz. 2021. "COVID-19 and Supreme Court Oral Argument: The Curious Case of Justice Clarence Thomas." *Journal of Appellate Practice and Process* 21: 113–62.

Johnson, Kelly M., Samuel L. Gaertner, John F. Dovidio, Missy A. Houlette, Blake M. Riek, and Eric W. Mania. 2006. "Emotional Antecedents and Consequences of Common Ingroup Identity." In *Social Identities: Motivational, Emotional, and Cultural Influences*, edited by Rupert Brown and Dora Capozza. New York: Psychology Press.

Jordan, Emma Coleman. 1992. "Race, Gender, and Social Class in the Thomas Sexual Harassment Hearings: The Hidden Fault Lines in Political Discourse." *Harvard Women's Law Journal* 15: 1–24.

Joyella, Mark. 2020. "Fox News Dominates Cable News Ratings for Barrett Hearings," Forbes, October 14, 2020. https://www.forbes.com/sites/markjoyella/2020/10/14/fox-news-dominates-cable-news-ratings-for-barrett-hearings/?sh=7c176dc3137b.

Kang, Chris. 2013. "President Obama Nominates Four Distinguished Women to Serve as Federal Judges." May 17, 2013. http://www.whitehouse.gov/blog/2013/05/17/president-obama-nominates-four-distinguished-women-serve-federal-judges.

Kang, Sonia K., Katherine A. DeCelles, Andras Tilcsik, and Sora Jun. 2016. "Whitened Resumes: Race and Self Presentation in the Labor Market." *Administrative Science Quarterly* 61: 469–502.

Kanter v. Barr, 919 F. 3d 437 (2019).

Kaplan, David A. 1991. "Anatomy of a Debacle." Newsweek, October 21, 1991. https://www.newsweek.com/anatomy-debacle-204540.

Kaplan, David A. 2018. "Does Kavanaugh-Ford Hearing Show Progress Has Been Made Since Anita Hill? Here's Newsweek's 1991 Cover Story." Newsweek, October 3, 2018. https://www.newsweek.com/2018/10/19/kavanaugh-ford-hearing-show-progress-anita-hill-1991-cover-story-1149466.html.

Kar, Rob. 2009. "Lawyer's Evaluations of Judge Sonia Sotomayor." *Prawfsblawg*, May 12, 2009. https://prawfsblawg.blogs.com/prawfsblawg/2009/05/lawyers-evaluations-of-judge-sonia-sotomayor.html.

Karakowsky, Leonard, Kenneth McBey, and Diane L. Miller. 2004. "Gender, Perceived Competence, and Power Displays: Examining Verbal Interruptions in a Group Context." *Small Group Research* 35: 407–39.

Karakowsky, Leonard, and J. P. Siegel. 1999. "The Effects of Proportional Representation and Gender Orientation of the Task on Emergent Leadership Behavior in Mixed-Gender Groups." *Journal of Applied Psychology* 84: 620–31.

Karl, Kristyn L., and Timothy J. Ryan 2016. "When Are Stereotypes about Black Candidates Applied? An Experimental Test." *Journal of Race, Ethnicity and Politics* 1: 253–279.

Karpowitz, Christopher F., Tali Mendelberg, and Lauren Mattioli. 2015. "Why Women's Numbers Elevate Women's Influence, and When They Do Not: Rules, Norms, and Authority in Political Discussion." *Politics, Groups, and Identities* 3: 149–77.

Kastellec, Jonathan P. 2013. "Racial Diversity and Judicial Influence on Appellate Courts." *American Journal of Political Science* 57: 167–83.

Kathlene, Lyn. 1994. "Power and Influence in State Legislative Policymaking: The Interaction of Gender and Position in Committee Hearing Debates." *American Political Science Review* 88: 560–76.

Katrompas, Alexander, and Vangelis Metsis. 2021. "Rate My Professors: A Study of Bias and Inaccuracies in Anonymous Self-Reporting." 2nd Internal Conference on Computing and Data Science 2021: 536–42.

Kavanaugh, Brett M. 2018. "Opinion: I Am an Independent, Impartial Judge." Wall Street Journal, October 5, 2018. https://www.wsj.com/articles/i-am-an-independent-impartial-judge-1538695822.

Kawakami, Kerry, John F. Dovidio, Jasper Moll, Sander Hermsen, and Abby Russin. 2000. "Just Say No (to Stereotyping): Effects of Training in the Negation of

Stereotype Associations on Stereotype Activation." *Journal of Personality and Social Psychology* 78: 871–88.

Keblusek, Lauren, Howard Giles, and Anne Maass. 2017. "Communication and Group Life: How Language and Symbols Shape Intergroup Relations." *Group Processes & Intergroup Relations* 20: 632–43.

Kenney, Sally J. 2014. "Judicial Women." In *Women and Elective Office: Past, Present, and Future*, edited by Sue Thomas and Clyde Wilcox. New York: Oxford University Press.

Kim, Jennifer Y., and Loriann Roberson. 2022. "I'm Biased and So Are You. What Should Organizations Do? A Review of Organizational Implicit-Bias Training Programs." *Consulting Psychology Journal* 74: 19–39.

Kinder, Donald R., and David O. Sears. 1981. "Prejudice and Politics: Symbolic Racism Versus Racial Threats to the Good Life." *Journal of Personality and Social Psychology* 40: 414–31.

King, Ryan D., and Michael T. Light. 2019. "Have Racial and Ethnic Disparities in Sentencing Declined?" *Crime and Justice* 48: 365–437.

Koch, Jeffrey W. 2000. "Do Citizens Apply Gender Stereotypes to Infer Candidates' Ideological Orientations?" *Journal of Politics* 62: 414–29.

Kurland, Phillip B. 1972. "The Appointment and Disappointment of Supreme Court Justices." *Law and the Social Order* 2: 183–237.

Kutateladze, Besiki L., Nancy R. Andiloro, Brian D. Johnson, and Cassia C. Spohn. 2014. "Cumulative Disadvantage: Examining Racial and Ethnic Disparity in Prosecution and Sentencing." *Criminology* 52: 514–51.

Lawless, Jennifer L. 2004. "Women, War, and Winning Elections: Gender Stereotyping in the Post-September 11th Era." *Political Research Quarterly* 57: 479–90.

Lawless, Jennifer L., and Kathryn Pearson. 2008. "The Primary Reason for Women's Underrepresentation? Reevaluating the Conventional Wisdom." *Journal of Politics* 70: 67–82.

Lazarus, Jeffrey, and Amy Steigerwalt. 2018. *Gendered Vulnerability: How Women Work Harder to Stay in Office*. Ann Arbor: University of Michigan Press.

Lee, Frances E. 2008. "Agreeing to Disagree: Agenda Content and Senate Partisanship, 1981–2004." *Legislative Studies Quarterly* 33: 199–22.

Lee, Frances E. 2009. *Beyond Ideology: Politics, Principles, and Partisanship in the U.S. Senate*. Chicago: University of Chicago Press.

Lee, I-Ching, and Wei-Fang Lin. 2022. "Us Versus Them: The Debates on the Legislation of Same-Sex Marriage (1994–2015) in Taiwan." *Journal of Homosexuality* 69: 655–76.

Leman, Patrick J., Shahina Ahmed, and Louise Ozarow. 2005. "Gender, Gender Relations, and the Social Dynamics of Children's Conversations." *Developmental Psychology* 41: 64–74.

Leman, Patrick, and Theresa Ikoko. 2010. "Interruption in Women's Conversations: The Effects of Context in Ethnic Majority and Minority Group Interactions." *Psychology of Language and Communication* 14: 61–70.

Lewis, Andrew R. 2014. "Staffing the Front Lines of the Culture War: Constituency Religious Effects on Assignment to the Senate Judiciary Committee." *Congress & the Presidency* 41: 167–89.

Lewis, Neil A. 1991. "The Supreme Court: Man in the News; From Poverty to the Bench; Clarence Thomas." New York Times, July 2, 1991. https://www.nytimes.com/1991/07/02/us/the-supreme-court-man-in-the-news-from-poverty-to-the-bench-clarence-thomas.html.

Liptak, Adam. 2021. "Supreme Court Tries to Tame Unruly Oral Arguments." New York Times, November 1, 2021. https://www.nytimes.com/2021/11/01/us/supreme-court-oral-arguments.html.

Litman, Leah. 2020. "Muted Justice." *University of Pennsylvania Law Review Online* 169: 134–66.

Livingston, Robert W., Ashley Shelby Rosette, and Ella F. Washington. 2012. "Can an Agentic Black Woman Get Ahead? The Impact of Race and Interpersonal Dominance on Perceptions of Female Leaders." *Psychological Science* 23: 354–58.

Lott, Bernice 1985. "The Devaluation of Women's Competence." *Journal of Social Issues* 41: 43–60.

Lowe, Will. 2002. *Software for Content Analysis–A Review*. Cambridge: Weatherhead Center for International Affairs and the Harvard Identity Project. https://dl.conjugateprior.org/preprints/content-review.pdf (accessed June 2, 2022).

Lugo-Lugo, Carmen R., and Mary K. Bloodsworth-Lugo. 2017. *Feminism After 9/11: Women's Bodies as Cultural and Political Threat*. New York: Palgrave Macmillan.

Lutler, David. 2018. "A Generation After Clarence Thomas, the Senate Heads for Another Battle Over Judging Allegations of Sexual Misconduct." Los Angeles Times, September 17, 2018. https://www.latimes.com/politics/la-na-pol-kavanaugh-debate-20180917-story.html.

Madera, Juan M., Michelle R. Hebl, and Randi C. Martin. 2009. "Gender and Letters of Recommendation for Academia: Agentic and Communal Differences." *Journal of Applied Psychology* 94: 1591–99.

Magee, Joe C., and Adam D. Galinsky. 2008. "Social Hierarchy: The Self-Reinforcing Nature of Power and Status" *The Academy of Management Annals* 2: 351–98.

Magee, Joe C., and Pamela K. Smith. 2013. "The Social Distance Theory of Power." *Personality and Social Psychology Review* 17: 158–86.

Maitner, Angela T., Eliot R. Smith, and Diane M. Mackie. 2017. "Intergroup Emotions Theory: Prejudice and Differentiated Emotional Reactions Toward Outgroups." In *The Cambridge Handbook of the Psychology of Prejudice.*, edited by Chris G. Sibley and Fiona Kate Barlow. Cambridge: Cambridge University Press.

Mak, Maxwell, Andrew H. Sidman, Vincent Palmeri, Nico Denise, and Ruben Huertero. 2021. "Judges' Race and the Voting Rights Act: Perceived Expertise in Three-Judge District Court Panels." *Justice System Journal* 42: 375–93.

Maltese, John Anthony. 1998. *The Selling of Supreme Court Nominees*. Baltimore, MD: Johns Hopkins University Press.

Marrero-Otero, Joel. 2011. "What Does a Wise Latina Look Like? An Intersectional Analysis of Sonia Sotomayor's Confirmation to the Supreme Court." *Chicana/o-Latina/o Law Review* 30: 177–216.

Martin, Betsy Fischer. 2020. "Gender at the South Carolina Primary." Gender on the Ballot, March 2, 2020. https://www.genderontheballot.org/gender-at-the-south-carolina-primary/.

Martin, Jonathan, and Mike Allen. 2009. "How, Why Obama Picked Sotomayor." *Politico*, May 26, 2009. https://www.politico.com/story/2009/05/how-why-obama-picked-sotomayor-022970.

Martin, Patricia Yancey, John R. Reynolds, and Shelley Keith. 2002 "Gender Bias and Feminist Consciousness among Judges and Attorneys: A Standpoint Theory Analysis." *Signs* 27: 665–701.

Mattei, Laura R. Winsky. 1998. "Gender and Power in American Legislative Discourse." *Journal of Politics* 60: 440–61.

Mauro, Tony. 2013. "The Supreme Court: Sotomayor and Kagan." *Judicature* 97: 57–60.

Mayer, Jane, and Jill Abramson. 1994. *Strange Justice: The Selling of Clarence Thomas*. Boston: Houghton Mifflin.

McClain, Paula D., Jessica D. Johnson Carew, Eugene Walton, Jr., and Candis S. Watts. 2009. "Group Membership, Group Identity, and Group Consciousness: Measures of Racial Identity in American Politics?" *Annual Review of Political Science* 12: 471–85.

McConnell, Mitch. 2017. "Judge Gorsuch 'Somebody Who Understands the West.'" March 20, 2017. https://www.republicanleader.senate.gov/newsroom/research/judge-gorsuch-somebody-who-understands-the-west.

McConnell, Mitch. 2022. "McConnell Statement on Judge Ketanji Brown Jackson." February 25, 2022. https://www.republicanleader.senate.gov/newsroom/press-releases/mcconnell-statement-on-judge-ketanji-brown-jackson.

McCleary, Kelly, and Amir Vera. 2018. "A Video of Black Men Being Arrested at Starbucks. Three Very Different Reactions." *CNN*, April 15, 2018. https://www.cnn.com/2018/04/14/us/philadelphia-police-starbucks-arrests/index.html.

McDermott, Monika L. 1998. "Race and Gender Cues in Low-Information Elections." *Political Research Quarterly* 51: 895–918.

McFeatters, Ann Carey. 2006. *Sandra Day O'Connor: Justice in the Balance*. Albuquerque: University of New Mexico Press.

McGinley, Ann C. 2019. "The Masculinity Mandate: #MeToo, Brett Kavanaugh, and Christine Blasey Ford." *Employee Rights and Employment Policy Journal* 23: 59–83.

Means, Taneisha N. 2016. "They're There, Now What?: The Identities, Behaviors, and Perceptions of Black Judges." Ph.D. diss., Duke University.

Means, Taneisha N. 2018. "Race, Gender, and the Battle to Confirm Judge Constance Baker Motley, the first Black Woman Federal Judge, to the Bench." In *Race, Gender, Sexuality, and the Politics of the American Judiciary*, edited by Sharon Navarro and Samantha Hernandez. New York: Cambridge University Press.

Means, Taneisha N., Andrew Eslich, and Kaitlin Prado. 2019. "Judicial Diversity in the United States Federal Judiciary." In *Research Handbook in Law and Courts*, edited by Susan M. Sterett and Lee Demetrius Walker. Cheltenham, UK: Elgar Publishing.

Mears, Bill. 2014. "Memo Reveals Clinton's Difficulty over Supreme Court Choice." *CNN*, April 15, 2014. https://www.cnn.com/2014/02/17/politics/clinton-breyer-s-election-memo/index.html.

Meltzer, Leo, William N. Morris, and Donald Hayes. 1971. "Interruption Outcomes and Vocal Amplitude: Explorations in Social Psychophysics." *Journal of Personality and Social Psychology* 18: 392–402.

Mendelberg, Tali, Christopher F. Karpowitz, and J. Baxter Oliphant. 2014. "Gender Inequality in Deliberation: Unpacking the Black Box of Interaction." *Perspectives on Politics* 12: 18–44.

Mersky, Roy M., and J. Myron Jacobstein. 1977. *The Supreme Court of the United States: Hearings and Reports on Successful and Unsuccessful Nominations of Supreme Court Justices by the Senate Judiciary Committee, 1916–1975.* Buffalo, NY: WS Hein.

Miller, Cheryl. 2020. "Judicial Council Mandates Anti-Bias Training for State Judges." Law.com, September 25, 2020. https://www.law.com/therecorder/2020/09/25/judicial-council-mandates-anti-bias-training-for-state-judges/.

Miller, Jake C. 2005. "The NAACP and the Confirmation of Supreme Court Justices, 1930–1991." *National Political Science Review* 10: 177–90.

Mitchell, Tara L., Ryann M. Haw, Jeffrey E. Pfeifer, and Christian A. Meissner. 2005. "Racial Bias in Mock Juror Decision-making: A Meta-analytic Review of Defendant Treatment." *Law and Human Behavior* 29: 621–37.

Molotsky, Irvin. 1986. "Hatch Backs Rehnquist on Medication." New York Times, August 14, 1986. https://www.nytimes.com/1986/08/14/us/hatch-backs-rehnquist-on-medication.html.

Montanaro, Domenico. 2019. "New Calls to Impeach Justice Kavanaugh: How It Would Work and Why It Likely Won't." *National Public Radio*, September 16, 2019. https://www.npr.org/2019/09/16/761193794/new-calls-to-impeach-justice-kavanaugh-how-it-would-work-and-why-it-likely-wont.

Morin, Jason L. 2014. "The Voting Behavior of Minority Judges in the U.S. Courts of Appeals: Does the Race of the Claimant Matter?" *American Politics Research* 42: 34–64.

Morrison, Toni, ed. 1992. *Race-ing Justice, En-Gendering Power: Essays on Anita Hill, Clarence Thomas, and the Construction of Social Reality.* New York: Pantheon.

Moyer, Laura P. 2021. "'She Blinded Me with Science': The Use of Science Frames in Abortion Litigation before the Supreme Court." *Justice System Journal* 43: 153–73.

Moyer, Laura, and Susan Haire. 2015. "Trailblazers and Those That Followed: Personal Experiences, Gender, and Judicial Empathy." *Law & Society Review* 49: 665–89.

Moyer, Laura P., John Szmer, Susan Haire, and Robert K. Christensen. 2021. "'All Eyes Are On You': Gender, Race, and Opinion Writing on the US Courts of Appeals." *Law & Society Review* 55: 452–72.

NALP. 2020. *Women of Color: A Study of Law School Experiences.* NALP Foundation for Law Career Research and Education and the Center for Women in Law. https://utexas.app.box.com/s/kvn7dezec99khii6ely9cve368q4gj90.

National Association for Legal Career Professionals. 2018. "Women and Minorities at Law Firms—What Has Changed and What Has Not in the Past 25 Years." NALP Bulletin, February 2018. https://www.nalp.org/0218research.

Nelson, Kjersten. 2015. "Double-Bind on the Bench: Citizen Perceptions of Judge Gender and the Court." *Politics & Gender* 11: 235–64.

Nelson, Robert L., Ioana Sendroiu, Ronit Dinovitzer, and Meghan Dawe. 2019. "Perceiving Discrimination: Race, Gender, and Sexual Orientation in the Legal Workplace." *Law & Social Inquiry* 44: 1051–82.

Nemacheck, Christine L. 2007. *Strategic Selection: Presidential Nomination of Supreme Court Justices from Herbert Hoover through George W. Bush.* Charlottesville: University of Virginia Press.

Nemacheck, Christine L. 2017. "Appointing Supreme Court Justices." In *The Oxford Handbook of U.S. Judicial Behavior,* edited by Lee Epstein and Stefanie A. Lindquist. New York: Oxford University Press.

Neuendorf, Kimberly A. 2011. "Content Analysis—A Methodological Primer for Gender Research." *Sex Roles* 64: 276–89.

Neuendorf, Kimberly A. 2014. "The Content Analysis Guidebook Online." http://academic.csuohio.edu/neuendorf_ka/content/cata.html (June 2, 2022).

Neuendorf, Kimberly A. 2017. *The Content Analysis Guidebook.* Thousand Oaks, CA: Sage.

New York Times. 1937a. "Radio Talk Is Brief," New York Times, October 2, 1937.

New York Times. 1937b. "Bar Asks Inquires on Future Judges," New York Times, October 2, 1937.

New York Times Archive. 1991. "The Supreme Court: Excerpts from News Conference Announcing Court Nominee." New York Times, July 2, 1991. https://www.nytimes.com/1991/07/02/us/the-supreme-court-excerpts-from-news-conference-announcing-court-nominee.html.

Neumann, Richard K., Jr. 2007. "The Revival of Impeachment as a Partisan Political Weapon." *Hastings Constitutional Law Quarterly* 34: 161–327.

Nicholson, Chris, and Paul M. Collins, Jr. 2008. "The Solicitor General's Amicus Curiae Strategies in the Supreme Court." *American Politics Research* 36: 382–415.

Ninth Circuit Public Information Office 2016. "Ninth Circuit Recalls Shirley M. Hufstedler." March 31, 2016. https://www.ca9.uscourts.gov/ninth-circuit-news/ninth-circuit-recalls-shirley-m-hufstedler/.

Obama, Barack. 2009. "Remarks by the President and Supreme Court Justice Sonia Sotomayor at Reception in Her Honor." August 12, 2009. https://obamawhitehouse.archives.gov/realitycheck/the-press-office/remarks-president-and-justice-sotomayor-reception-her-honor.

Obama, Barack. 2010. "Remarks on Senate Confirmation of Elena Kagan as a Supreme Court Associate Justice in Chicago." The American Presidency Project, August 5, 2010. https://www.presidency.ucsb.edu/node/288623.

Obama, Barack. 2011. "Remarks at a Democratic National Committee Fundraiser in Orlando." American Presidency Project, October 11, 2011. https://www.presidency.ucsb.edu/documents/remarks-democratic-national-committee-fundraiser-orlando.

O'Brien, David M. 1991. "The Politics of Professionalism: President Gerald R. Ford's Appointment of Justice John Paul Stevens." *Presidential Studies Quarterly* 21: 103–26.

O'Brien, David M. 1986. "Packing the Supreme Court." *Virginia Quarterly Review* 62: 189–212.

Omnibus Judgeship Act, H.R. 7843, Pub. L. No. 95–486, 92 Stat. 1629 (1978).

Ono, Yoshikuni, and Michael A. Zilis. 2022. "Ascriptive Characteristics and Perceptions of Impropriety in the Rule of Law: Race, Gender, and Public Assessments of Whether Judges Can Be Impartial." *American Journal of Political Science* 66: 43–58.

Orth, John V. 2002. "How Many Judges Does It Take to Make a Supreme Court?" *Constitutional Commentary* 536: 681–92.

Overbeck, Jennifer R., and Bernadette Park 2006. "Powerful Perceivers, Powerless Objects: Flexibility of Powerholders' Social Attention." *Organizational Behavior and Human Decision Processes* 99: 227–43.

Overby, L. Marvin, Beth M. Henschen, Julie Strauss, and Michael H. Walsh. 1994. "African American Constituents and Supreme Court Nominees: An Examination of the Senate Confirmation of Thurgood Marshall." *Political Research Quarterly* 47: 839–55.

Painter, Neil Irvin. 1992. "Hill, Thomas, and the Use of Racial Stereotype." In *Race-ing Justice, En-Gendering Power: Essays on Anita Hill, Clarence Thomas, and the Construction of Social Reality*, edited by Toni Morrison. New York: Pantheon.

Palmer, Barbara. 2002. "Ten Years Later, Anita Hill Revisits the Clarence Thomas Controversy." Stanford Report, April 3, 2002. https://news.stanford.edu/news/2002/april3/anitahill-43.html.

Palmer, Barbara, and Dennis Simon. 2006. *Breaking the Political Glass Ceiling: Women and Congressional Elections*. New York: Routledge.

Papke, Leslie E., and Jeffrey M. Wooldridge. 1996. "Econometric Methods for Fractional Response Variables with an Application to 401(K) Plan Participation Rates." *Journal of Applied Econometrics* 11: 619–32.

Parry-Giles, Trevor. 1996. "Character, the Constitution, and the Ideological Embodiment of 'Civil Rights' in the 1967 Nomination of Thurgood Marshall to the Supreme Court." *Quarterly Journal of Speech* 82: 364–82.

Patton, Dana, and Joseph L. Smith. 2017. "Lawyer, Interrupted: Gender Bias in Oral Arguments at the US Supreme Court." *Journal of Law and Courts* 5: 337–61.

Peffley, Mark, Jon Hurwitz, and Paul M. Sniderman. 1997. "Racial Stereotypes and Whites' Political Views of Blacks in the Context of Welfare and Crime." *American Journal of Political Science* 41: 30–60.

Pellish, Aaron, and Sonnet Swire. 2022. "Republican Sen. Graham Heaps Praise on Fellow South Carolinian and Potential Supreme Court Nominee J. Michelle Childs." *CNN*, January 30, 2022. https://www.cnn.com/2022/01/30/politics/lindsey-graham-j-michelle-childs-supreme-court/index.html.

Pennebaker, James W., Matthias R. Mehl, and Kate G. Niederhoffer. 2003. "Psychological Aspects of Natural Language Use: Our Words, Our Selves." *Annual Review of Psychology* 54: 547–77.

Peresie, Jennifer L. 2005. "Female Judges Matter: Gender and Collegial Decision Making in the Federal Appellate Courts." *Yale Law Journal* 114: 1759–90.

Perlin, Adam A. 2010. "The Impeachment of Samuel Chase: Redefining Judicial Independence." *Rutgers Law Review* 62: 725–89.

Perry, Barbara A. 1991. *A 'Representative' Supreme Court? The Impact of Race, Religion, and Gender on Appointments*. Westport, CT: Greenwood.

Pfander, James E. 2004. "Article I Tribunals, Article III Courts, and the Judicial Power of the United States." *Harvard Law Review* 118: 643–776.

Plessy v. Ferguson, 163 U.S. 537 (1896).

Post, Robert, and Reva Siegel 2006. "Originalism as a Political Practice: The Right's Living Constitution." *Fordham Law Review* 75: 545–74.

Presidential Commission on the Supreme Court of the United States. 2021. "Final Report." https://www.whitehouse.gov/wp-content/uploads/2021/12/SCOTUS-Report-Final-12.8.21-1.pdf.

Pretorious, Richard. 2009. "Even for Justices, It's All Politics." The National, July 16, 2009. https://www.thenational.ae/world/the-americas/even-for-justices-it-s-all-politics-1.550811.

Primus, Richard. 2016. "The Unexpected Importance of Clarence Thomas," Politico Magazine, October 4, 2016. https://www.politico.com/magazine/story/2016/10/supreme-court-2016-clarence-thomas-legacy-214319/.

Pritlove, Cheryl, Clara Juando-Prats, Kari Ala-leppilampi, and Janet A. Parsons. 2019. "The Good, the Bad, and the Ugly of Implicit Bias." *The Lancet* 393: 502–4.

Purushothaman, Deepa. 2022. "Women of Color Can No Longer Buy into the 'Inclusion Delusion.'" Fortune, March 28, 2022. https://fortune.com/2022/03/28/women-careers-color-inclusion-delusion-kbj-supreme-court-gender-power-business-corporate-culture-deepa-purushothaman/.

Quillian, Lincoln. 2006. "New Approaches to Understanding Racial Prejudice and Discrimination." *Annual Review of Sociology* 32: 299–328.

Quillian, Lincoln, Devah Pager, Ole Hexel, and Arnfinn H. Midtbøen. 2017. "Meta-analysis of Field Experiments Shows no Change in Racial Discrimination in Hiring Over Time." *PNAS* 114: 10870–75.

Quadlin, Natasha. 2018. "The Mark of a Woman's Record: Gender and Academic Performance in Hiring." *American Sociological Review* 83: 331–60.

R Street Institute. 2019. "Supreme Court Confirmation Hearing Transcripts, As Data." April 4, 2019. https://www.rstreet.org/2019/04/04/supreme-court-confirmation-hearing-transcripts-as-data/.

Redman, Shane M. 2017. "Descriptive Gender Representation and Legitimacy in US Trial Courts." *Justice System Journal* 38: 311–31.

Rehnquist, William H. 1992. *Grand Inquests: The Historic Impeachments of Justice Samuel Chase and President Andrew Johnson*. New York: Quill, William Morrow & Co.

Reid, Scott A., and Sik Hung Ng. 1999. "Language, Power, and Intergroup Relations." *Journal of Social Issues* 55: 119–39.

Remiche, Adelaide 2015. "When Judging Is Power: A Gender Perspective on the French and American Judiciaries." *Journal of Law and Courts* 3: 95–114.

Ricci v. DeStefano, 530 F.3d 88 (2d Cir. 2008).

Rice, Douglas, and Christopher Zorn. 2019. "Corpus-based Dictionaries for Sentiment Analysis of Specialized Vocabularies." *Political Science Research & Methods* 9: 20–35.

Ringhand, Lori A. 2010. "Aliens on the Bench: Identity, Race and Politics from the First Modern Supreme Court Confirmation Hearing." *Michigan State Law Review* 3: 795–835.

Ringhand, Lori A., and Paul M. Collins, Jr. 2011. "May It Please the Senate: An Empirical Analysis of the Senate Judiciary Committee Hearings of Supreme Court Nominees, 1939–2009." *American University Law Review* 60: 589–641.

Ringhand Lori A., and Paul M. Collins, Jr. 2021. "Improving the Senate Judiciary Committee's Role in the Confirmation of Supreme Court Justices." *British Journal of American Legal Studies* 10: 363–78.

Roberts, Steven B. 1987. "Ginsberg Withdraws Name as Supreme Court Nominee Citing Marijuana 'Clamor.'" New York Times, November 8, 1987. https://www .nytimes.com/1987/11/08/us/ginsburg-withdraws-name-as-supreme-court-nomi nee-citing-marijuana-clamor.html.

Roe v. Wade, 410 U.S. 113 (1973).

Rogers, Alex. 2020. "Takeaways from Day 3 of the Amy Coney Barrett Confirmation Hearings." *CNN*, October 14, 2020. https://www.cnn.com/2020/10/14/politics/ amy-coney-barrett-hearing-takeaways-wednesday/index.html.

Roosevelt, Franklin D. 1937. "On 'Court-Packing,'" radio, 34:46, March 9, 1937. Miller Center. https://millercenter.org/the-presidency/presidential-speeches/ march-9-1937-fireside-chat-9-court-packing.

Rosen, Jeffrey. 2009. "The Case Against Sotomayor." The New Republic, May 4, 2009. https://newrepublic.com/article/60740/the-case-against-sotomayor.

Rosenthal, Andrew. 1991. "Marshall Retires from High Court; Blow to Liberals." New York Times, June 28, 1991. https://www.nytimes.com/1991/06/28/us/marshall-re tires-from-high-court-blow-to-liberals.html.

Ross, David A., Dowin Boatright, Marcella Nunez-Smith, Ayana Jordan, Adam Chek-roud, and Edward Z. Moore. 2017. "Differences in Words Used to Describe Racial and Gender Groups in Medical Student Performance Evaluations." *PLOS ONE* 12: e0181659.

Rubini, Monica, and Arie W. Kruglanski. 1997. "Brief Encounters Ending in Estrange-ment: Motivated Language Use and Interpersonal Rapport in the Question-Answer Paradigm." *Journal of Personality and Social Psychology* 72: 1047–60.

Ruger, Todd. 2019. "Democrats See Loss of Senate Power in Latest Judicial Vote." Roll Call, February 27, 2019. https://rollcall.com/2019/02/27/democrats-see-loss-of-sen ate-power-in-latest-judicial-vote/.

Ruger, Todd. 2022. "Seeking Court that Looks 'Like America,' Biden Picks Ketanji Brown Jackson," Roll Call, February 25, 2022. https://rollcall.com/2022/02/25/ seeking-court-that-looks-like-america-biden-picks-ketanji-brown-jackson/.

Rutkus, Denis Steven. 2010. "Supreme Court Appointment Process: Roles of the President, Judiciary Committee, and Senate." CRS Report for Congress RL31989. https://www.everycrsreport.com/reports/RL31989.html.

Rutkus, Denis Steven, and Maureen Bearden. 2009. *Supreme Court Nominations, 1789–2009: Actions by the Senate, the Judiciary Committee, and the President.* CRS Report for Congress RL33225. https://crsreports.congress.gov/product/ details?prodcode=RL33225.

Saad, Lydia. 2020. "More Americans Cite COVID-19 as Most Important U.S. Prob-lem." Gallup, August 5, 2020. https://news.gallup.com/poll/316751/americans-cite -covid-important-problem.aspx.

Sanchez-Hucles, Janis V., and Donald D. Davis. 2010. "Women and Women of Color in Leadership: Complexity, Identity, and Intersectionality." *American Psychologist* 65: 171–81.

Saucedo, Selena, and Iris Hentze. 2020. "Raising Awareness About Diversity, Equity and Inclusion." *National Conference of State Legislatures LegisBrief* Volume 28, October 6, 2020. https://www.ncsl.org/research/about-state-legislatures/raising-awareness-about-diversity-equity-and-inclusion.aspx.

Schaffner, Brian F., and Mark Gadon. 2004. "Reinforcing Stereotypes? Race and Local Television News Coverage of Congress." *Social Science Quarterly* 85: 604–23.

Scherer, Nancy. 2011. "Diversifying the Federal Bench: Is Universal Legitimacy for the U.S. Justice System Possible?" *Northwestern University Law Review* 105: 587–633.

Scherer, Nancy, and Brett Curry. 2010. "Does Descriptive Race Representation Enhance Institutional Legitimacy? The Case of the U.S. Courts." *Journal of Politics* 72: 90–104.

Schmader, Toni, Jessica Whitehead, and Vicki H. Wysocki. 2007. "A Linguistic Comparison of Letters of Recommendation for Male and Female Chemistry and Biochemistry Job Applicants." *Sex Roles* 57: 509–14.

Schneider, Andrea Kupfer, Catherine H. Tinsley, Sandra Cheldelin, and Emily T. Amanatullah. 2010. "Likeability v. Competence: The Impossible Choice Faced by Female Politicians, Attenuated by Lawyers." *Duke Journal of Gender Law & Policy* 17: 363–84.

Schneider, Monica C., and Bos, Angela L. 2011. "An Exploration of the Content of Stereotypes of Black Politicians." *Political Psychology* 32: 205–33.

Schoenherr, Jessica A., Elizabeth A. Lane, and Miles T. Armaly. 2020. "The Purpose of Senatorial Grandstanding during Supreme Court Confirmation Hearings." *Journal of Law and Courts* 8: 333–58.

Schuette v. Coalition to Defend Affirmative Action, 572 U.S. 291 (2014).

Sears, David O., Jim Sidanius, James Sidanius, and Lawrence Bobo, eds. 2000. *Racialized Politics: The Debate about Racism in America*. Chicago: University of Chicago Press.

Segal, Jeffrey. 1987. "Senate Confirmation of Supreme Court Justices: Partisan and Institutional Politics." *Journal of Politics* 49: 998–1015.

Sen, Maya. 2014. "How Judicial Qualification Ratings May Disadvantage Minority and Female Candidates." *Journal of Law and Courts* 2: 33–65.

Sen, Maya. 2017. "Diversity, Qualifications, and Ideology: How Female and Minority Judges Have Changed, or Not Changed, over Time." *Wisconsin Law Review* 2017: 367–99.

Senate Democrats. 2022. "Majority Leader Schumer Statement on President Biden's Nomination of Judge Ketanji Brown Jackson to the United States Supreme Court." February 25, 2022. https://www.democrats.senate.gov/newsroom/press-releases/majority-leader-schumer-statement-on-president-bidens-nomination-of-judge-ketanji-brown-jackson-to-the-united-states-supreme-court.

Senate Judiciary Committee. 2021. "Rules of Procedure United States Senate Committee on the Judiciary." https://www.judiciary.senate.gov/about/rules.

Serwer, Adam. 2022. "Republicans Seem to Think Putting a Black Woman on the Supreme Court Is the Real Racism." The Atlantic, February 2, 2022. https://www.theatlantic.com/ideas/archive/2022/02/biden-supreme-court-nominee-smear-campaign/621408/.

Shah, Paru. 2015. "Stepping Up: Black Political Ambition and Success." *Politics, Groups and Identities* 3: 278–94.

Shipan, Charles R. 2008. "Partisanship, Ideology, and Senate Voting on Supreme Court Nominees." *Journal of Empirical Legal Studies* 5: 55–76.

Sigelman, Lee, Christopher J. Deering, and Burdett A. Loomis. 2001. "'Wading Knee Deep in Words, Words, Words': Senatorial Rhetoric in the Johnson and Clinton Impeachment Trials." *Congress & the Presidency* 28: 119–39.

Sigelman, Carol K., Lee Sigelman, Barbara J. Walkosz, and Michael Nitz. 1995. "Black Candidates, White Voters: Understanding Racial Bias in Political Perceptions." *American Journal of Political Science* 39: 243–65.

Sinclair, Lisa, and Ziva Kunda. 2000. "Motivated Stereotyping of Women: She's Fine If She Praised Me but Incompetent If She Criticized Me." *Personality and Social Psychology Bulletin* 26: 1329–42.

Smelcer, Susan Navarro, Amy Steigerwalt, and Richard L. Vining Jr. 2012. "Bias and the Bar: Evaluating the ABA Ratings of Federal Judicial Nominees." *Political Research Quarterly* 65: 827–40.

Smith, Barbara. 1992. "Ain't Gonna Let Nobody Turn Me Around." *The Black Scholar* 22: 90–93.

Smith, David G., Judith E. Rosenstein, Margaret C. Nikolov, and Darby A. Chaney. 2019. "The Power of Language: Gender, Status, and Agency in Performance Evaluations." *Sex Roles* 80: 159–71.

Smith, Pamela K., and Joe C. Magee. 2015. "The Interpersonal Nature of Power and Status." *Current Opinion in Behavioral Sciences* 3: 152–56.

Smith, Terry. 2020. *Whitelash: Unmasking White Grievance at the Ballot Box*. Cambridge: Cambridge University Press.

Smith-Lovin, Lynn, and Charles Brody. 1989. "Interruptions in Group Discussions: The Effects of Gender and Group Composition." *American Sociological Review* 54: 424–35.

Sneed, Tierney. 2022. "Judiciary Committee Senators Spar Over the Tone of Questions Directed at Nominees of Color." *CNN*, February 10, 2022. https://www.cnn .com/2022/02/10/politics/senate-judiciary-racial-bias-nominees-of-color/index .html.

Snyder, Kieran. 2014. "How to Get Ahead as a Woman in Tech: Interrupt Men." Slate, July 23, 2014. http://www.slate.com/blogs/lexicon_valley/2014/07/23/study _men_interrupt_women_more_in_tech_workplaces_but_high_ranking_women .html.

Solowiej, Lisa, and Thomas L. Brunell. 2003. "The Entrance of Women to the U.S. Congress: The Widow Effect." *Political Research Quarterly* 56: 283–92.

Sotomayor, Sonia. 2017. "A Tribute to Justice Scalia." *Yale Law Journal* 126: 1609–11.

Sotomayor Sonia. 2002. "A Latina Judge's Voice." *Berkeley La Raza Law Journal* 13: 87–93.

Stabile, Bonnie, Aubrey Grant, Hemant Purohit, and Kelsey Harris. 2019. "Sex, Lies, and Stereotypes: Gendered Implications of Fake News for Women in Politics." *Public Integrity* 21: 491–502.

Stanzione, Melissa Heelan. 2020. "ABA Group Urges Implicit Bias Training for Judges, Lawyers." Bloomberg Law, July 28, 2020. https://news.bloomberglaw.com/us-law-week/proposal-seeks-implicit-bias-training-for-judges-lawyers.

State of California. 2021. "SB-263 Real Estate Applicants and Licensees: Education Requirements: Fair Housing and Implicit Bias Training." September 29, 2021. https://leginfo.legislature.ca.gov/faces/billTextClient.xhtml?bill_id=202120220SB263.

State of Michigan. 2021. "FAQs for Implicit Bias Training." Bureau of Professional Licensing, September 24, 2021. https://www.michigan.gov/documents/lara/Implicit_Bias_FAQs_FINAL_7.22.2021_731300_7.pdf.

Steffensmeier, Darrell, and Chester L. Britt. 2001. "Judges' Race and Judicial Decision Making: Do Black Judges Sentence Differently?" *Social Science Quarterly* 82: 749–64.

Steigerwalt, Amy, Richard L. Vining, Jr., and Tara W. Stricko. 2013. "Minority Representation, the Electoral Connection, and the Confirmation Vote of Sonia Sotomayor." *Justice System Journal* 34: 189–207.

Stephan, Walter G. 2014. "Intergroup Anxiety: Theory, Research, and Practice." *Personality and Social Psychology Review* 18: 239–55.

Stolberg, Sheryl Gay. 2018. "Democrats Grilling Kavanaugh Have Their Eyes on 2020." New York Times, September 6, 2018. https://www.nytimes.com/2018/09/06/us/politics/kavanaugh-hearings-kamala-harris-cory-booker.html.

Stolberg, Sheryl Gay, and Nicholas Fandos. 2018. "Brett Kavanaugh and Christine Blasey Ford Duel with Tears and Fury." New York Times, September 27, 2018. https://www.nytimes.com/2018/09/27/us/politics/brett-kavanaugh-confirmation-hearings.html.

Stolberg, Sheryl Gay, and Carl Hulse. 2019. "Joe Biden Expresses Regret to Anita Hill, but She Says 'I'm Sorry' Is Not Enough." New York Times, April 25, 2019. https://www.nytimes.com/2019/04/25/us/politics/joe-biden-anita-hill.html.

Stolzenberg, Ross M., and James Lindgren. 2010. "Retirement and Death in Office of U.S. Supreme Court Justices." *Demography* 47: 269–98.

Stubbs, Jonathan K. 2016. "A Demographic History of Federal Judicial Appointments by Sex and Race: 1789–2016." *Berkeley La Raza Law Journal* 26: 92–128.

Sullivan, Sean, Josh Dawsey, Rosalind S. Helderman, and Michelle Ye Hee Lee. 2018. "Arizona Prosecutor Rachel Mitchell Is GOP Choice to Question Kavanaugh and Accuser at Hearing." Washington Post, September 25, 2018. https://www.washingtonpost.com/powerpost/arizona-prosecutor-rachel-mitchell-emerges-as-gop-choice-to-question-kavanaugh-and-accuser-at-hearing/2018/09/25/47964afa-c0ff-11e8-9005-5104e9616c21_story.html.

Swire, Sonnet, and Veronica Stracqualursi. 2022. "GOP Senator Says Black Woman Supreme Court Pick Would Be 'Beneficiary" of Affirmative Action." *CNN*, January 29, 2022. https://www.cnn.com/2022/01/29/politics/roger-wicker-supreme-court-biden-nominee-affirmative-action/index.html.

Szmer, John J., Tammy A. Sarver, and Erin B. Kaheny. 2010. "Have We Come a Long Way, Baby? The Influence of Attorney Gender on Supreme Court Decision Making." *Politics & Gender* 6: 1–36.

Taaffe, Gideon, and Mia Gingerich. 2022. "Biden Pledged to Nominate a Black Woman to the Supreme Court. Right-wing Media Are Rushing to Dismiss the Idea." Media Matters for America, January 28, 2022. https://www.mediamatters .org/supreme-court/biden-pledged-nominate-black-woman-supreme-court-right -wing-media-are-rushing-dismiss.

Talbot, Margaret. 2022. "Amy Coney Barrett's Long Game." *The New Yorker*, February 14 and 21, 2022. https://www.newyorker.com/magazine/2022/02/14/amy -coney-barretts-long-game.

Talmadge, John E. 1960. *Rebecca Latimer Felton: Nine Stormy Decades*. Athens: University of Georgia Press.

Tausczik, Yla R., and James W. Pennebaker. 2010. "The Psychological Meaning of Words: LIWC and Computerized Text Analysis Methods." *Journal of Language and Social Psychology* 29: 24–54.

Tinkler, Justine E. 2012. "Controversies in Implicit Race Bias Research." *Sociology Compass* 6: 987–97.

Toobin, Jeffrey. 2007. *The Nine: Inside the Secret World of the Supreme Court*. New York: Doubleday.

Totenberg, Nina. 2011. "Thomas Confirmation Hearings Had Ripple Effect." National Public Radio, October 11, 2011. https://www.npr.org/2011/10/11/141213260/ thomas-confirmation-hearings-had-ripple-effect.

Totenberg, Nina. 2018. "A Timeline of Clarence Thomas-Anita Hill Controversy as Kavanaugh to Face Accuser." *National Public Radio*, September 23, 2018. https:// www.npr.org/2018/09/23/650138049/a-timeline-of-clarence-thomas-anita-hill -controversy-as-kavanaugh-to-face-accuse.

Totenberg, Nina. 2020. "Justice Ruth Bader Ginsburg, Champion of Gender Equality, Dies at 87," *National Public Radio*, September 18, 2020. https://www.npr. org/2020/09/18/100306972/justice-ruth-bader-ginsburg-champion-of-gender -equality-dies-at-87.

Towner, Terri L., and Rosalee A. Clawson. 2016. "A Wise Latina or a Baffled Rookie? Media Coverage of Justice Sonia Sotomayor's Ascent to the Bench." *Journal of Women, Politics & Policy* 37: 316–40.

Trix, Frances, and Carolyn Psenka. 2003. "Exploring the Color of Glass: Letters of Recommendation for Female and Male Medical Faculty." *Discourse & Society* 14: 191–220.

Trope, Yaacov, and Nira Liberman. 2003. "Temporal Construal." *Psychological Review* 110: 403–21.

Trope, Yaacov, and Nira Liberman. 2010. "Construal-level Theory of Psychological Distance." *Psychological Review* 117: 440–63.

Truong, Khiet P. 2013. "Classification of Cooperative and Competitive Overlaps in Speech Using Cues from the Context, Overlapper, and Overlappee." *Interspeech* 2013: 1404–8.

Turner, John C. 1982. "Towards a Cognitive Redefinition of the Social Group." In *Social Identity and Intergroup Relations*, edited by Henri Tajfel. Cambridge: Cambridge University Press.

UltraViolet. 2022a. "Reporting in an Era of Disinformation: Fairness Media Guide for Covering Women and People of Color without Bias." https://weareuv.us/mediagu ide2022 (February 2022).

UltraViolet. 2022b. "Women's Disinfo Defense Project Announces Major Effort to Defend Biden's Supreme Court Nominee from Racist or Sexist Attacks & Disinformation." Press Release, February 15, 2022. https://weareultraviolet.org/press-rel/womens-disinfo-defense-project-announces-major-effort-to-defend-bidens-su preme-court-nominee-from-racist-or-sexist-attacks-disinformation/.

Umoh, Ruth. 2018. "Why All Companies Should Have Racial Bias Training—Before Public Outcry." *CNBC*, May 30, 2018. https://www.cnbc.com/2018/05/30/3-rea sons-all-companies-should-have-racial-bias-training.html.

U.S. Courts. 2019. March 12, 2019. https://www.uscourts.gov/news/2019/03/12/ judicial-conference-approves-package-workplace-conduct-reforms.

U.S. Senate. 2013. S. Doc. No. 113–18.

United States Senate. 1991. "Nomination of Judge Clarence Thomas to Be Associate Justice of the Supreme Court of the United States." https://www.senate.gov/refer ence/Supreme_Court_Nomination_Hearings.htm.

United States Senate. 2021a. "Women of the Senate." https://www.senate.gov/artand history/history/People/Women/Women-of-the-Senate.htm.

United States Senate. 2021b. "Minorities in the Senate." https://www.senate.gov/refer ence/reference_index_subjects/Minorities_vrd.htm.

United States Senate. 2022a. "Women in the Senate." https://www.senate.gov/artand history/history/common/briefing/women_senators.htm.

United States Senate. 2022b. "Ethnic Diversity in the Senate." http://www.senate.gov/ artandhistory/history/common/briefing/minority_senators.htm.

United States Senate. 2022c. "Biographical Directory of the United States Congress." https://bioguide.congress.gov/.

United States Supreme Court. 2021. "Guide for Counsel in the Cases to Be Argued before the Supreme Court of the United States." October Term 2021. https://www .supremecourt.gov/Guide%20for%20Counsel%202021.pdf

Uscinski, Joseph E., and Lilly J. Goren. 2011. "What's in a Name? Coverage of Senator Hillary Clinton during the 2008 Democratic Primary." *Political Research Quarterly* 64: 884–96.

Van der Pas, Daphne Joanna, and Loes Aaldering. 2020. "Gender Differences in Political Media Coverage: A Meta-analysis." *Journal of Communication* 70: 114–43.

van Diggelen, Alison. 2010. "Jeffrey Toobin: Kagan, Supreme Court & Environment." *Fresh Dialogues*, April 12, 2010. https://www.freshdialogues.com/2010/04/12/ jeffrey-toobin-supreme-court-environment/.

Vining, Richard L., Jr. 2011. "Grassroots Mobilization in the Digital Age: Interest Group Response to Supreme Court Nominees." *Political Research Quarterly* 64: 790–802.

Vorauer, Jacquie D., and Matthew Quesnel. 2017. "Antecedents and Consequences of Evaluative Concerns Experienced During Intergroup Interaction: When and How Does Group Status Matter?" In *The Cambridge Handbook of the Psychology of Prejudice.*, edited by Chris G. Sibley and Fiona Kate Barlow. Cambridge: Cambridge University Press.

Vought, Russell. 2020. "Memorandum for the Heads of Executive Departments and Agencies." Executive Office of the President, Office of Management and Budget, September 4, 2020. https://www.whitehouse.gov/wp-content/up loads/2020/09/M-20-34.pdf?fbclid=IwAR1r7Ej2VogZ8pNhIEjLtHDDNlfeYvB kzEgUfbrU3cXfot7RP2XKPwnCDe4.

Ward, Artemus. 2012. *Deciding to Leave: The Politics of Retirement from the United States Supreme Court.* Albany: State University of New York Press.

Ward, Stephanie Francis. 2011. "Female Judicial Candidates Are Held to Different Standards, Sotomayor Tells Students." ABA Journal, http://www.abajournal.com/ news/article/female_judicial_candidates_are_held_to_different_standards_soto mayor_tells_/ (March 2018).

Waldman, Paul. 2022. "An Ugly Racist Attack on Ketanji Brown Jackson Makes Its Inevitable Return." Washington Post, March 3, 2022. https://www.washingtonpost .com/opinions/2022/03/03/ugly-racist-attack/.

Walsh, Deirdre. 2020. "Takeaways from Amy Coney Barrett's Judiciary Confirmation Hearings," *NPR*, October 15, 2020. https://www.npr.org/2020/10/15/923637375/ takeaways-from-amy-coney-barretts-judiciary-confirmation-hearings.

Ware, Gilbert. 1984. *William Hastie: Grace Under Pressure.* New York: Oxford University Press.

Washington, Linn. 1994. *Black Judges on Justice: Perspectives from the Bench.* New York: New Press.

Watson, George, and John Stookey. 1987. "Supreme Court Confirmation Hearings: A View from the Senate." *Judicature* 71: 186–96.

Weinberg, Jill D., and Laura Beth Nielsen. 2012. "Examining Empathy: Discrimination, Experience, and Judicial Decisionmaking." *Southern California Law Review* 85: 313–52.

Weitzer, Ronald, and Steven A. Tuch. 1999. "Race, Class, and Perceptions of Discrimination by the Police." *Crime & Delinquency* 45: 494–507.

Welch, Susan, Michael Combs, and John Gruhl. 1988. "Do Black Judges Make a Difference?" *American Journal of Political Science* 32: 126–36.

West, Paul. 2005. "Loyalty Is Key in Choice of Miers." Baltimore Sun, October 4, 2005. https://www.baltimoresun.com/news/bal-te.analysis04oct04-story.html.

Wheelock, Darren, Meghan S. Stroshine, and Michael O'Hear. 2019. "Disentangling the Relationship between Race and Attitudes toward the Police: Police Contact, Perceptions of Safety, and Procedural Justice." *Crime & Delinquency* 65: 941–68.

Williams, Linda F. 1990. "White/Black Perceptions of the Electability of Black Political Candidates." *National Political Science Review* 2: 45–64.

Williams, Margaret S. 2008. "Ambition, Gender, and the Judiciary." *Political Research Quarterly* 61: 68–78.

Williams, Margaret, and Lawrence Baum. 2006. "Supreme Court Nominees Before the Senate Judiciary Committee." *Judicature* 90: 73–80.

Wolf, Richard. 2020. "Justice Ruth Bader Ginsburg's Top Opinions and Dissents, from VMI to Voting Rights Act," USA Today, September 18, 2020. https://www.usatoday.com/story/news/politics/2020/09/18/i-dissent-justice-ruth-bader-gins burgs-most-memorable-opinions/2661426002/.

Wolf, Richard, and Maureen Groppe. 2020. "Amy Coney Barrett: Talented Judge, Popular Professor Brings Solid Conservative Credentials." USA Today, September 26, 2020. https://www.usatoday.com/story/news/politics/2020/09/26/who-amy -coney-barrett-talented-judge-conservative-credentials/3494471001/.

Wolfartsberger, Anita. 2011. "ELF Business/Business ELF: Form and Function in Simultaneous Speech." In *Latest Trends in ELF Research.*, edited by Alasdair Archibald, Alessia Cogo, and Jennifer Jenkins. Newcastle upon Tyne, UK: Cambridge Scholars.

Wright, James E., and Andrea M. Headley. 2020. "Police Use of Force Interactions: Is Race Relevant or Gender Germane?" *American Review of Public Administration* 50: 851–64.

Zeldon, Charles L., ed. 2007. *The Judicial Branch of Federal Government: People, Process, and Politics*. Santa Barbara, CA: ABC-CLIO.

Zimmerman, Don H., and Candace West. 1975. "Sex Roles, Interruptions and Silences in Conversations." In *Language and Sex: Difference and Dominance*, edited by Barrie Thorne and Nancy Henley. Rowley, MA: Newbury House.

Zhou, Li. 2020. "What's Next for Amy Coney Barrett's Supreme Court Nomination," Vox, October 15, 2020. https://www.vox.com/21517484/amy-coney-barrett -senate-vote.

# INDEX

Page numbers in *italics* refer to figures.

Abramson, Jill, 174–75
abortion: *Roe v. Wade*, 31, 62, 65, 135, 230n5; subject matter stereotype, 98, 101, 109–10, 112–14, 119; topic at confirmation hearings, 65–67; influences on questions at confirmation hearings, *113, 119*; topic at confirmation hearings, by gender, race, and partisanship, 109–14
affirmative action: cases, 40, 62; issue competency stereotypes and, 92, 98; nominees questioned about, 62, 65; nominees suggested to be "beneficiaries" of, 24
Affordable Care Act, 43, 53, 56, 230n4
Alito, Samuel, 30, 69, 96–97
Allen, Florence, 13, 14, 24–25; considered for Supreme Court by Truman, 13; Eisenhower and, 25, 228n6; first Ohio Supreme Court female justice, 24; legacy of, 14, 24–25; shortlisted for Supreme Court by Roosevelt, 25; Sixth Circuit Court of Appeals nomination, 25

American Bar Association (ABA): on bias training, 218; definition of judicial temperament, 73; rating of Barrett, 32; rating of Ginsburg, 29; rating of Kagan, 31; rating of Sotomayor, 23, 74; ratings of female and person of color nominees, 33, 94–95, 228n7; ratings of potential Supreme Court nominees, 27, 50; role in history of open, public confirmation hearings, 55
Angelou, Maya, 22
appointment process. *See* Supreme Court confirmation process
Article I judges, 227–28n1
Article III judges, 17–18, 25, 227–28n1

Bacon, Sylvia, 25, 27
Barrett, Amy Coney: ABA rating, 32; confirmation vote, 43–44; questioning of at confirmation hearing, 2–3, 7, 8, 43, 53, 56, 67, 209–10; as role model, 8, 32, 225; Trump's nomination process, 32
Bayh, Evan, 63

O'Connor, Sandra Day: education and
   legal career, 28, 33; historic nature
   of nomination, 15, 17, 37; language
   choices by media when referring to,
   5; questioning of at confirmation
   hearing, 65, 67; Reagan's nomination
   process, 28–29, 51; retirement, 29, 48;
   as role model, 225
Omnibus Judgeship Act, 36
out-group theory, 82, 91–92, 95, 100, 117

Padilla, Alex, 219–20
panel effects, 40
Patton, Dana, 126
Peffley, Mark, 98
*Plessy v. Ferguson,* 61
Powell, Lewis, 5, 27, 33, 50, 65

Quillian, Lincoln, 93

racial discrimination: discussed at confirmation hearings, 59–63; subject matter
   stereotype, 101, 109, 111–16, 120
Reagan, Ronald: gubernatorial backing
   of Lillie, 27; Kennedy nomination,
   48; O'Connor nomination, 15, 28–29,
   48, 51, 65; percentage of female
   judicial appointments, 37; promise to
   nominate a woman to Supreme Court,
   27–28, 37
Rehnquist, William, 5, 27; death of,
   29, 48; judicial career, 33; personal
   misconduct allegations against, 173;
   questioning of during confirmation
   hearing, 63, 65
Reid, Harry, 30
résumés, job, 5–7
Revels, Hiram, 202
*Ricci v. DeStefano,* 62
Roberts, John, 29, 126, 149–50, 221, 223
*Roe v. Wade,* 31, 62, 65, 135, 230n5
role models, judges as, 8, 32, 39, 63, 65, 215,
   224–25, 229n17
Romney, Mitt, 24

Roosevelt, Franklin D., 224, 230n4;
   Allen nomination to U.S. Court of
   Appeals, 25; Allen shortlisted for
   Supreme Court, 25; Black nomina-
   tion, 54; "court packing" plan, 46;
   Frankfurter nomination, 54; Hastie
   appointment to Virgin Islands District
   Court, 17
Rutledge, John, 173
Rymer, Pamela A., 21

Scalia, Antonin, 5, 32, 42–43, 48, 75
Schneider, Monica C., 98
Schumer, Chuck, 1, 53, 96, 150
Schweers, Dylan, 126, 128
Scott, Rick, 53
Scott, Tim, 203
Second Amendment, 43, 129, 209
Segal, Jeffrey, 231n17
segregation, 17–18, 60, 235n2
Sen, Maya, 39, 94–95
Senate Judiciary Committee, 3–5, 52–68;
   behavior of women senators and
   senators of color, 203–17; confirmation
   hearing process, 54–59; confirmation
   process reforms, 221–22; discussion of
   gender at hearings, 63–69; discussion
   of race at hearings, 59–63; diversification of membership, 201–3; gender
   and sexual orientation discrimination
   discussed at confirmation hearings,
   63–68; interruptions by, 208–14; language used toward nominees, 214–17;
   racial discrimination discussed at
   confirmation hearings, 59–63; senators
   of color and women senators, *202. See
   also* abortion; gender and sexual orientation discrimination; interruptions;
   language choices
Senate Rule XXVI, 196
Sessions, Jeff, 96, 100, 149, 150
sexual orientation discrimination.
   *See* gender and sexual orientation
   discrimination

Printed in the USA
CPSIA information can be obtained
at www.ICGtesting.com
JSHW081932100823
46299JS00001B/1